"WORKING HARD FOR SOMETHING WE DON'T CARE ABOUT IS CALLED STRESSED; WORKING HARD FOR SOMETHING WE LOVE IS CALLED PASSION."

Simon Sinek

Copyright © HGV Publishing
November 2022

HGV DRIVERS DIARY 2022

Name:

Surname:

Company:

Phone Number:

USEFUL TELEPHONE NUMBERS

Printable Emergency Contact List

Emergency Contacts

Contact 1 Name		Relationship	
Phone 1		Phone 2	
Address			

Contact 2 Name		Relationship	
Phone 1		Phone 2	
Address			

Contact 3 Name		Relationship	
Phone 1		Phone 2	
Address			

Neighbors / Landlord / HOA

Neighbor 1 Name		Phone	
Neighbor 2 Name		Phone	
Neighbor 3 Name		Phone	
Landlord / HOA		Phone	

Medical Contact Info

Doctor Name		Phone	
Dentist Name		Phone	
Preferred Hospital		Phone	

Police / Ambulance / Fire: 9-1-1

Police		Phone	
Fire Department		Phone	
Electric Company		Phone	
Gas Company		Phone	
Water Company		Phone	
Poison Control		Phone	
Animal Control		Phone	

Other Telephone Numbers

Name	No.	Comment
1.		
2.		
3.		
4.		
5.		
6.		
7.		
8.		
9.		
10.		
11.		
12.		
13.		
14.		
15.		
16.		
17.		
18.		
19.		
20.		
21.		

Name	No.	Comment
22.		
23.		
23.		
24.		
25.		
26.		
27.		
28.		
29.		
30.		
31.		
32.		
33.		
34.		
35.		
36.		
37.		
38.		
39.		
40.		
41.		
42.		
43.		
44.		
45.		
46.		
47.		
48.		
49.		
50.		

CPR

CPR

1. Call Emergency Number

2. Check Vital Signs
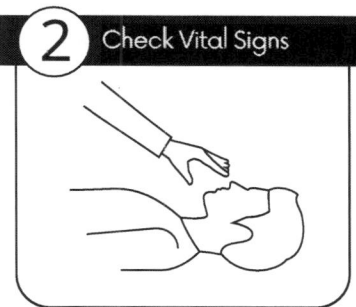

3. Check Breathing
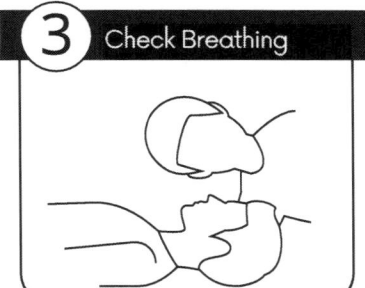

4. Give Rescure Breaths

5. Perform CPR
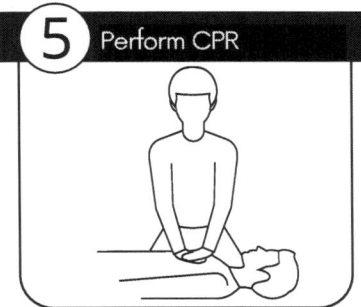

6. Turn On Side
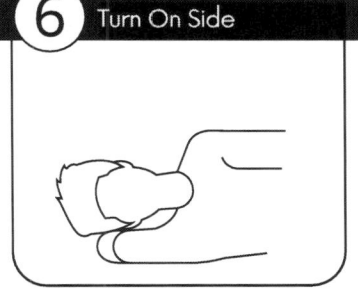

Learn the steps to perform this lifesaving technique on adults and children.

Cardiopulmonary resuscitation (CPR) is a lifesaving technique that's useful in many emergencies, such as a heart attack or near drowning, in which someone's breathing or heartbeat has stopped. The American Heart Association recommends starting CPR with hard and fast chest compressions. This hands-only CPR recommendation applies to both untrained bystanders and first responders.

If you're afraid to do CPR or unsure how to perform CPR correctly, know that it's always better to try than to do nothing at all. The difference between doing something and doing nothing could be someone's life

Here's advice from the American Heart Association:

- Untrained. If you're not trained in CPR or worried about giving rescue breaths, then provide hands-only CPR. That means uninterrupted chest compressions of 100 to 120 a minute until paramedics arrive (described in more detail below). You don't need to try rescue breathing.

- Trained and ready to go. If you're well-trained and confident in your ability, check to see if there is a pulse and breathing. If there is no pulse or breathing within 10 seconds, begin chest compressions. Start CPR with 30 chest compressions before giving two rescue breaths.

- Trained but rusty. If you've previously received CPR training but you're not confident in your abilities, then just do chest compressions at a rate of 100 to 120 a minute (details described below).

The above advice applies to situations in which adults, children, and infants need CPR, but not newborns (infants up to 4 weeks old).

CPR can keep oxygen-rich blood flowing to the brain and other organs until emergency medical treatment can restore a normal heart rhythm. When the heart stops, your body no longer gets oxygen-rich blood. The lack of oxygen-rich blood can cause brain damage in only a few minutes.

If you are untrained and have immediate access to a phone, call 911 or your local emergency number before beginning CPR. The dispatcher can instruct you in the proper procedures until help arrives. To learn CPR properly, take an accredited first-aid training course, including CPR and how to use an automated external defibrillator (AED).

Before you begin.

Before starting CPR, check:

- Is the environment safe for the person?
- Is the person conscious or unconscious?
- If the person appears unconscious, tap or shake his or her shoulder and ask loudly, "Are you OK?"
- If the person doesn't respond and you're with another person who can help, have one person call 911 or the local emergency number and get the AED if one is available. Have the other person begin CPR.
- If you are alone and have immediate access to a telephone, call 911 or your local emergency number before beginning CPR. Get the AED if one is available.
- As soon as an AED is available, deliver one shock if instructed by the device, then begin CPR.

Scan the QR code and open the instructional video on how to make a CRP step by step.

EMERGENCY NUMBERS

EMERGENCY NUMBERS

911
Emergency

111
national non-emergency medical number

112
112 will work on any mobile phone anywhere in the world

101
non-emergency number for the police

EMERGENCY NUMBERS

It used to be just 999 for emergency services, but now there are many numbers we can use to summon help. But which is which, and when should we use them?

999 – The main emergency number

This is the emergency number for police, ambulance, fire brigade, coastguard, cliff rescue, mountain rescue, cave rescue, etc. Note the important word 'EMERGENCY'. This number should be used only when urgent attendance by the emergency services is required – for example, someone is seriously ill or injured, or a crime is in progress.

Calls are free, and 999 can be dialled from a locked mobile phone.

112 – Another emergency number

This operates the same as 999 and directs you to the same emergency call center. The important thing about 112 is that it will work on a mobile phone anywhere in the world. Incidentally, an EU requirement is that emergency call centers must provide a translations service.

101 – The non-emergency number for the police

Use 101 when you want to contact the police, but it's not an emergency – i.e. an immediate response is not necessary and/or will not serve any purpose.

For example, your car has been stolen, your property has been damaged, your home has been broken into.

A general rule is "if the crime is not currently in progress, use 101." Yes, we would love an immediate response, but the police have to concentrate their emergency resources on where the criminals are now, not where they were two hours ago.

101 can also be used to give information about a crime committed, or to contact the police with a general inquiry.

111 – The non-emergency medical number

This is available nationwide and replaced and expanded on the former NHS Direct service. Use this for illnesses and minor injuries where life isn't threatened, but you would like some advice on what to do next.

Calls are free.

HGV ALLIANCE

HGV ALLIANCE

Logistics Directory of Low Bridges, Truck Stops, Weighbridge Locations.

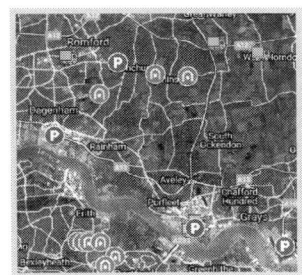

Use the ready-made google map and find what you are looking for.

Scan the QR code and open the map on your phone or tablet.

WAZE NAVIGATION

Always know what's happening on the road with Waze. Even if you know the way, Waze tells you instantly about traffic, roadworks, police, accidents & more. If traffic is bad on your route, Waze will change it to save you time.

- See what's happening - Alerts about traffic, police, hazards, and more on your drive
- Get there faster - Instant routing changes to avoid traffic and save you time
- Easily listen to music - play your favorite apps for music, podcasts & more right from Waze
- Know when you'll arrive - your Arrival Time is based on live traffic data
- Pay less for fuel - find the cheapest fuel along your route
- Always find the way - choose from a variety of voices to guide you while you drive

Scan the QR code and open the Waze Navigation on your phone or tablet.

Apple Android

UNIT CONVERTER

Unit Converter is an app that lets you do exactly what its name suggests: convert all kinds of units, regardless of what you're trying to measure. You can convert measurement units of length, weight, temperature, speed, power, voltage, and many others.

In total, Unit Converter has 29 different categories, which let you convert miles into kilometers, ounces into grams, or euros into dollars. To make accessing each category easier, the app has divided the different types of converters into different categories: basic, life, science, and others. Like this, you can quickly access whatever you're interested in.

One of Unit Converter's really great features automatically adapts to the country you're in, offering you the most common units of measure. So, if you're in Spain, for instance, it automatically detects that the euro is your currency.

Android

Scan the QR code and open the Unit Converter on your phone or tablet.

MOTORWAY BUDDY

MotorWayBuddy is the first and only complete guide to all of the Truck Stops that operate in the UK.

As well as the address and telephone numbers the app provides information regarding the facilities, spaces, and costs of parking at the Truck Stops.

The application also provides a real-time view of all incidents on the roads of the UK provided by the highways agency.

Scan the QR code and open the Motorway Buddy on your phone or tablet.

Apple   Android

TRUCKER TIMER

Truck drivers: save yourself a fine and maximise your driving hours with this advanced tachograph and driving log.

TruckerTimer is the only application designed specifically for truck, lorry, and HGV drivers in the UK and Europe that will help you track your driving hours and alert you to impending fatigue violations. TruckerTimer is designed to keep you legal within the many complex rules of the EU driver's hours regulations.

Scan the QR code and open the TruckerTimer on your phone or tablet.

Apple

Android

HGVparking

HGVparking is the most comprehensive guide to overnight lorry parking in the UK. Find a variety of different parking areas near you now!

HGVparking makes it easy to locate parking areas anywhere in the UK. It's perfect if you're not familiar with an area or want an alternative to a busy service area, it's dead simple to use and a great tool to have with you in the cab.

Scan the QR code and open the HGVparking on your phone or tablet.

Apple

Android

Live Traffic Info

Check how the traffic is flowing on motorways and major A roads in England with official information live from the Highways England National Traffic Control Centre.

This app only contains information about the roads we manage in England. Other smaller roads in England are managed by local authorities. Trunk roads and motorways in Scotland are the responsibility of Transport Scotland; those in Wales of the Welsh Assembly Government.

Official data is collected from thousands of vehicle monitors, CCTV and patrol reports to show where the Highways England network is flowing well and to keep you up-to-date with traffic incidents as they break throughout the day.

Scan the QR code and open the Live Traffic Info on your phone or tablet.

Apple

Android

STANDARD SPEEDS LIMITS IN EUROPE

Standard speeds limits in Europe

Country	Heavy goods vehicles over 3.5t - urban roads	Heavy goods vehicles over 3.5t - non-urban roads	Heavy goods vehicles over 3.5t - expressways	Heavy goods vehicles over 3.5t - motorways
Austria	50 km/h	70 km/h	80 km/h	80 km/h
Belgium	50 km/h 20 km/h in residential areas. 30 km/h near schools and in streets with cycle paths	90 km/h	90 km/h	90 km/h
Bulgaria	50 km/h 40 km/h - maximum speed for vehicles carrying dangerous goods	80 km/h 70 km/h for heavy goods vehicles with semitrailers or trailers (Type O3, O4). 50 km/h for heavy goods vehicles carrying dangerous goods.	90 km/h 90 km/h for heavy goods vehicles with semitrailers or trailers (Type O3, O4). 90 km/h for heavy goods vehicles carrying dangerous goods.	100 km/h 90 km/h for heavy goods vehicles with semitrailers or trailers (Type O3, O4) .90 km/h for heavy goods vehicles carrying dangerous goods.
Croatia	50 km/h	80 km/h	90 km/h	90 km/h
Cyprus	50 km/h	64 km/h	80 km/h	80 km/h
Czech Republic	50 km/h	64 km/h	80 km/h	80 km/h
Denmark	50 km/h	70 km/h	80 km/h	80 km/h
Estonia	50 km/h	90 km/h	90 km/h	90 km/h
Finland	50 km/h	80 km/h	80 km/h	80 km/h On any other highways, the speed is restricted to 60 km/h for vehicles over 7.5 t

Standard speeds limits in Europe

Country	Heavy goods vehicles over 3.5t - urban roads	Heavy goods vehicles over 3.5t - non-urban roads	Heavy goods vehicles over 3.5t - expressways	Heavy goods vehicles over 3.5t - motorways
France	50 km/h	80 km/h 60 km/h for combination of vehicles over 12t	80 km/h	90 km/h
Germany	50 km/h	50 km/h 60 km/h Vehicle over 7.5t 80 km/h Vehicle up to 7.5t 60 km/h Vehicle up to 7.5t with trailer 60 km/h Vehicle over 7.5t with trailer	60 km/h Vehicle over 7.5t 80 km/h Vehicle up to 7.5t 60 km/h Vehicle up to 7.5t with trailer 60 km/h Vehicle over 7.5t with trailer	80 km/h Vehicle with trailer & Towing vehicle with two trailers
Greece	50 km/h	80 km/h 70 km/h for heavy goods vehicles with semitrailers or trailers (Type O3, O4)	80 km/h 80-70 km/h for heavy goods vehicles with semitrailers or trailers (Type O3, O4)	80 km/h 85 km/h 80-70 km/h for heavy goods vehicles with semitrailers or trailers (Type O3, O4)
Hungary	50 km/h	70 km/h	80 km/h	80 km/h
Ireland	50 km/h	80 km/h	90 km/h	90 km/h
Italy	50 km/h	80 km/h 80 km/h for vehicles up to 12 t. 70 km/h for vehicles over 12t	80/100 km/h 100 km/h for vehicles up to 12 t. 80 km/h for vehicles over 12t	80/100 km/h 100 km/h for vehicles up to 12 t. 80 km/h for vehicles over 12t
Latvia	50 km/h	80 km/h	-	-

Standard speeds limits in Europe

Country	Heavy goods vehicles over 3.5t - urban roads	Heavy goods vehicles over 3.5t - non-urban roads	Heavy goods vehicles over 3.5t - expressways	Heavy goods vehicles over 3.5t - motorways
Liechtenstein	50 km/h	80 km/h	-	-
Lithuania	50 km/h	80 km/h Roads with asphalt and concrete cover – 80 km/h Other roads – 70 km/h	80 km/h	90 km/h
Luxembourg	50 km/h	75 km/h	90 km/h	90 km/h
Malta	40 km/h	60 km/h	60 km/h	60 km/h
Netherlands	50 km/h	80 km/h	80 km/h	80 km/h
Norway	50 km/h	80 km/h	80 km/h	80 km/h
Poland	50 km/h	70 km/h 80 km/h on dual carriageway with at least 2 lanes for every direction	80 km/h	80 km/h
Portugal	50 km/h	80 km/h	80 km/h	90 km/h
Romania	50 km/h	90/80 km/h	110 km/h	110 km/h
Slovakia	50 km/h	90 km/h	90 km/h	90 km/h
Slovenia	50 km/h 30 km/h – in speed limit zones 10 km/h – in pedestrian zones where traffic is allowed	80 km/h	80 km/h	90 km/h
Sweden	50 km/h	70 km/h	90 km/h	90 km/h

Standard speeds limits in Europe

Country	Heavy goods vehicles over 3.5t - urban roads	Heavy goods vehicles over 3.5t - non-urban roads	Heavy goods vehicles over 3.5t - expressways	Heavy goods vehicles over 3.5t - motorways
Liechtenstein	50 km/h	80 km/h	-	-
Spain	50 km/h	70 km/h Roads with no/narrow hard shoulder (<1.5 m) 10 km/h slower than the normal speed limit if carrying dangerous goods 80 km/h roads with hard shoulder (>1.5 m) or dual carriageway 10 km/h slower than the normal speed limit if carrying dangerous goods	80 km/h 10 km/h slower than the normal speed limit if carrying dangerous goods	80 km/h 10 km/h slower than the normal speed limit if carrying dangerous goods
Switzerland	50 km/h	80 km/h	80 km/h	90 km/h
United Kingdom	48 km/h	80 km/h	112 km/h 96 km/h on motorways and dual carriageways if articulated or towing a trailer	112 km/h 96 km/h on motorways and dual carriageways if articulated or towing a trailer

ALCOHOL LIMITS IN EUROPE

Alcohol limits in Europe

Country	Vehicle registration plates	Maximum blood alcohol content - **Standard drivers**	Maximum blood alcohol content - **Novice drivers**	Maximum blood alcohol content - **Professional drivers**
Austria	A	< 0,5 ‰ (from 0.8 ‰, withdrawal of driving licence)	0,1 ‰ (less than 2 years' driving experience)	0,1 ‰
Belgium	B	0.5 ‰	0.5 ‰	0.2 ‰
Bulgaria	BG	0,0 ‰	0,0 ‰	0,0 ‰
Croatia	HR	0,5 ‰	0,0 ‰	0,0 ‰
Cyprus	CY	0.5 ‰	0.5 ‰	0.5 ‰
Czech Republic	CZ	0,0 ‰	0,0 ‰	0,0 ‰
Denmark	DK	0,5 ‰	0,5 ‰	0,5 ‰
Estonia	EST	0,2 ‰	0,2 ‰	0,2 ‰
Finland	FIN	0,5 ‰	0,5 ‰	0,5 ‰
France	F	0,5 ‰	0,2 ‰ (who have held a driving licence for (a) less than 3 years, or (b) less than 2 years if the driver – in addition to completing 20 hours of hands-on driving lessons with an instructor - has driven at least 3000 km over a minimum of 2 years, accompanied by an experienced driver, before passing the driving test)	0,5 ‰ (For bus and coach drivers the limit is 0.2 ‰)

Alcohol limits in Europe

Country	Vehicle registration plates	Maximum blood alcohol content - Standard drivers	Maximum blood alcohol content - Novice drivers	Maximum blood alcohol content - Professional drivers
Germany	D	0,5 ‰ above 1.1 ‰ is treated as a crime, 0.5-1.0 ‰ the penalty is a fine	0,0 ‰ less than 2 years' driving experience and under 21's	0,0 ‰ offenders can be sacked
Greece	GR	0,5 ‰ (0,2 ‰ for motorbike and moped drivers)	0,2 ‰	0,2 ‰
Hungary	H	0,0 ‰	0,0 ‰	0,0 ‰
Ireland	IRL	0.5 ‰ Maximum penalties on conviction for drink or drug driving is €5 000 and/or 6 months imprisonment.	0.2 ‰ Maximum penalties on conviction for drink or drug driving is €5 000 and/or 6 months imprisonment.	0.5 ‰ Maximum penalties on conviction for drink or drug driving is €5 000 and/or 6 months imprisonment.
Italy	I	0,5 ‰	0,0 ‰	0,0 ‰
Latvia	LV	0,5 ‰	0,2 ‰	0,5 ‰
Liechtenstein	L	0,8 ‰	0,8 ‰	0,8 ‰ Prohibited from drinking alcohol either during working hours or 6 hours before their work starts
Lithuania	LT	0,4 ‰	0,0 ‰ less than 2 years' driving experience) and moped, motorcycle, tricycle, all kind of quadricycle drivers	0,0 ‰ vehicles weighing more than 3.5 tonnes or with more than 9 seats, taxi drivers, drivers of vehicles transporting dangerous goods

Alcohol limits in Europe

Country	Vehicle registration plates	Maximum blood alcohol content - Standard drivers	Maximum blood alcohol content - Novice drivers	Maximum blood alcohol content - Professional drivers
Luxembourg	L	0,5 ‰	0,2 ‰	0,2 ‰
Malta	M	0,8 ‰	0,8 ‰	0,8 ‰
Netherlands	NL	0,5 ‰	0,2 ‰ Less than 5 years' driving experience	0,5 ‰
Norway	N	0,2 ‰	0,2 ‰	0,2 ‰
Poland	PL	< 0,2 ‰	< 0,2 ‰	< 0,2 ‰
Portugal	P	0,5 ‰	0,5 ‰	0,5 ‰
Romania	RO	0,0 ‰	0,0 ‰	0,0 ‰
Slovakia	SK	0,0 ‰	0,0 ‰	0,0 ‰
Slovenia	SLO	0,5 ‰ 0,24 mg/l breath	0,0 ‰	0,0 ‰
Spain	E	0.5 ‰	0.3 ‰	0.3 ‰ Drivers are given two tests with (minimum) 10 minutes between.
Sweden	S	0,2 ‰	0,2 ‰	0,2 ‰
Switzerland	CH	0,5 ‰	0,5 ‰	0,1 ‰ trucks, buses, transport of dangerous goods
United Kingdom	GB	0,8 ‰ 0,5 ‰ in Scotland	0,8 ‰ 0,5 ‰ in Scotland	0,8 ‰ 0,5 ‰ in Scotland

HGV DAILY WALKAROUND CHECKS

Carry out HGV daily walkaround checks ✓

You're **responsible** for making sure your vehicle is safe to drive. Carry out a walkaround check of the vehicle before your journey to make sure it's safe. Report any defects in writing to the person in charge of sorting out vehicle defects in your organisation.

The police and Driver and Vehicle Standards Agency (DVSA) officers can **stop you** to do checks on your vehicles.

⚠️ You can be stopped from driving until you fix any problems they find, or they can issue you with a fine.

Read guidance about how to make walkaround checks part of your processes for keeping your vehicles safe to drive.

Watch a video showing what checks to do ✓

This short video shows some of the checks that you should do. Read the full list in this guide for more details.

Scan Me

Topside checks, Diesel emissions check, Under vehicle checks, Headlamp aim, Brake testing.

The film does not show the inspection of every item in detail and must not be interpreted as demonstrating a complete and exhaustive inspection.

Check INSIDE the vehicle

1. Mirrors and glass

Check that the windscreen is not:

- **cracked**
- **scratched**
- **discoloured**

Check that the windscreen and front side windows are not excessively tinted.

Check that all mirrors are in place and not:

- **damaged or missing glass**
- **obscured**
- **insecure**

If a camera system is used instead of a mirror, check that it works and the view is correct.

2. Windscreen wipers and washers

Make sure the windscreen wipers work. Check that they are not:

- **missing**
- **damaged or worn**

Make sure the windscreen washer is working.

3. Front view

Check that no objects get in the way of your front view.

As a general rule, there should be nothing in the swept area of the windscreen wipers.

Some official stickers and road safety items are allowed, as long as they do not seriously block your view of the road, for example, operator licence disc.

Check inside the vehicle ✓

4. Dashboard warning lights and gauges

Check that all of these are working correctly:

- instruments
- gauges
- warning lights - including the engine warning, emissions system, anti-lock braking system (ABS), and electronic braking system (EBS)

5. Steering

Check that the steering wheel:

- **moves properly and that the power-assisted steering works correctly**
- **has no excessive play**
- **does not jam**

Check that there's no excessive lift or movement in the steering column.

6. Horn

Check that the horn works and is easily accessible from the driver's seat.

7. Brakes and air build-up

Check that:

- the air builds up correctly and the warning system works
- there are no air leaks
- the footwell is clear
- the service brake operates both the tractor and trailer brakes
- the parking brake for the tractor works
- the service brake pedal does not have excessive side play or missing loose or incomplete anti-slip tread

Check inside the vehicle ☑

8. Height marker

Check the correct vehicle height is displayed on the vehicle height marker in the cab.

Remember, the height can change, for example, when the fifth wheel is adjusted, or if the trailer is loaded, unloaded or reloaded.

9. Seatbelts

Check those seatbelts:

- **do not have any cuts, damage, or fraying that may stop them from working**
- **stay secure when you plug them in**
- **retract against you when fitted, and fully retract when you take them off**

Check OUTSIDE the vehicle ☑

10. Lights and indicators

Check that:

- **all lights and indicators work correctly**
- **all lenses are fitted, clean, and in the right colour**
- **stop lamps come on when you apply the service brake and go out when you release it**
- **marker lights are fitted and work**

11. Fuel and oil leaks

Check that the fuel filler cap is fitted correctly.

Turn on the engine and check underneath the vehicle for any fuel or oil leaks.

Check OUTSIDE the vehicle ✓

12. Battery security and conditions

Check that your battery is:

- secure
- in good condition
- not leaking

13. Diesel exhaust fluid (AdBlue)

Check that your diesel vehicle has enough AdBlue diesel exhaust fluid and top up if necessary.

14. Excessive engine exhaust smoke

Check that the exhaust does not emit an excessive amount of smoke.

15. Security of body and wings

Check that:

- all fastening devices work
- cab doors and trailer doors are secure when closed
- body panels on tractor or trailer are secure and not likely to fall off
- landing legs (if fitted) are secure and not likely to fall off while driving
- side guards and rear under-run guards are fitted if required and that they're not insecure or damaged

15. Security of body and wings

If spray suppression flaps are required, check that they are:

- fitted
- secure
- not damaged
- not clogged with mud or debris

Check OUTSIDE the vehicle ✓

12. Battery security and conditions

Check that your battery is:

- secure
- in good condition
- not leaking

13. Diesel exhaust fluid (AdBlue)

Check that your diesel vehicle has enough AdBlue diesel exhaust fluid and top up if necessary.

14. Excessive engine exhaust smoke

Check that the exhaust does not emit an excessive amount of smoke.

15. Security of body and wings

Check that:

- all fastening devices work
- cab doors and trailer doors are secure when closed
- body panels on tractor or trailer are secure and not likely to fall off
- landing legs (if fitted) are secure and not likely to fall off while driving
- side guards and rear under-run guards are fitted if required and that they're not insecure or damaged

16. Spray suppression

If spray suppression flaps are required, check that they are:

- fitted
- secure
- not damaged
- not clogged with mud or debris

Check OUTSIDE the vehicle

17. Tyres and wheel fixing

Check that:

- the tyres and wheels are secure
- the tyres have a tread depth of at least 1mm
- the tyres are inflated correctly
- there are no deep cuts in the tyre's sidewall
- there is no cord visible anywhere on the tyre
- all-wheel nuts are tight enough - you can check if wheel nut indicators (if fitted) have moved to do this
- there are no objects or debris trapped between the twin wheels

18. Brake lines and trailer parking brake

Check that:

- couplings are free from debris and are in the right place
- there are no leaks
- there is no damage or wear to the brake lines
- the parking brake for the trailer works

After the initial brake test, leave the engine running so pressure can build up. This will make it easier to hear any leaks as you carry out the rest of the walkaround check.

19. Electrical connections

Check each connection and make sure that all:

- visible wiring is insulated
- visible wiring is not likely to get caught or damaged
- all electrical trailer couplings are connected securely
- all electrical switches work correctly

Check OUTSIDE the vehicle ✓

20. Coupling security

Check that your vehicle is securely attached to your trailer and that the:

- trailer is located correctly in the fifth wheel or coupling
- secondary locking devices are in the correct position

21. Security of load

Check that the load does not move and is not likely to move.

Make sure you use the right type of load securing system for the load.

- **get a competent person to assess it**
- **reload or resecure it if necessary**

22. Number plate

Check that the number plate is not:

- broken or incomplete
- incorrect or spaced incorrectly
- dirty
- faded
- covered over by anything

23. Reflectors

Check that the reflectors (including side reflectors) are not:

- missing
- broken
- insecure
- fitted incorrectly
- the wrong colour
- obscured by dirt or other objects

Check OUTSIDE the vehicle

24. Markings and warning plates

Check that the vehicle's markings (including conspicuity markings) are:

- the right colour
- visible
- securely fastened
- not obscured by dirt or other objects

Record and REPORT the result of your check

Record and report all defects that you:

- find during the daily walkaround check
- become aware of during your journe

Record:

- the vehicle registration (number plate) or identification mark
- the date
- details of the defects or symptoms
- your assessment of the defects (for example, 'dangerous')
- your name
- whom it was reported to

Use a form that includes a list of the items checked each day. Record 'nil' defects if you do not find any.

> DVSA can ask for a record of your walkaround check at a roadside check.

If you become aware of defects during your journey

Find a safe place to stop to assess and report any defects you become aware of during your journey.

> ⓘ You can get an unlimited fine and a prison sentence for using an HGV in a dangerous condition.

HGV walkaround check defect report form on LAST PAGE the book

HEALTHY EATING TIPS TRUCK DRIVERS

Healthy Eating Tips Truck Drivers

Maintaining a healthy lifestyle can be hard for truck drivers with long hours, lack of exercise, and eating meals away from home. However, you can eat a healthy diet and be more active. It takes planning. Making healthy choices may mean better quality of life. Here are a few tips:

- **Consider Buying a Power Inverter.** This would allow you to use a small microwave, a mini-refrigerator, or an electric cooler. You could make some of your own meals and healthier snacks. With the money saved from eating out 2 - 3 times per day, it would pay for itself quickly.

- **Plan Ahead.** Packing meals and snacks will **help your waistline** and budget. Keep in mind balance, variety, and moderation.

	Fruits	Fresh and canned fruit (packed in its own natural juice or with no added sugar)
	Breads/Grains	Whole grain breads and cereals, whole grain crackers, English muffin, and mini bagels
	Vegetables	Fresh vegetables already washed and cut up in small plastic bags or containers
	Milk/Dairy	Low-fat cheeses such as mozzarella, string cheese, farmer's cheese, low-fat cottage cheese; low-fat yogurt, and small containers of skim or 1% milk
	Meat/Protein	Salmon and tuna packed in water or low-fat meats like roasted chicken, turkey, ham, and lean roast beef

- **Fuel Up Often (and not just your truck).** Start your day with a balanced breakfast. Eating **3 smaller meals** and 2- 3 healthy snacks is a better choice than eating 2-3 large fast-food meals each day.

- **Hydrate, Hydrate, Hydrate.** Keep a supply of water in the truck and drink a glass before each meal. It is a **zero-calorie** drink and will prevent excess snacking. Try a lemon or lime slice to add flavor.

Healthy Eating Tips Truck Drivers

- **Snack Smart.** Eating out of **bags or boxes** can lead to overeating. Pre-filling small plastic bags with snacks is helpful. Instead of potato chips or candy choose:

  1. raw veggies or low sodium vegetable juice
  2. fresh fruit, dried fruit, or fruit canned in its own juice or with no added sugar
  3. 100 calorie® snack packs
  4. low-fat granola bar, or high fiber bar
  5. low-fat or light yogurt (add a high fiber cereal for a creamy but crunchy snack)
  6. whole-grain pretzels
  7. whole-grain crackers with a thin layer of peanut butter or reduced-fat cheese
  8. nuts (be mindful of portion size). A serving of nuts is a small handful (¼ cup or ~250 calories). Some of the healthier nuts are almonds, pistachios, walnuts, and pecans.
  9. hummus with pita crisps

- **Walk Break.** After you gas up or use the facilities, walk around the outside of the parking lot. Even a 15-minute walk will help stretch your legs, burn some calories, and combat fatigue. Doing this twice a day would be an investment in your health. Be sure you are in a safe area and are aware of your surroundings.

- **Shop Around.** If you don't have much room in your truck, you may only be able to bring 2- 3 days worth of food. Take the time to go to a store to restock your cab. It takes time but you are worth it!

Healthy Snacks

- **Apples and peanut butter** – a childhood treat that we know and love. Protein, healthy fats, and sustained energy.
- **Yogurt** – contains vitamin B-12 that helps with mental clarity and depression and probiotics which help gut bacteria to have a stronger immune system.
- **Trail mix** – is made up of dried fruits, granola, and nuts. Others may contain pumpkin and sunflower seeds. All these contain potassium and vitamin C, which are good for heart health.
- **Popcorn** – contains antioxidants called polyphenols that can help your body fight osteoporosis, cancer, and diabetes. However, avoid toppings and opt for the plain or lightly salted options.
- **Tuna Pouch** – high in Omega-3 fatty acids, it will protect your body from coronary diseases while providing a great source of protein.
- **Hard-boiled eggs** – a rich source of protein; a single egg can yield 70 calories of energy and 6 grams of protein.

Top 8 must-have cooking equipment

Cooking food on the road is a great way for truck drivers to eat healthy and save money. However, limited space and electricity are just two of the many roadblocks that drivers encounter when cooking in their cab.
The following are our **top ten picks** for the best cooking equipment for truck drivers:

1. Refrigerator - Keeping things cool

Mini-fridges and electric coolers are great semi-truck appliances for truck drivers. Portable refrigeration is game-changing because it expands drivers' ability to meal prep and eat healthy food while on the road.

Mini-fridges and electric coolers are great semi-truck appliances for truck drivers. Portable refrigeration is game-changing because it expands drivers' ability to meal prep and eat healthy food while on the road.

Scan the code and find the device on Amazon.

2. Dash Mini Waffle Maker - Maximizing space and versatility

The Dash Mini Waffle Maker provides a 4-inch non-stick cooking surface that heats in minutes and allows drivers to cook a variety of quick meals. The Dash Mini Waffle Maker is inexpensive, versatile, and only uses 350 watts.

Scan the code and find the device on Amazon.

Top 10 must-have cooking equipment

3. 12-volt portable stove - Turning up the heat

This little 12-volt portable stove packs a punch and can cook food at up to 300 degrees Fahrenheit. Maybe the most impressive part about this stove is that it generates heat through a 12-volt power port, making it one of the best cooking equipment options for truck drivers.

Scan the code and find the device on Amazon.

4. Crockpot - Cooking low and slow

There's nothing nicer than having a hot, ready-to-eat meal prepared at the end of a long day of driving. A crockpot is a great solution for truck drivers who don't have the time to prepare a freshly cooked meal at lunch or dinner time. Drivers can simply add their ingredients in the crockpot before they start driving and have a ready-to-eat meal by the end of the day.

Crockpots are an ideal appliance for truck drivers because they are affordable, convenient and come in small size options to accommodate limited storage space.

Scan the code and find the device on Amazon.

Top 10 must-have cooking equipment

5. Ninja Foodi pressure cooker - Combining cooking capabilities

Can't decide whether you want a presser cooker or air fryer for your truck? Get the best of both worlds with the Ninja Foodi. This appliance combines the cooking capabilities of a pressure cooker and air fryer and can steam, slow cook, make yogurt, sear, sauté, bake, roast, broil and dehydrate food.

The 5-quart Ninja Foodi uses approximately 1460 watts, has **14 safety features**, and comes with a booklet of delicious **45 recipe ideas**.

Scan the code and find the device on Amazon.

6. Electric skillet - Adding some sizzle

Having an electric skillet broadens drivers' cooking abilities and makes it easy to cook meals that would usually require a stove. Electric skillets are convenient because, unlike an electric stove, the skillet comes with a built-in pan.

Skillets are a great semi-truck appliance because they provide easy temperature control and allow truck drivers to cook a large amount of food evenly. Making on-the-road meal prep a snap.

Scan the code and find the device on Amazon.

Top 10 must-have cooking equipment

7. Personal blender - Maintaining a well-blended diet

Blenders are a great appliance for truck drivers who are looking to eat more fruits and veggies. Drivers can use a blender to make healthy foods and drinks like smoothies, sauces, soups and so much more.

Scan the code and find the device on Amazon.

8. Travel spice rack - Spicing up your recipes

It is easy for truck drivers to fall into a rut when it comes to what they eat on the road. Fast food may be convenient, but after a while, the food all starts to taste the same. Packing a travel sized spice rack can make a major difference.

Drivers can expand their pallets by experimenting with new recipes and flavors. There are a variety of portable spice rack options ranging from stackable styles to spice containers with their own storage cases.

Scan the code and find the device on Amazon.

CALENDAR PLANNER SHIFT LOG

DECEMBER 2021

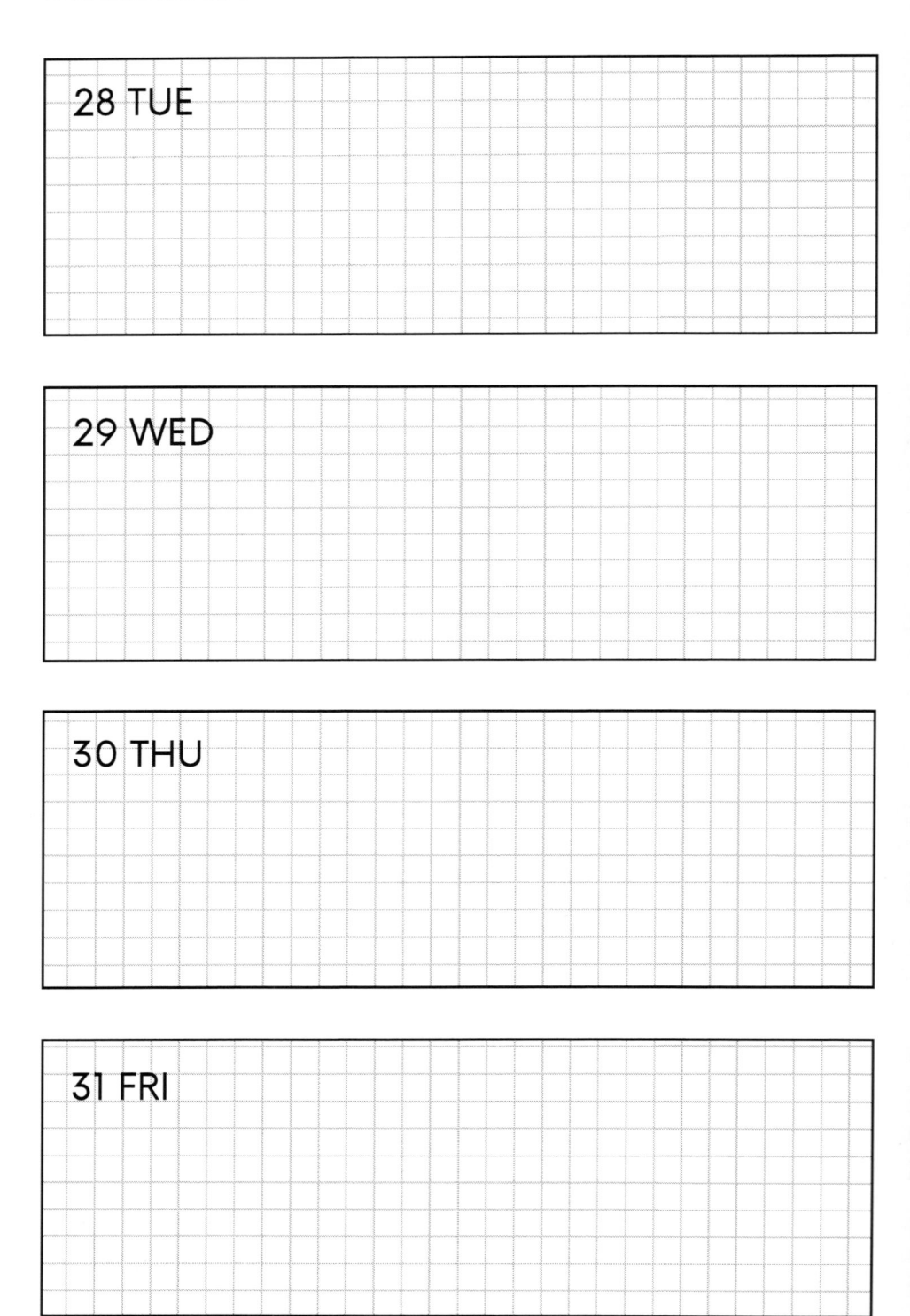

28 TUE

29 WED

30 THU

31 FRI

DATE	START	BREAK	BREAK	FINISH	TOTAL HOURS

- VEHICLE INFORMATION
- START LOCATION
- END LOCATION
- PURPOSE

START	END	BUSINESS MILES	PERSONAL MILES

DATE	START	BREAK	BREAK	FINISH	TOTAL HOURS

- VEHICLE INFORMATION
- START LOCATION
- END LOCATION
- PURPOSE

START	END	BUSINESS MILES	PERSONAL MILES

DATE	START	BREAK	BREAK	FINISH	TOTAL HOURS

- VEHICLE INFORMATION
- START LOCATION
- END LOCATION
- PURPOSE

START	END	BUSINESS MILES	PERSONAL MILES

DATE	START	BREAK	BREAK	FINISH	TOTAL HOURS

- VEHICLE INFORMATION
- START LOCATION
- END LOCATION
- PURPOSE

START	END	BUSINESS MILES	PERSONAL MILES

JANUARY 2022

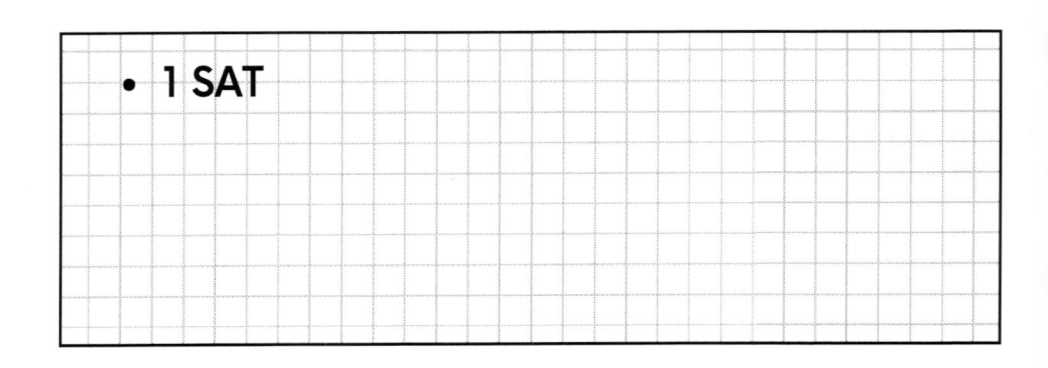

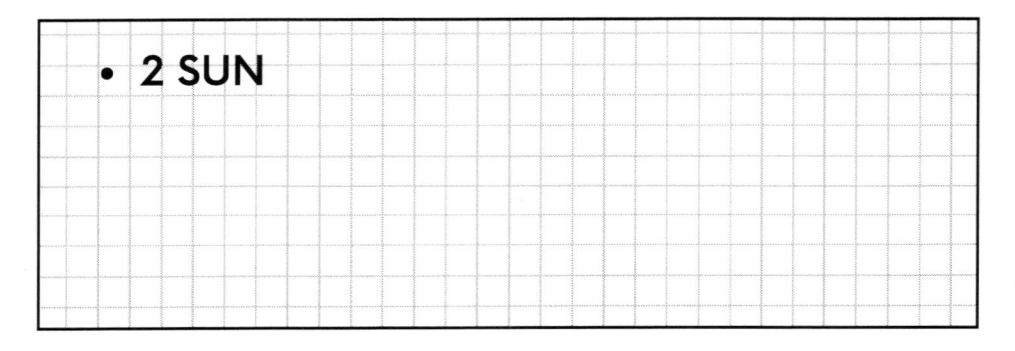

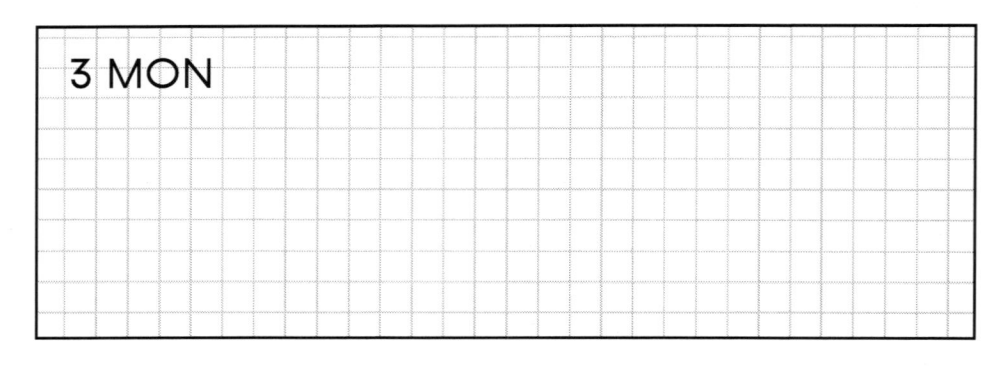

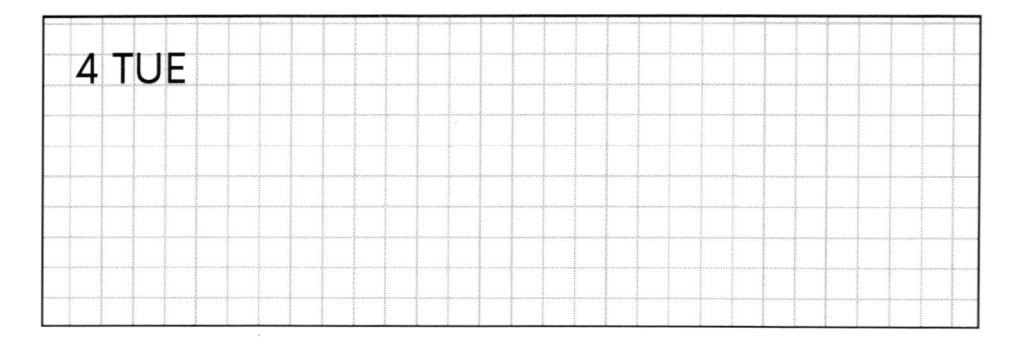

- **1 SAT**

- **2 SUN**

3 MON

4 TUE

DATE	START	BREAK	BREAK	FINISH	TOTAL HOURS

- VEHICLE INFORMATION
- START LOCATION
- END LOCATION
- PURPOSE

START	END	BUSINESS MILES	PERSONAL MILES

DATE	START	BREAK	BREAK	FINISH	TOTAL HOURS

- VEHICLE INFORMATION
- START LOCATION
- END LOCATION
- PURPOSE

START	END	BUSINESS MILES	PERSONAL MILES

DATE	START	BREAK	BREAK	FINISH	TOTAL HOURS

- VEHICLE INFORMATION
- START LOCATION
- END LOCATION
- PURPOSE

START	END	BUSINESS MILES	PERSONAL MILES

DATE	START	BREAK	BREAK	FINISH	TOTAL HOURS

- VEHICLE INFORMATION
- START LOCATION
- END LOCATION
- PURPOSE

START	END	BUSINESS MILES	PERSONAL MILES

JANUARY 2022

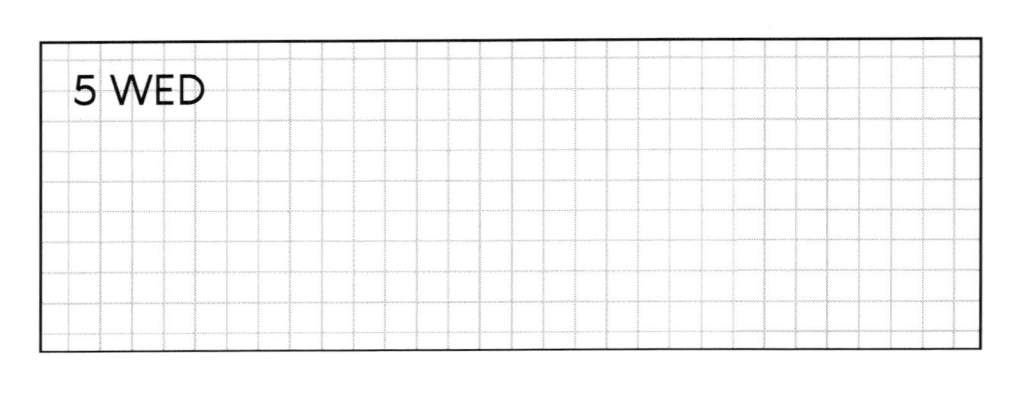

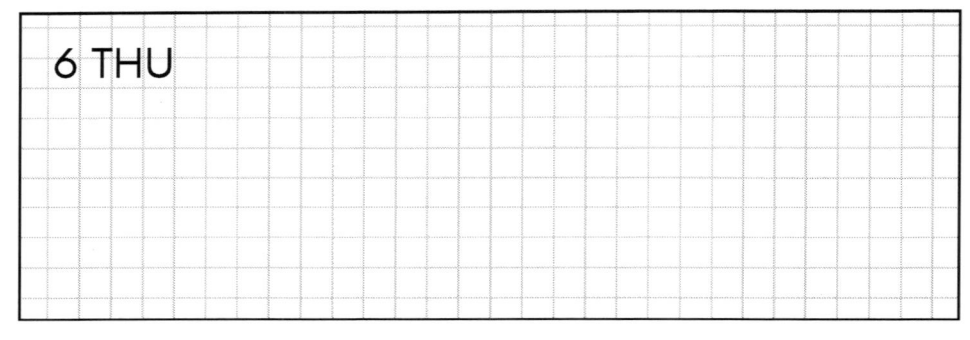

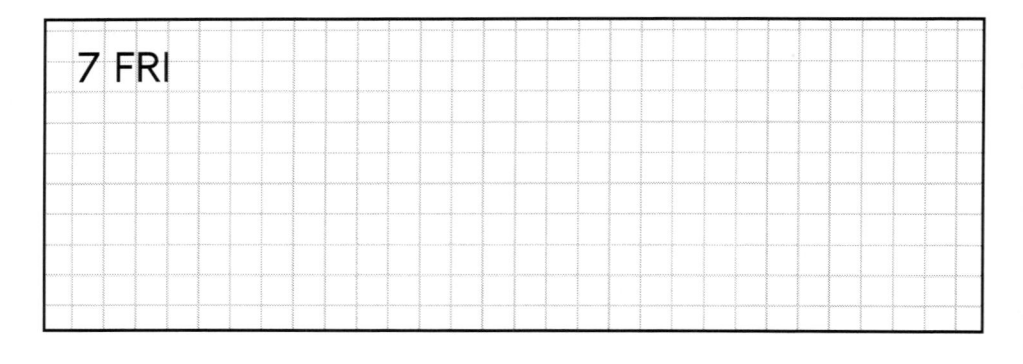

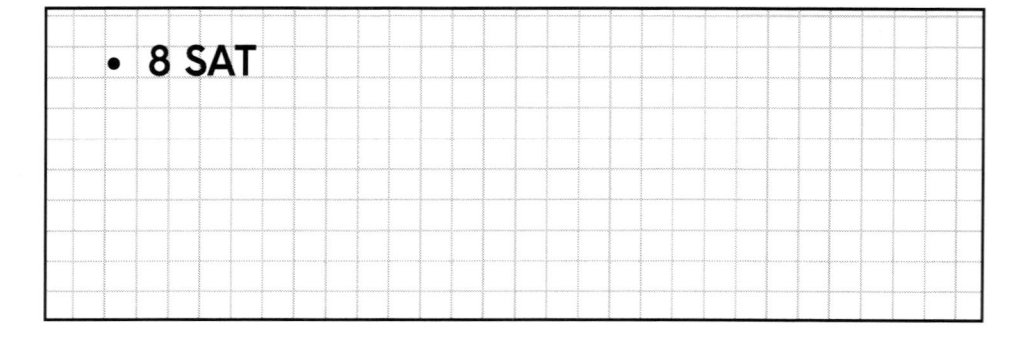

5 WED

6 THU

7 FRI

• 8 SAT

DATE	START	BREAK	BREAK	FINISH	TOTAL HOURS

- VEHICLE INFORMATION
- START LOCATION
- END LOCATION
- PURPOSE

START	END	BUSINESS MILES	PERSONAL MILES

DATE	START	BREAK	BREAK	FINISH	TOTAL HOURS

- VEHICLE INFORMATION
- START LOCATION
- END LOCATION
- PURPOSE

START	END	BUSINESS MILES	PERSONAL MILES

DATE	START	BREAK	BREAK	FINISH	TOTAL HOURS

- VEHICLE INFORMATION
- START LOCATION
- END LOCATION
- PURPOSE

START	END	BUSINESS MILES	PERSONAL MILES

DATE	START	BREAK	BREAK	FINISH	TOTAL HOURS

- VEHICLE INFORMATION
- START LOCATION
- END LOCATION
- PURPOSE

START	END	BUSINESS MILES	PERSONAL MILES

JANUARY 2022

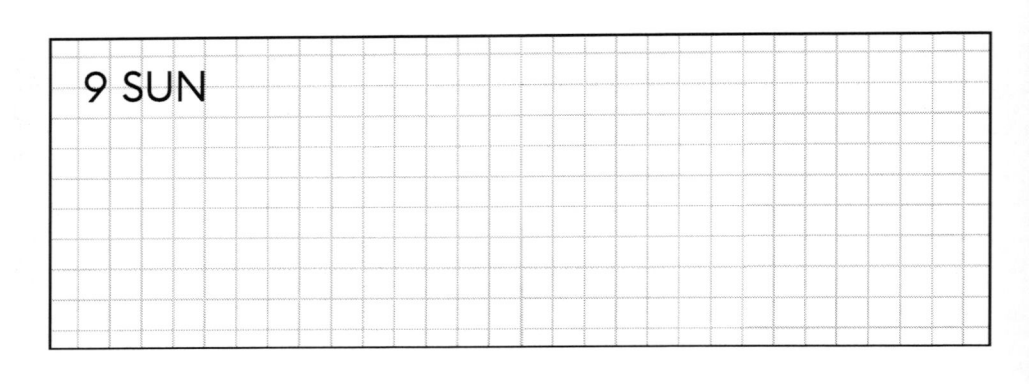

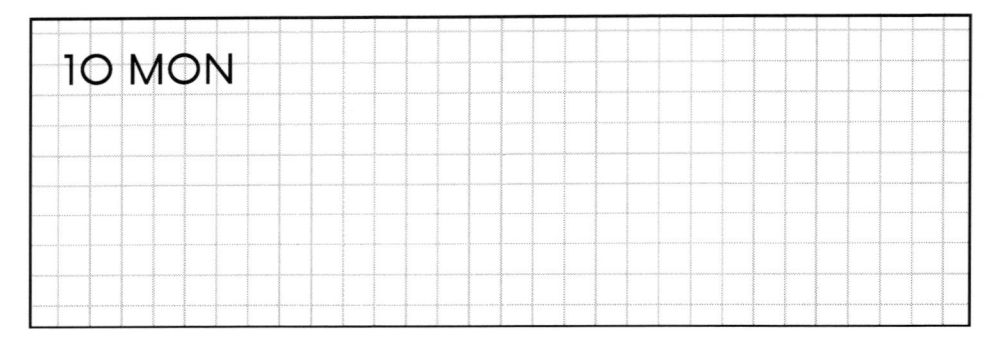

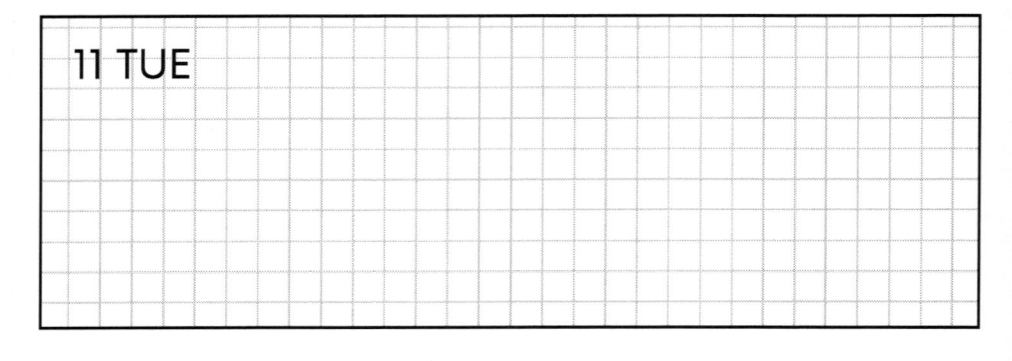

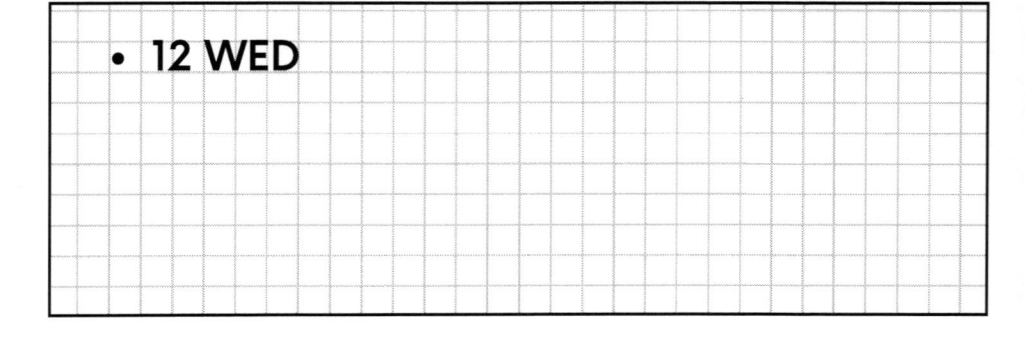

9 SUN

10 MON

11 TUE

- **12 WED**

DATE	START	BREAK	BREAK	FINISH	TOTAL HOURS

- VEHICLE INFORMATION
- START LOCATION
- END LOCATION
- PURPOSE

START	END	BUSINESS MILES	PERSONAL MILES

DATE	START	BREAK	BREAK	FINISH	TOTAL HOURS

- VEHICLE INFORMATION
- START LOCATION
- END LOCATION
- PURPOSE

START	END	BUSINESS MILES	PERSONAL MILES

DATE	START	BREAK	BREAK	FINISH	TOTAL HOURS

- VEHICLE INFORMATION
- START LOCATION
- END LOCATION
- PURPOSE

START	END	BUSINESS MILES	PERSONAL MILES

DATE	START	BREAK	BREAK	FINISH	TOTAL HOURS

- VEHICLE INFORMATION
- START LOCATION
- END LOCATION
- PURPOSE

START	END	BUSINESS MILES	PERSONAL MILES

JANUARY 2022

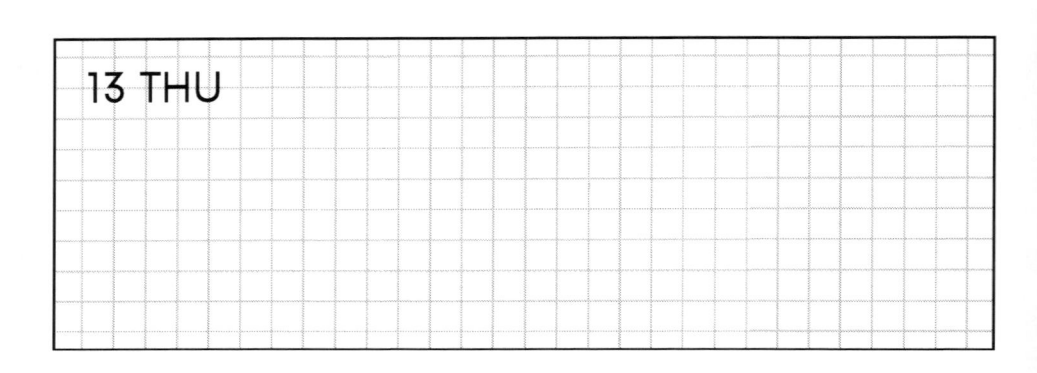

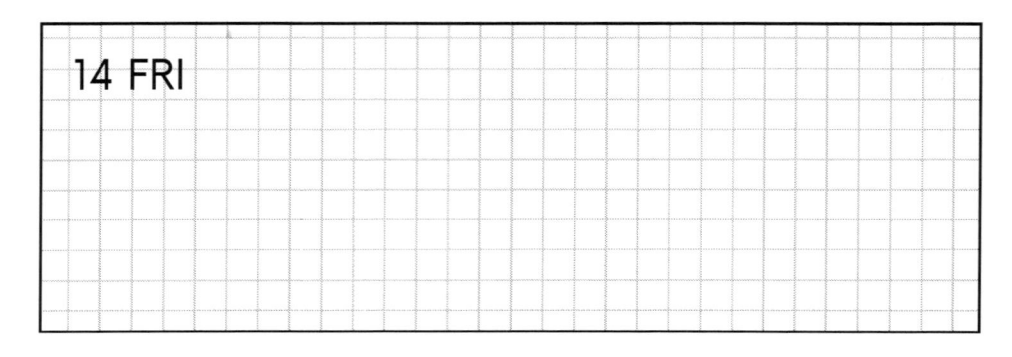

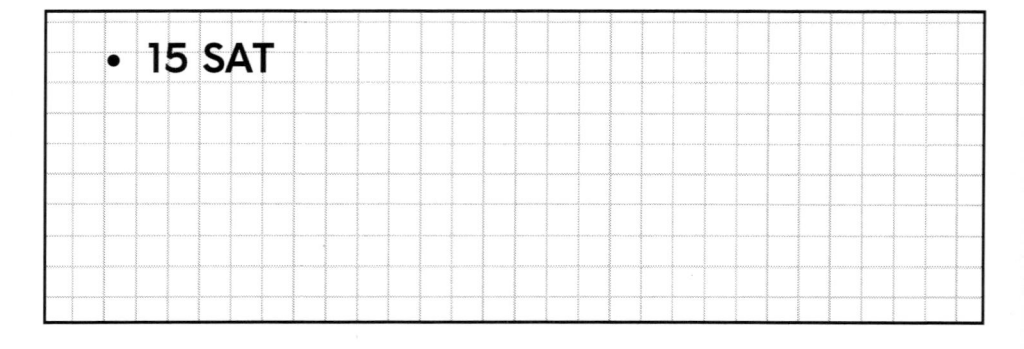

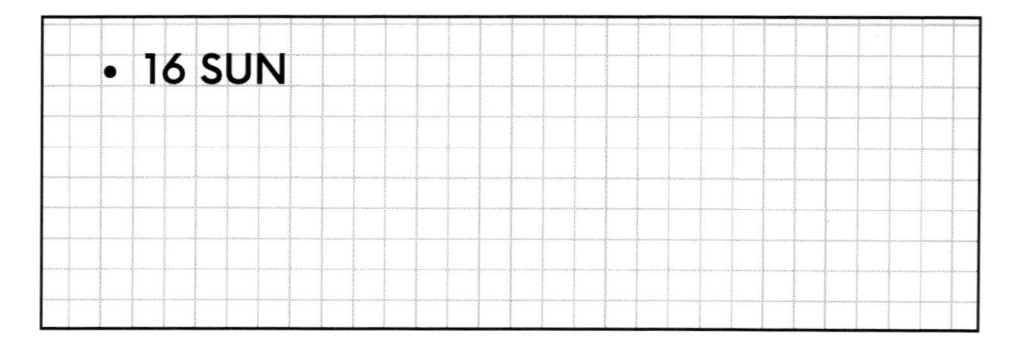

13 THU

14 FRI

- **15 SAT**

- **16 SUN**

DATE	START	BREAK	BREAK	FINISH	TOTAL HOURS

- VEHICLE INFORMATION
- START LOCATION
- END LOCATION
- PURPOSE

START	END	BUSINESS MILES	PERSONAL MILES

DATE	START	BREAK	BREAK	FINISH	TOTAL HOURS

- VEHICLE INFORMATION
- START LOCATION
- END LOCATION
- PURPOSE

START	END	BUSINESS MILES	PERSONAL MILES

DATE	START	BREAK	BREAK	FINISH	TOTAL HOURS

- VEHICLE INFORMATION
- START LOCATION
- END LOCATION
- PURPOSE

START	END	BUSINESS MILES	PERSONAL MILES

DATE	START	BREAK	BREAK	FINISH	TOTAL HOURS

- VEHICLE INFORMATION
- START LOCATION
- END LOCATION
- PURPOSE

START	END	BUSINESS MILES	PERSONAL MILES

JANUARY 2022

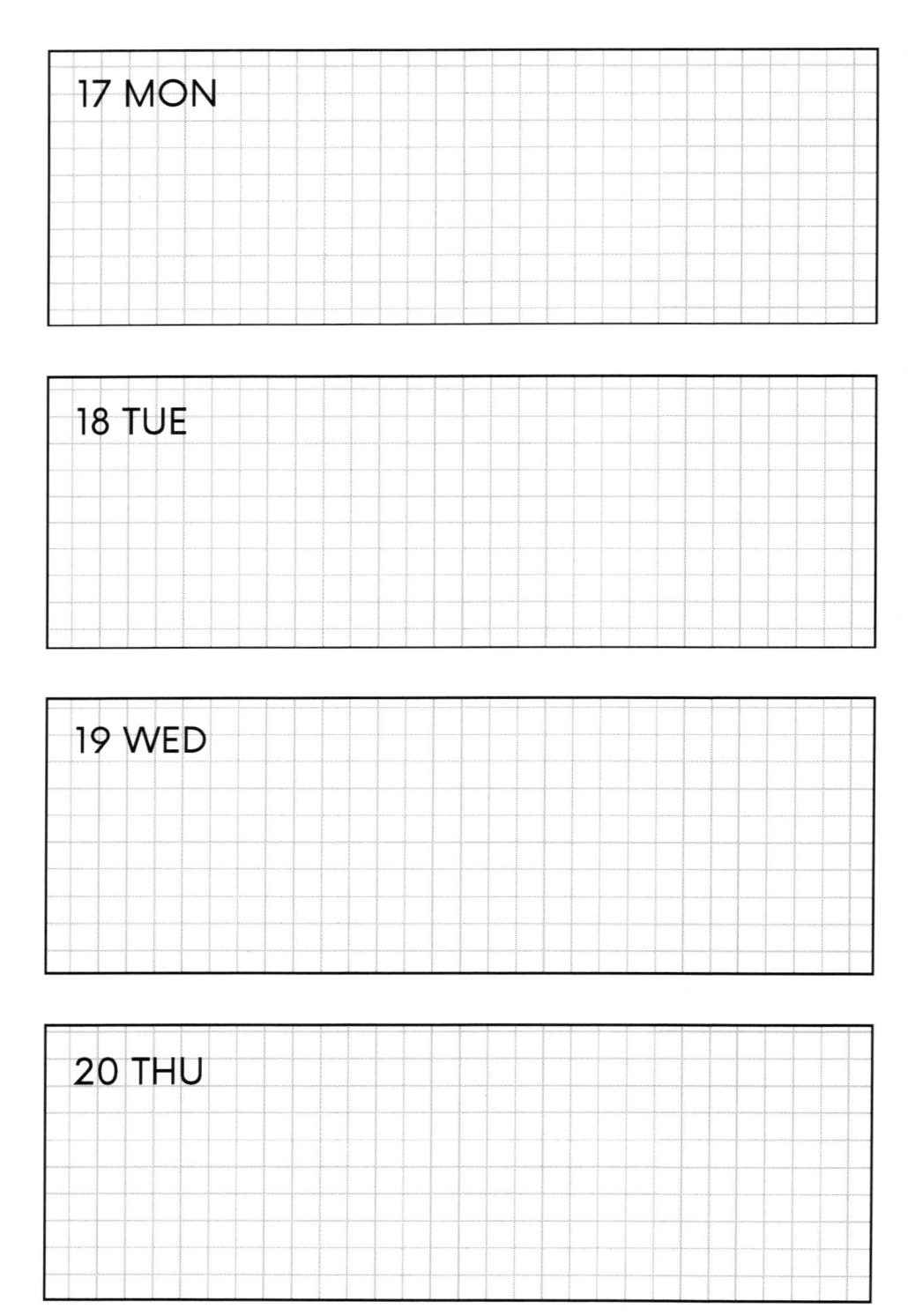

17 MON

18 TUE

19 WED

20 THU

DATE	START	BREAK	BREAK	FINISH	TOTAL HOURS

- VEHICLE INFORMATION
- START LOCATION
- END LOCATION
- PURPOSE

START	END	BUSINESS MILES	PERSONAL MILES

DATE	START	BREAK	BREAK	FINISH	TOTAL HOURS

- VEHICLE INFORMATION
- START LOCATION
- END LOCATION
- PURPOSE

START	END	BUSINESS MILES	PERSONAL MILES

DATE	START	BREAK	BREAK	FINISH	TOTAL HOURS

- VEHICLE INFORMATION
- START LOCATION
- END LOCATION
- PURPOSE

START	END	BUSINESS MILES	PERSONAL MILES

DATE	START	BREAK	BREAK	FINISH	TOTAL HOURS

- VEHICLE INFORMATION
- START LOCATION
- END LOCATION
- PURPOSE

START	END	BUSINESS MILES	PERSONAL MILES

JANUARY   2022

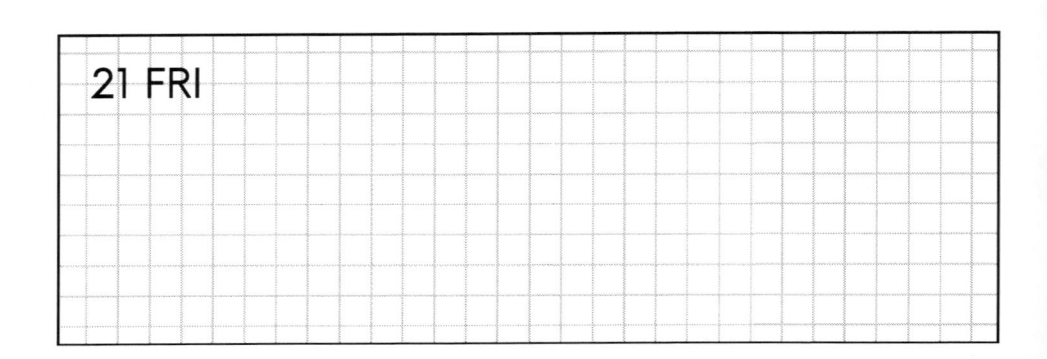

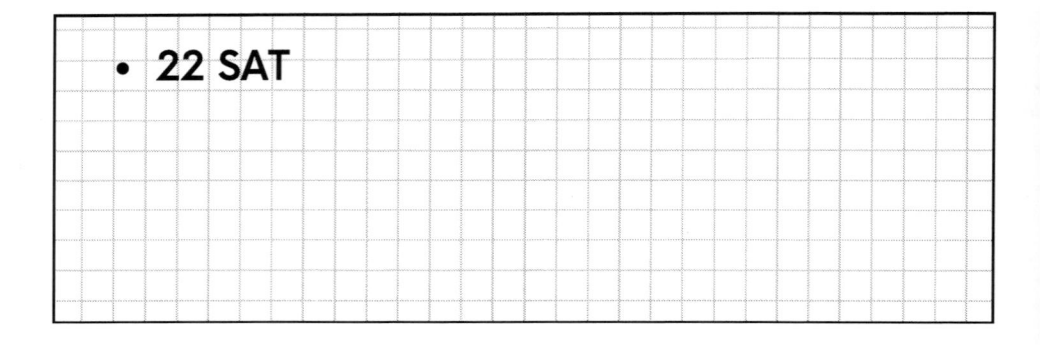

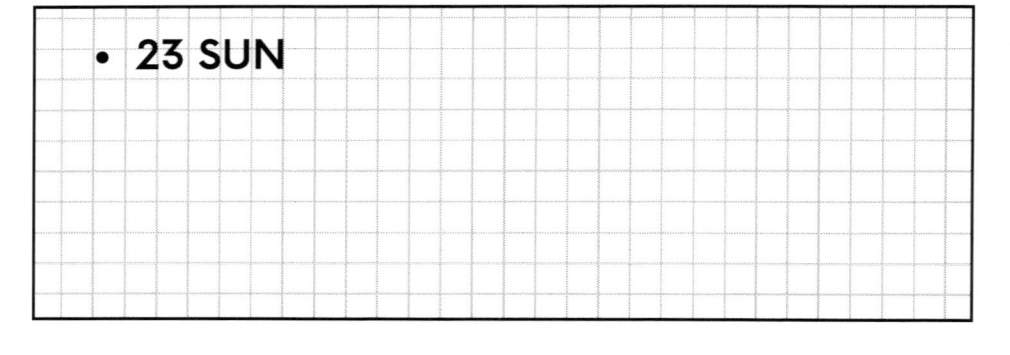

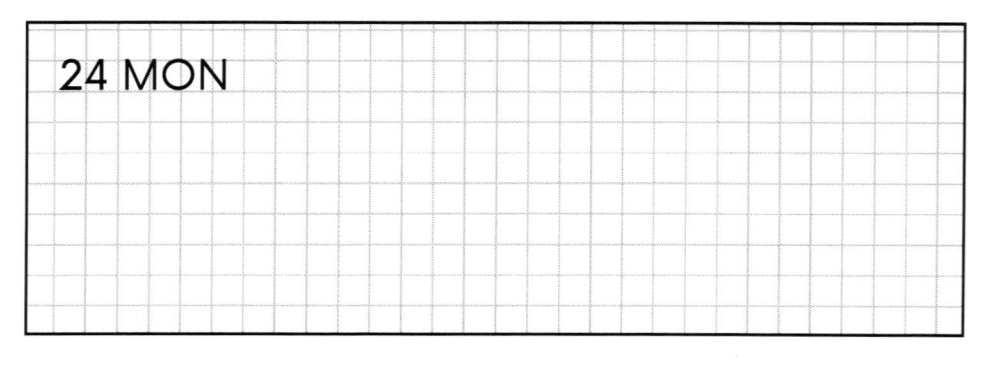

21 FRI

• 22 SAT

• 23 SUN

24 MON

DATE	START	BREAK	BREAK	FINISH	TOTAL HOURS

- VEHICLE INFORMATION
- START LOCATION
- END LOCATION
- PURPOSE

START	END	BUSINESS MILES	PERSONAL MILES

DATE	START	BREAK	BREAK	FINISH	TOTAL HOURS

- VEHICLE INFORMATION
- START LOCATION
- END LOCATION
- PURPOSE

START	END	BUSINESS MILES	PERSONAL MILES

DATE	START	BREAK	BREAK	FINISH	TOTAL HOURS

- VEHICLE INFORMATION
- START LOCATION
- END LOCATION
- PURPOSE

START	END	BUSINESS MILES	PERSONAL MILES

DATE	START	BREAK	BREAK	FINISH	TOTAL HOURS

- VEHICLE INFORMATION
- START LOCATION
- END LOCATION
- PURPOSE

START	END	BUSINESS MILES	PERSONAL MILES

JANUARY 2022

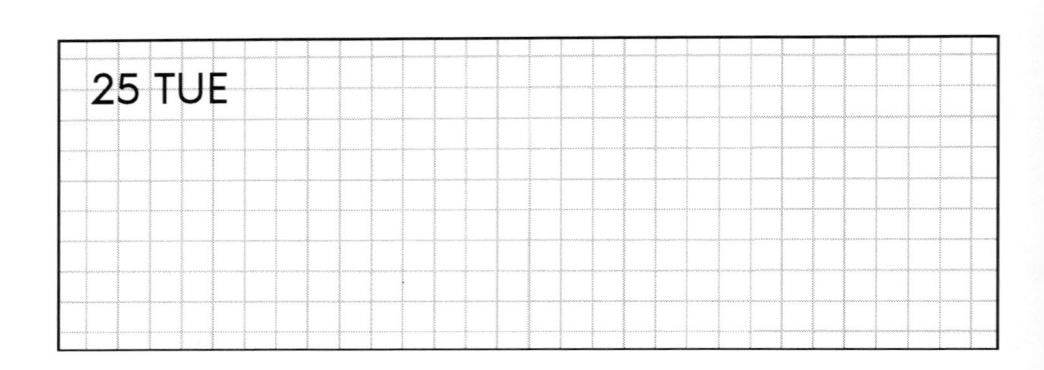

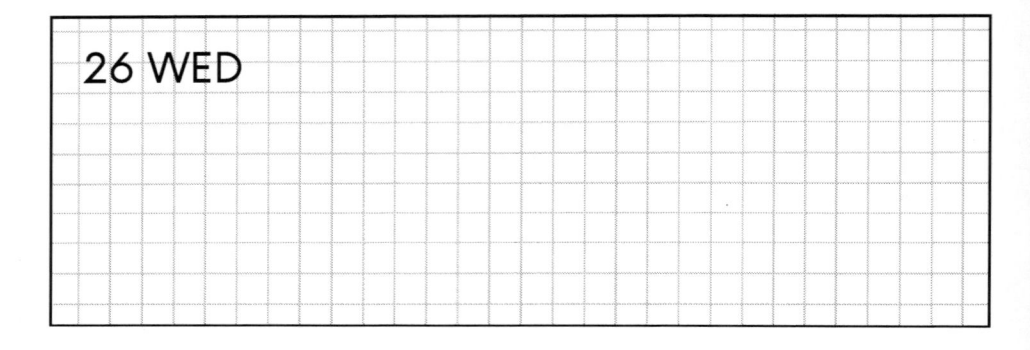

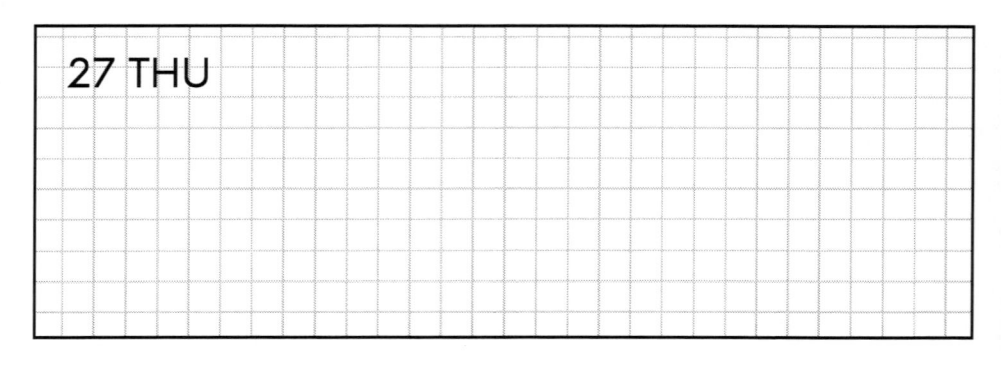

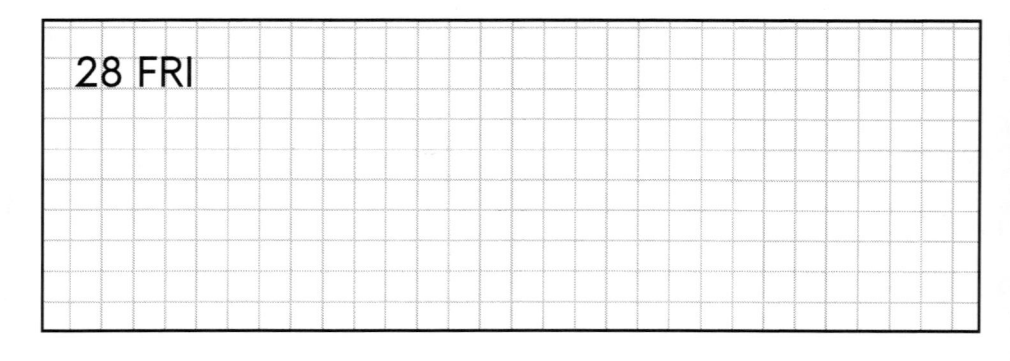

25 TUE

26 WED

27 THU

28 FRI

DATE	START	BREAK	BREAK	FINISH	TOTAL HOURS

- VEHICLE INFORMATION
- START LOCATION
- END LOCATION
- PURPOSE

START	END	BUSINESS MILES	PERSONAL MILES

DATE	START	BREAK	BREAK	FINISH	TOTAL HOURS

- VEHICLE INFORMATION
- START LOCATION
- END LOCATION
- PURPOSE

START	END	BUSINESS MILES	PERSONAL MILES

DATE	START	BREAK	BREAK	FINISH	TOTAL HOURS

- VEHICLE INFORMATION
- START LOCATION
- END LOCATION
- PURPOSE

START	END	BUSINESS MILES	PERSONAL MILES

DATE	START	BREAK	BREAK	FINISH	TOTAL HOURS

- VEHICLE INFORMATION
- START LOCATION
- END LOCATION
- PURPOSE

START	END	BUSINESS MILES	PERSONAL MILES

JANUARY/FEBRUARY 2022

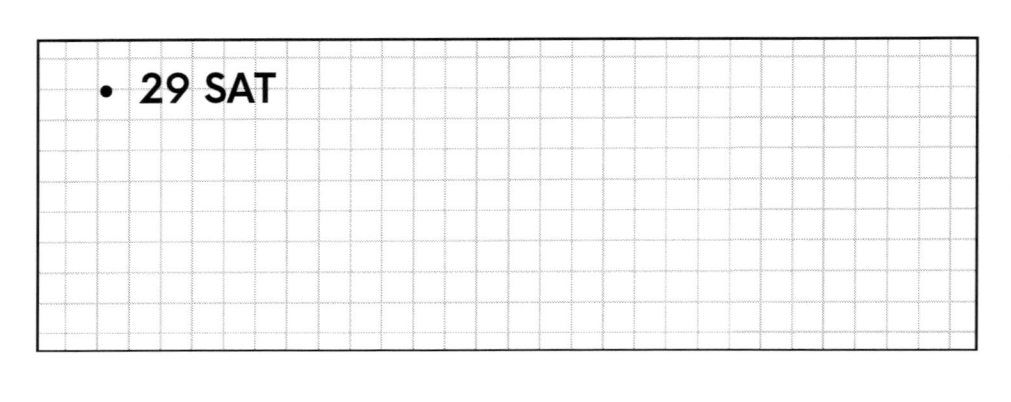

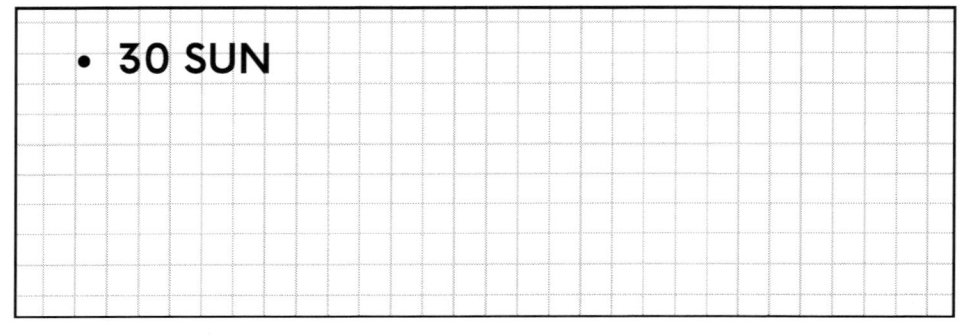

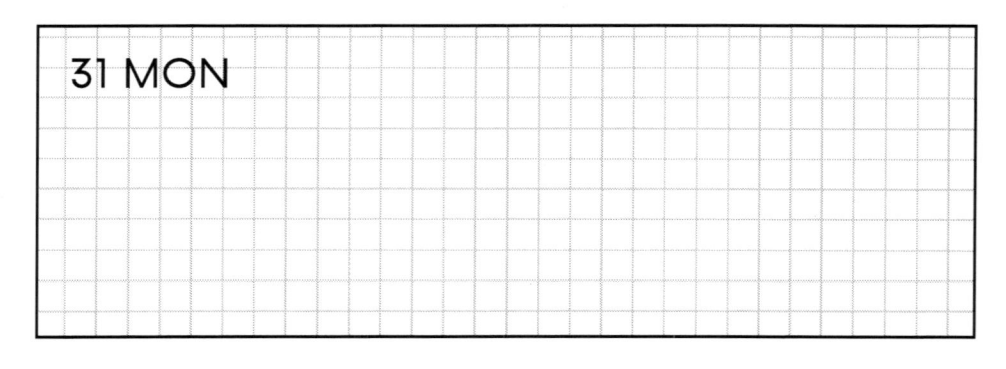

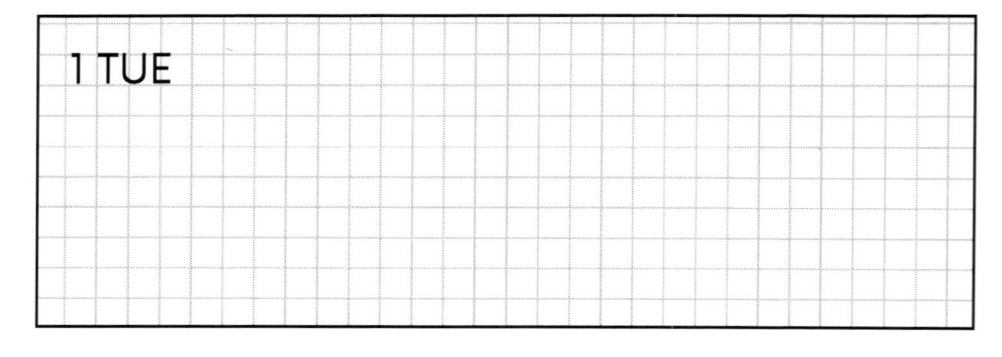

- **29 SAT**

- **30 SUN**

31 MON

1 TUE

DATE	START	BREAK	BREAK	FINISH	TOTAL HOURS

- VEHICLE INFORMATION
- START LOCATION
- END LOCATION
- PURPOSE

START	END	BUSINESS MILES	PERSONAL MILES

DATE	START	BREAK	BREAK	FINISH	TOTAL HOURS

- VEHICLE INFORMATION
- START LOCATION
- END LOCATION
- PURPOSE

START	END	BUSINESS MILES	PERSONAL MILES

DATE	START	BREAK	BREAK	FINISH	TOTAL HOURS

- VEHICLE INFORMATION
- START LOCATION
- END LOCATION
- PURPOSE

START	END	BUSINESS MILES	PERSONAL MILES

DATE	START	BREAK	BREAK	FINISH	TOTAL HOURS

- VEHICLE INFORMATION
- START LOCATION
- END LOCATION
- PURPOSE

START	END	BUSINESS MILES	PERSONAL MILES

FEBRUARY 2022

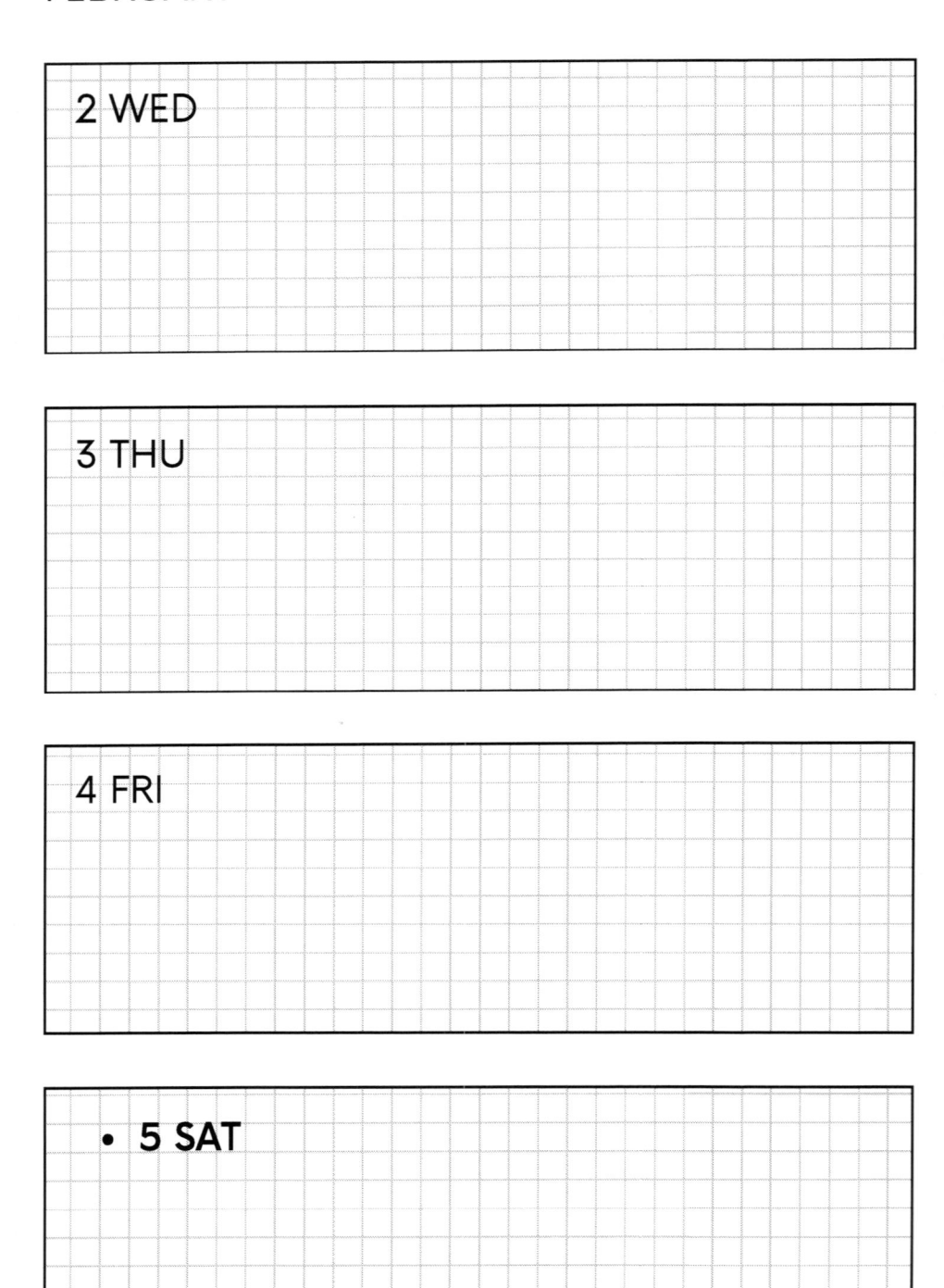

2 WED

3 THU

4 FRI

- **5 SAT**

DATE	START	BREAK	BREAK	FINISH	TOTAL HOURS

- VEHICLE INFORMATION
- START LOCATION
- END LOCATION
- PURPOSE

START	END	BUSINESS MILES	PERSONAL MILES

DATE	START	BREAK	BREAK	FINISH	TOTAL HOURS

- VEHICLE INFORMATION
- START LOCATION
- END LOCATION
- PURPOSE

START	END	BUSINESS MILES	PERSONAL MILES

DATE	START	BREAK	BREAK	FINISH	TOTAL HOURS

- VEHICLE INFORMATION
- START LOCATION
- END LOCATION
- PURPOSE

START	END	BUSINESS MILES	PERSONAL MILES

DATE	START	BREAK	BREAK	FINISH	TOTAL HOURS

- VEHICLE INFORMATION
- START LOCATION
- END LOCATION
- PURPOSE

START	END	BUSINESS MILES	PERSONAL MILES

FEBRUARY   2022

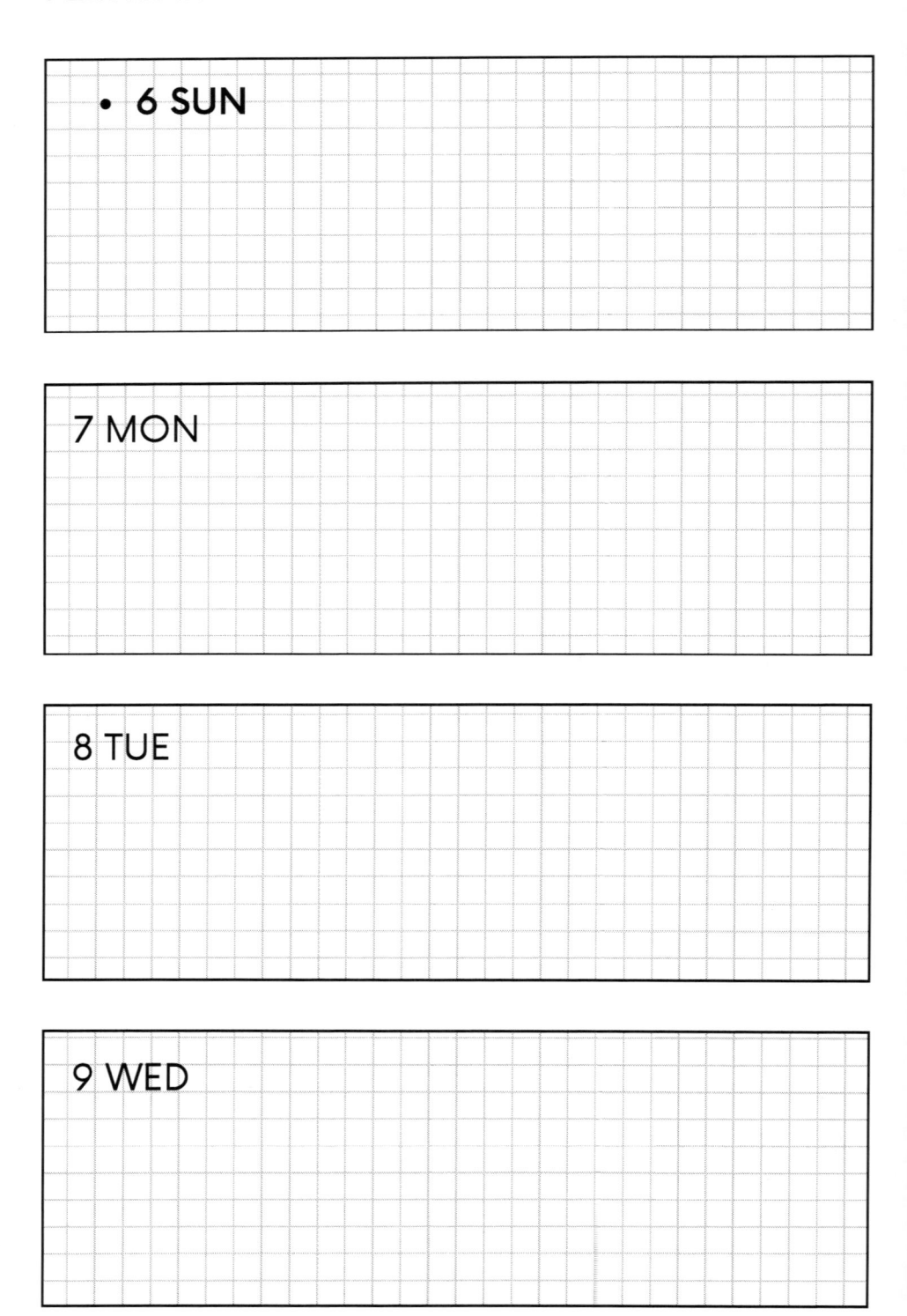

- **6 SUN**

7 MON

8 TUE

9 WED

DATE	START	BREAK	BREAK	FINISH	TOTAL HOURS

- VEHICLE INFORMATION
- START LOCATION
- END LOCATION
- PURPOSE

START	END	BUSINESS MILES	PERSONAL MILES

DATE	START	BREAK	BREAK	FINISH	TOTAL HOURS

- VEHICLE INFORMATION
- START LOCATION
- END LOCATION
- PURPOSE

START	END	BUSINESS MILES	PERSONAL MILES

DATE	START	BREAK	BREAK	FINISH	TOTAL HOURS

- VEHICLE INFORMATION
- START LOCATION
- END LOCATION
- PURPOSE

START	END	BUSINESS MILES	PERSONAL MILES

DATE	START	BREAK	BREAK	FINISH	TOTAL HOURS

- VEHICLE INFORMATION
- START LOCATION
- END LOCATION
- PURPOSE

START	END	BUSINESS MILES	PERSONAL MILES

FEBRUARY 2022

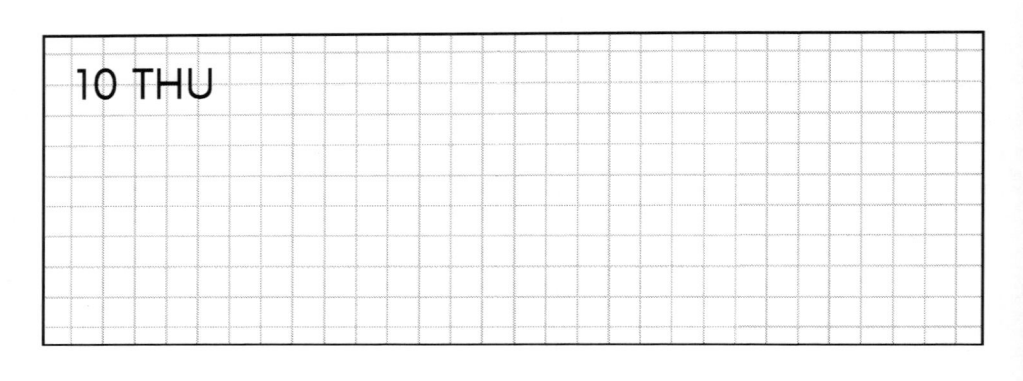

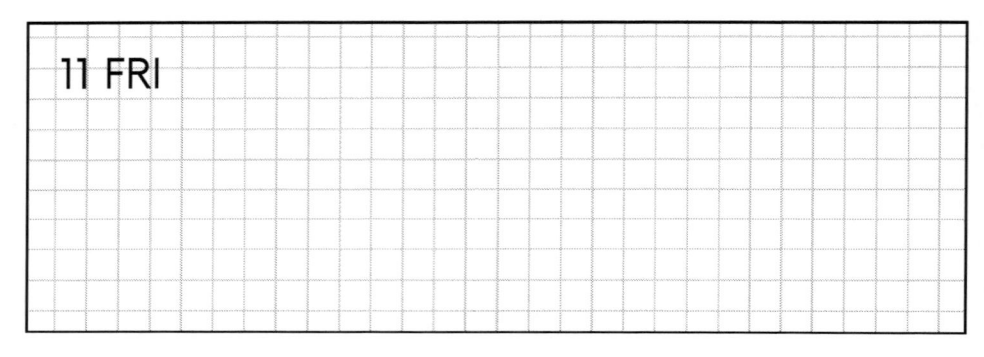

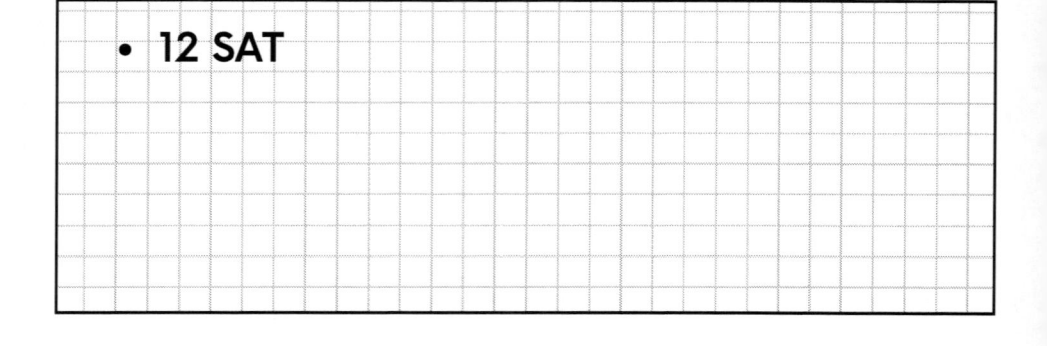

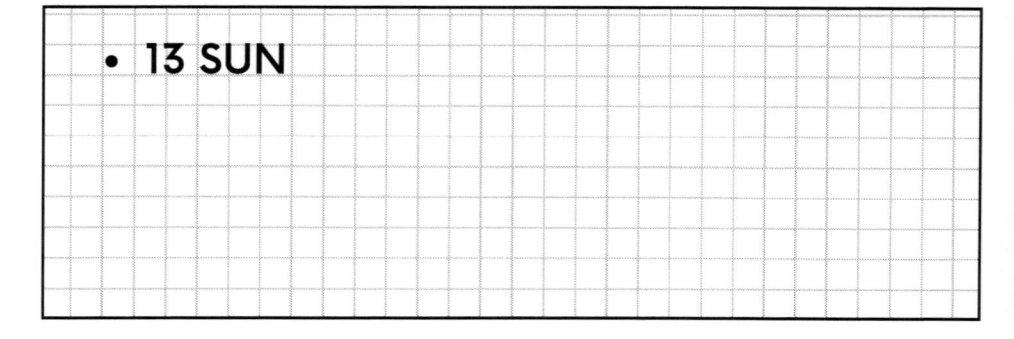

10 THU

11 FRI

- **12 SAT**

- **13 SUN**

DATE	START	BREAK	BREAK	FINISH	TOTAL HOURS

- VEHICLE INFORMATION
- START LOCATION
- END LOCATION
- PURPOSE

START	END	BUSINESS MILES	PERSONAL MILES

DATE	START	BREAK	BREAK	FINISH	TOTAL HOURS

- VEHICLE INFORMATION
- START LOCATION
- END LOCATION
- PURPOSE

START	END	BUSINESS MILES	PERSONAL MILES

DATE	START	BREAK	BREAK	FINISH	TOTAL HOURS

- VEHICLE INFORMATION
- START LOCATION
- END LOCATION
- PURPOSE

START	END	BUSINESS MILES	PERSONAL MILES

DATE	START	BREAK	BREAK	FINISH	TOTAL HOURS

- VEHICLE INFORMATION
- START LOCATION
- END LOCATION
- PURPOSE

START	END	BUSINESS MILES	PERSONAL MILES

FEBRUARY 2022

14 MON

15 TEU

16 WED

17 THU

DATE	START	BREAK	BREAK	FINISH	TOTAL HOURS

- VEHICLE INFORMATION
- START LOCATION
- END LOCATION
- PURPOSE

START	END	BUSINESS MILES	PERSONAL MILES

DATE	START	BREAK	BREAK	FINISH	TOTAL HOURS

- VEHICLE INFORMATION
- START LOCATION
- END LOCATION
- PURPOSE

START	END	BUSINESS MILES	PERSONAL MILES

DATE	START	BREAK	BREAK	FINISH	TOTAL HOURS

- VEHICLE INFORMATION
- START LOCATION
- END LOCATION
- PURPOSE

START	END	BUSINESS MILES	PERSONAL MILES

DATE	START	BREAK	BREAK	FINISH	TOTAL HOURS

- VEHICLE INFORMATION
- START LOCATION
- END LOCATION
- PURPOSE

START	END	BUSINESS MILES	PERSONAL MILES

FEBRUARY 2022

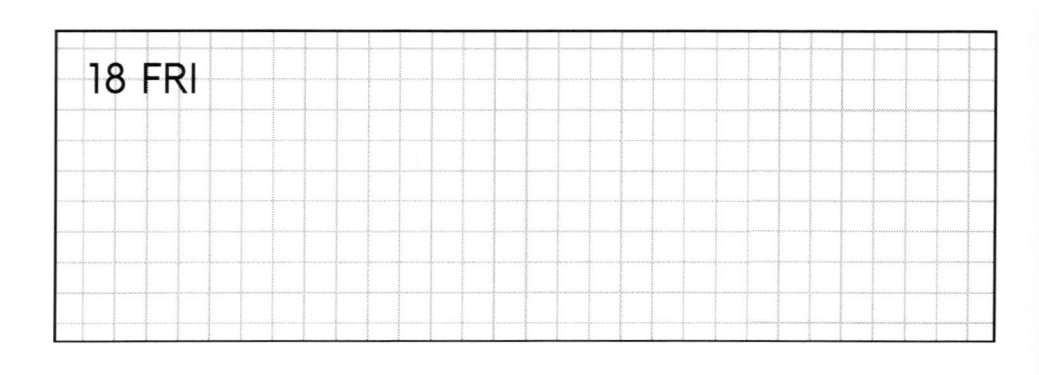

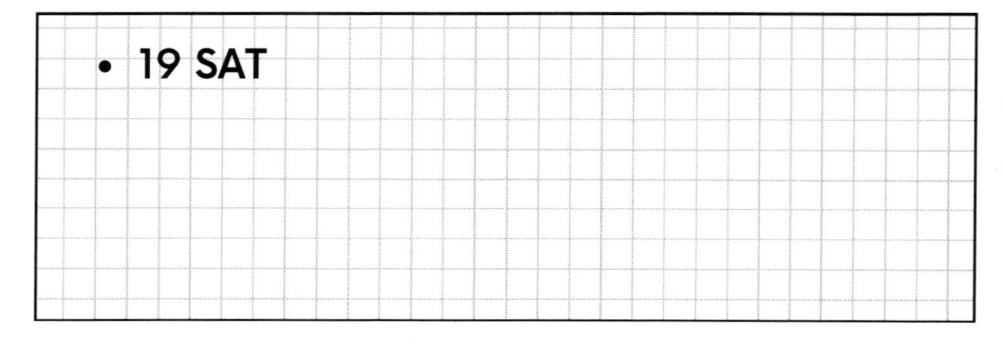

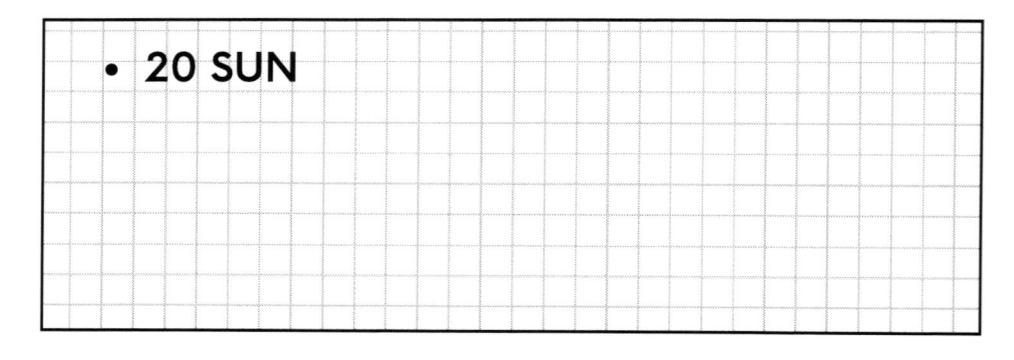

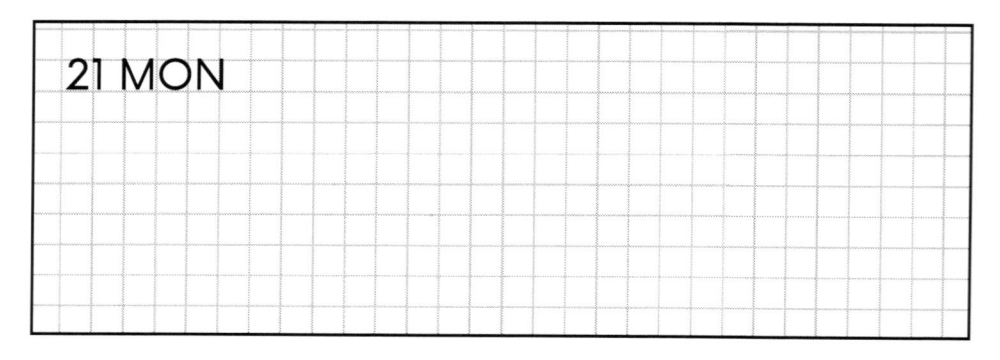

18 FRI

- **19 SAT**

- **20 SUN**

21 MON

DATE	START	BREAK	BREAK	FINISH	TOTAL HOURS

- VEHICLE INFORMATION
- START LOCATION
- END LOCATION
- PURPOSE

START	END	BUSINESS MILES	PERSONAL MILES

DATE	START	BREAK	BREAK	FINISH	TOTAL HOURS

- VEHICLE INFORMATION
- START LOCATION
- END LOCATION
- PURPOSE

START	END	BUSINESS MILES	PERSONAL MILES

DATE	START	BREAK	BREAK	FINISH	TOTAL HOURS

- VEHICLE INFORMATION
- START LOCATION
- END LOCATION
- PURPOSE

START	END	BUSINESS MILES	PERSONAL MILES

DATE	START	BREAK	BREAK	FINISH	TOTAL HOURS

- VEHICLE INFORMATION
- START LOCATION
- END LOCATION
- PURPOSE

START	END	BUSINESS MILES	PERSONAL MILES

FEBRUARY 2022

22 TUE

23 WED

24 THU

25 FRI

DATE	START	BREAK	BREAK	FINISH	TOTAL HOURS

- VEHICLE INFORMATION
- START LOCATION
- END LOCATION
- PURPOSE

START	END	BUSINESS MILES	PERSONAL MILES

DATE	START	BREAK	BREAK	FINISH	TOTAL HOURS

- VEHICLE INFORMATION
- START LOCATION
- END LOCATION
- PURPOSE

START	END	BUSINESS MILES	PERSONAL MILES

DATE	START	BREAK	BREAK	FINISH	TOTAL HOURS

- VEHICLE INFORMATION
- START LOCATION
- END LOCATION
- PURPOSE

START	END	BUSINESS MILES	PERSONAL MILES

DATE	START	BREAK	BREAK	FINISH	TOTAL HOURS

- VEHICLE INFORMATION
- START LOCATION
- END LOCATION
- PURPOSE

START	END	BUSINESS MILES	PERSONAL MILES

FEBRUARY/MARCH 2022

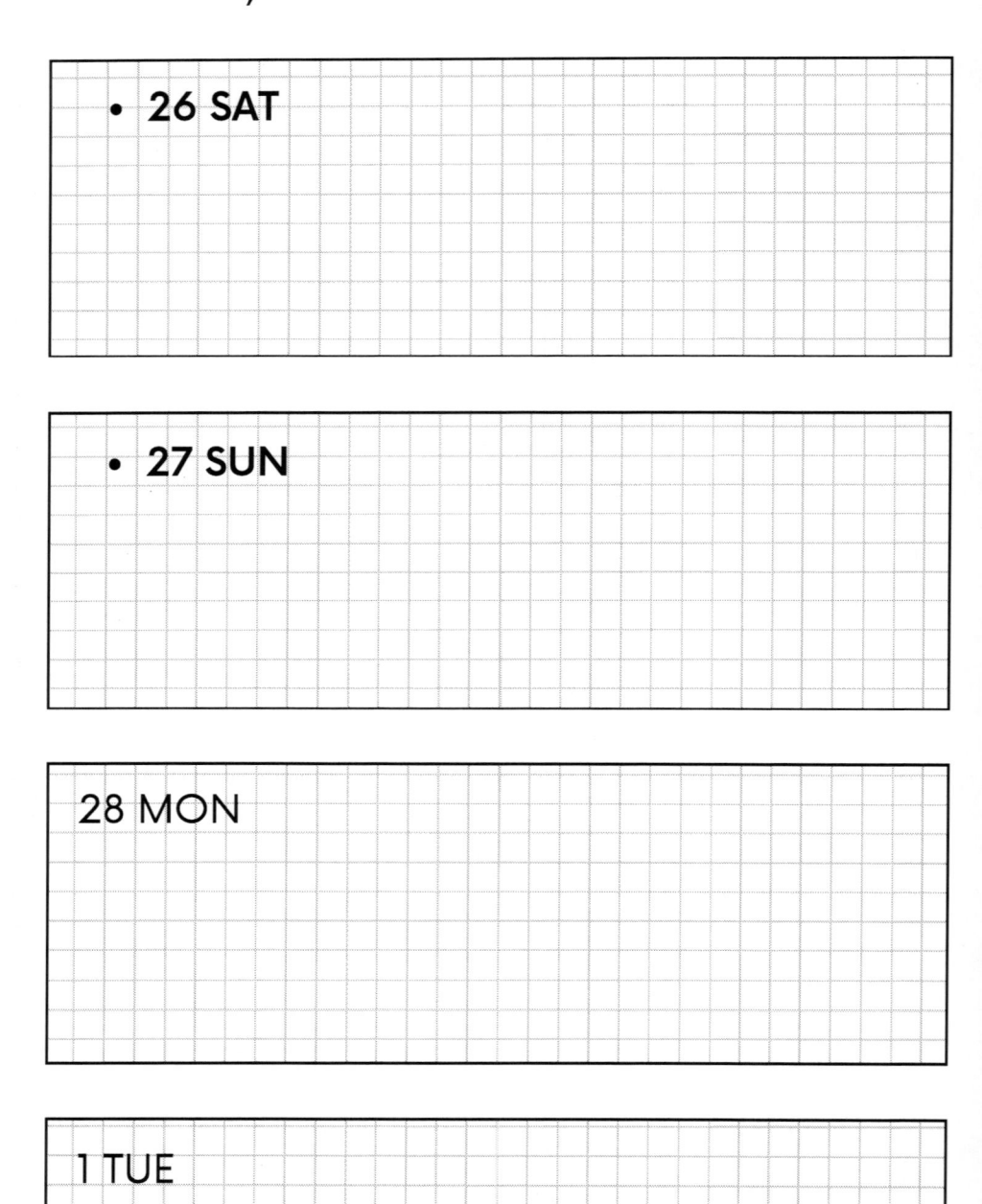

- **26 SAT**

- **27 SUN**

28 MON

1 TUE

DATE	START	BREAK	BREAK	FINISH	TOTAL HOURS

- VEHICLE INFORMATION
- START LOCATION
- END LOCATION
- PURPOSE

START	END	BUSINESS MILES	PERSONAL MILES

DATE	START	BREAK	BREAK	FINISH	TOTAL HOURS

- VEHICLE INFORMATION
- START LOCATION
- END LOCATION
- PURPOSE

START	END	BUSINESS MILES	PERSONAL MILES

DATE	START	BREAK	BREAK	FINISH	TOTAL HOURS

- VEHICLE INFORMATION
- START LOCATION
- END LOCATION
- PURPOSE

START	END	BUSINESS MILES	PERSONAL MILES

DATE	START	BREAK	BREAK	FINISH	TOTAL HOURS

- VEHICLE INFORMATION
- START LOCATION
- END LOCATION
- PURPOSE

START	END	BUSINESS MILES	PERSONAL MILES

MARCH 2022

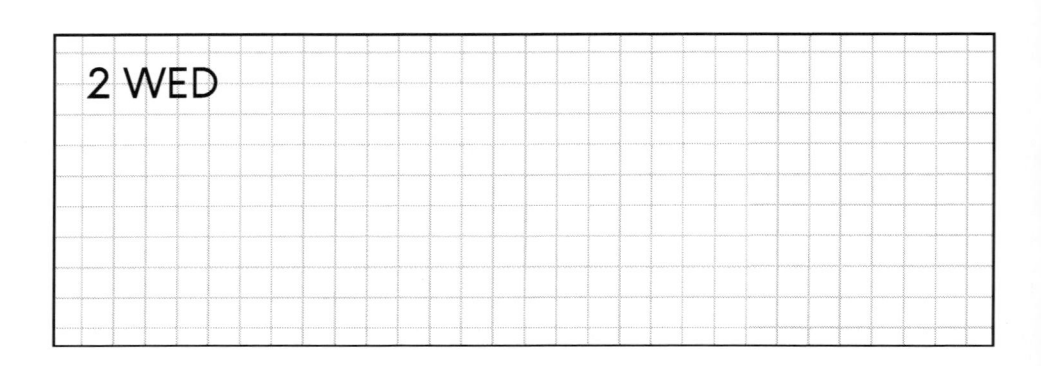

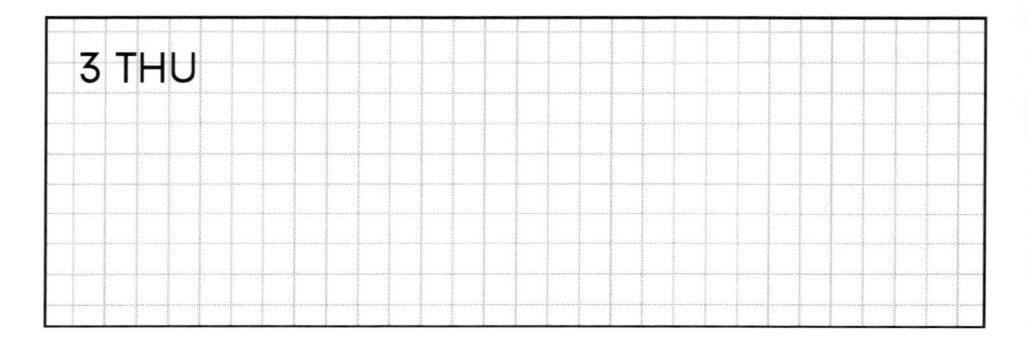

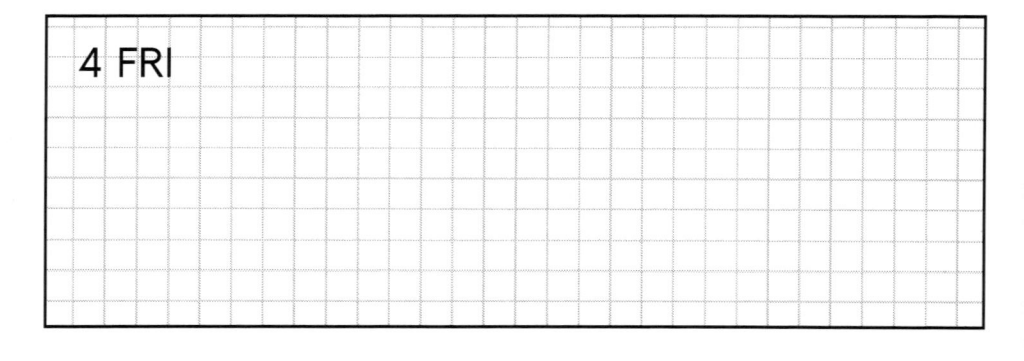

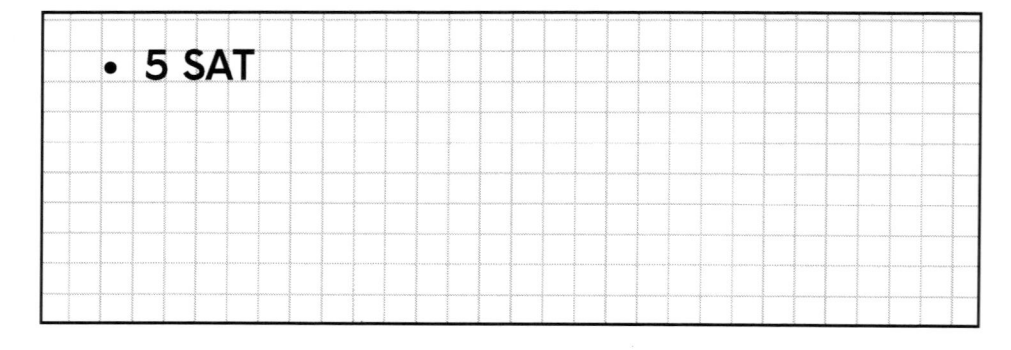

2 WED

3 THU

4 FRI

- **5 SAT**

DATE	START	BREAK	BREAK	FINISH	TOTAL HOURS

- VEHICLE INFORMATION
- START LOCATION
- END LOCATION
- PURPOSE

START	END	BUSINESS MILES	PERSONAL MILES

DATE	START	BREAK	BREAK	FINISH	TOTAL HOURS

- VEHICLE INFORMATION
- START LOCATION
- END LOCATION
- PURPOSE

START	END	BUSINESS MILES	PERSONAL MILES

DATE	START	BREAK	BREAK	FINISH	TOTAL HOURS

- VEHICLE INFORMATION
- START LOCATION
- END LOCATION
- PURPOSE

START	END	BUSINESS MILES	PERSONAL MILES

DATE	START	BREAK	BREAK	FINISH	TOTAL HOURS

- VEHICLE INFORMATION
- START LOCATION
- END LOCATION
- PURPOSE

START	END	BUSINESS MILES	PERSONAL MILES

MARCH 2022

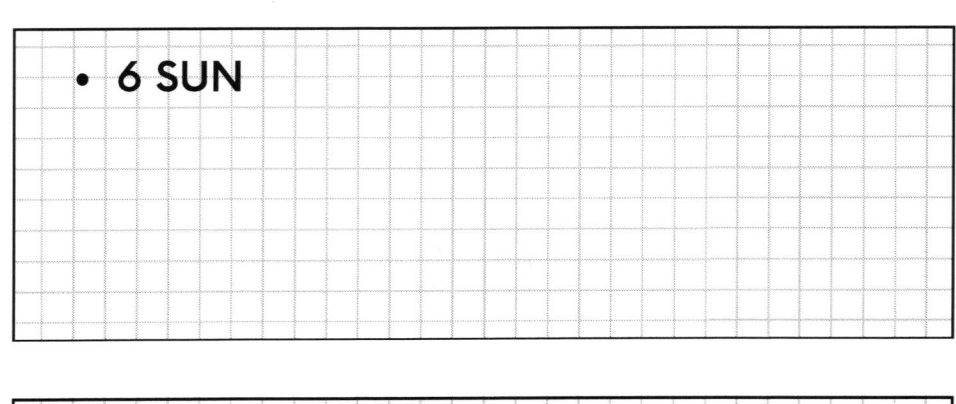

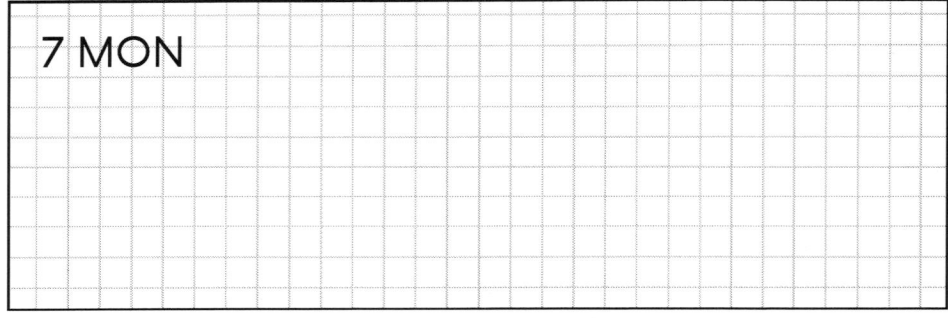

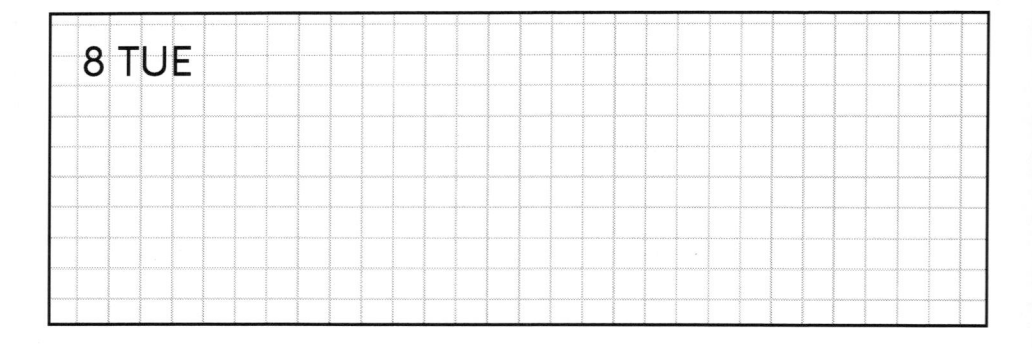

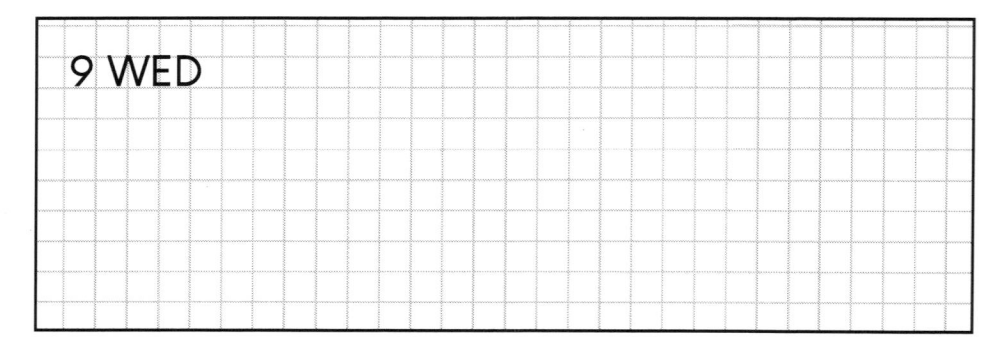

- **6 SUN**

7 MON

8 TUE

9 WED

DATE	START	BREAK	BREAK	FINISH	TOTAL HOURS

- **VEHICLE INFORMATION**
- **START LOCATION**
- **END LOCATION**
- **PURPOSE**

START	END	BUSINESS MILES	PERSONAL MILES

DATE	START	BREAK	BREAK	FINISH	TOTAL HOURS

- **VEHICLE INFORMATION**
- **START LOCATION**
- **END LOCATION**
- **PURPOSE**

START	END	BUSINESS MILES	PERSONAL MILES

DATE	START	BREAK	BREAK	FINISH	TOTAL HOURS

- **VEHICLE INFORMATION**
- **START LOCATION**
- **END LOCATION**
- **PURPOSE**

START	END	BUSINESS MILES	PERSONAL MILES

DATE	START	BREAK	BREAK	FINISH	TOTAL HOURS

- **VEHICLE INFORMATION**
- **START LOCATION**
- **END LOCATION**
- **PURPOSE**

START	END	BUSINESS MILES	PERSONAL MILES

MARCH 2022

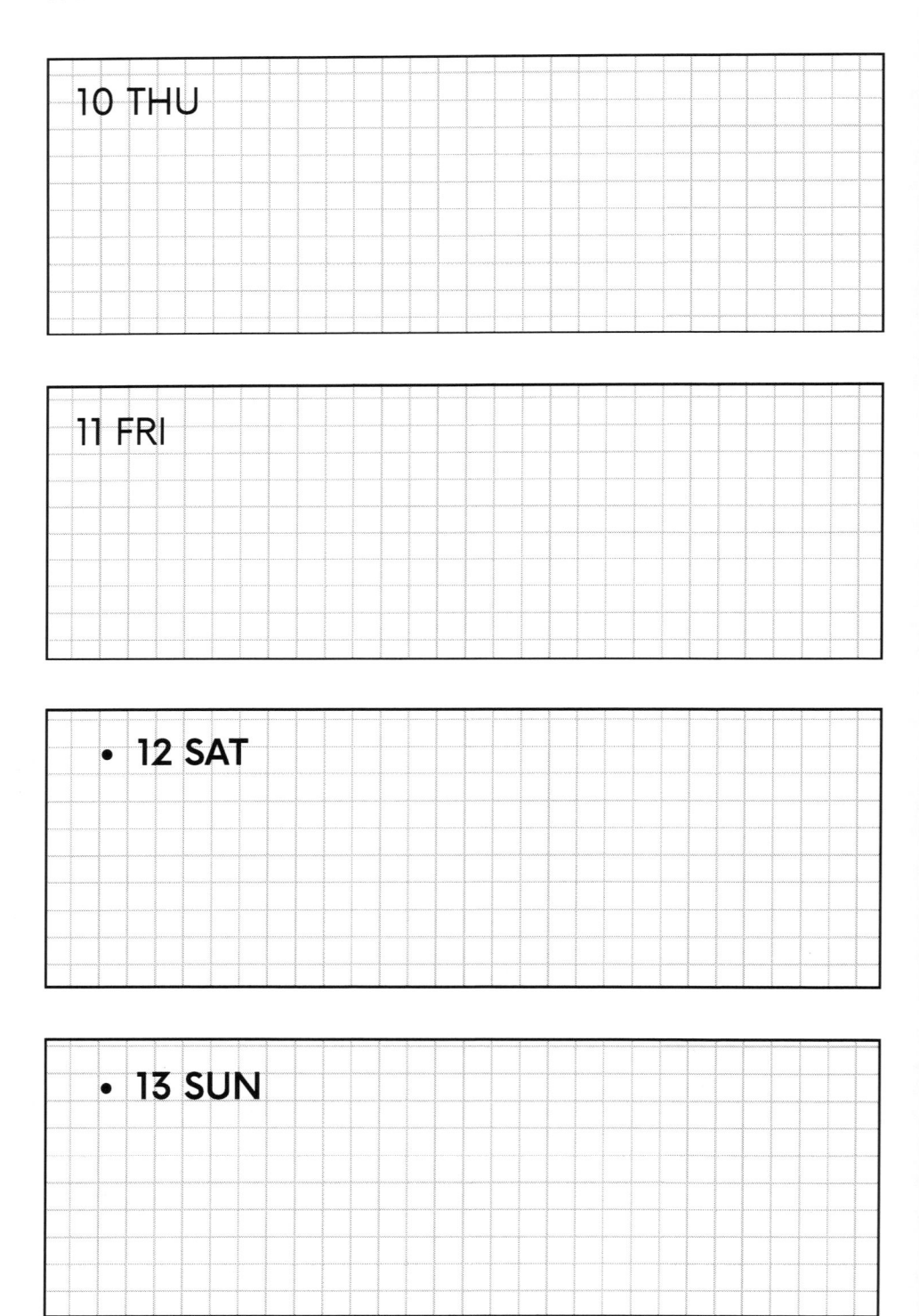

10 THU

11 FRI

- **12 SAT**

- **13 SUN**

DATE	START	BREAK	BREAK	FINISH	TOTAL HOURS

- VEHICLE INFORMATION
- START LOCATION
- END LOCATION
- PURPOSE

START	END	BUSINESS MILES	PERSONAL MILES

DATE	START	BREAK	BREAK	FINISH	TOTAL HOURS

- VEHICLE INFORMATION
- START LOCATION
- END LOCATION
- PURPOSE

START	END	BUSINESS MILES	PERSONAL MILES

DATE	START	BREAK	BREAK	FINISH	TOTAL HOURS

- VEHICLE INFORMATION
- START LOCATION
- END LOCATION
- PURPOSE

START	END	BUSINESS MILES	PERSONAL MILES

DATE	START	BREAK	BREAK	FINISH	TOTAL HOURS

- VEHICLE INFORMATION
- START LOCATION
- END LOCATION
- PURPOSE

START	END	BUSINESS MILES	PERSONAL MILES

MARCH 2022

14 MON

15 TUE

16 WED

17 THU

DATE	START	BREAK	BREAK	FINISH	TOTAL HOURS

- VEHICLE INFORMATION
- START LOCATION
- END LOCATION
- PURPOSE

START	END	BUSINESS MILES	PERSONAL MILES

DATE	START	BREAK	BREAK	FINISH	TOTAL HOURS

- VEHICLE INFORMATION
- START LOCATION
- END LOCATION
- PURPOSE

START	END	BUSINESS MILES	PERSONAL MILES

DATE	START	BREAK	BREAK	FINISH	TOTAL HOURS

- VEHICLE INFORMATION
- START LOCATION
- END LOCATION
- PURPOSE

START	END	BUSINESS MILES	PERSONAL MILES

DATE	START	BREAK	BREAK	FINISH	TOTAL HOURS

- VEHICLE INFORMATION
- START LOCATION
- END LOCATION
- PURPOSE

START	END	BUSINESS MILES	PERSONAL MILES

MARCH 2022

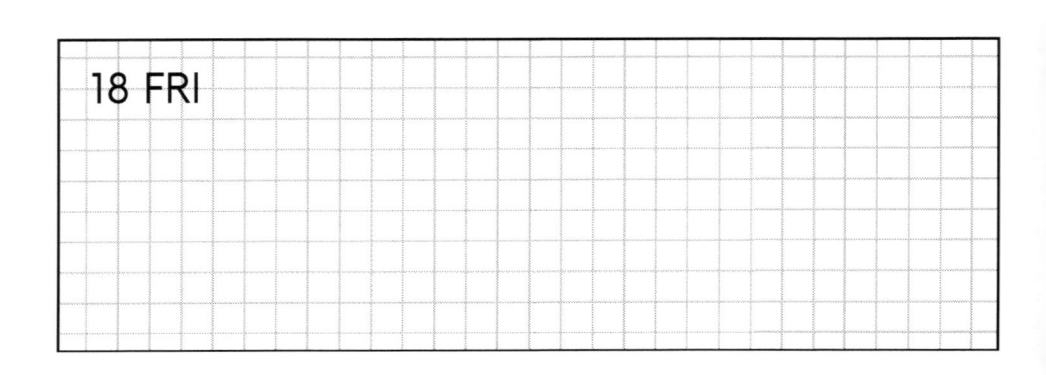

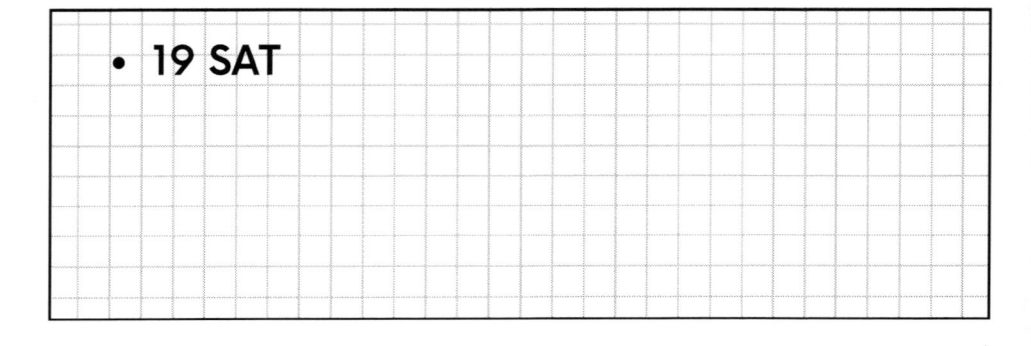

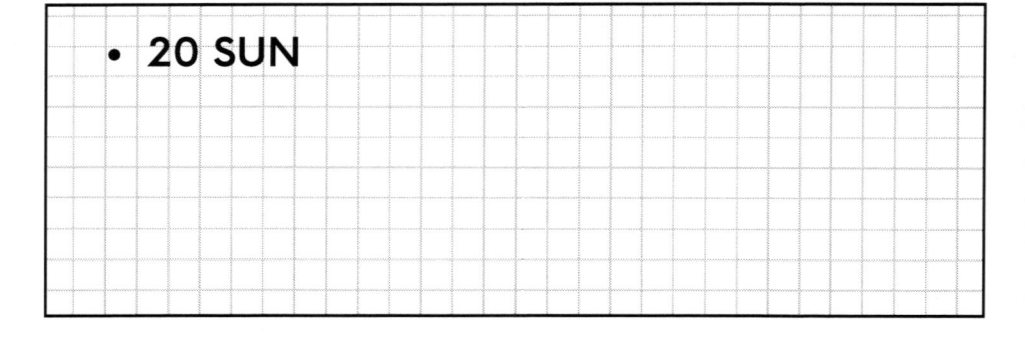

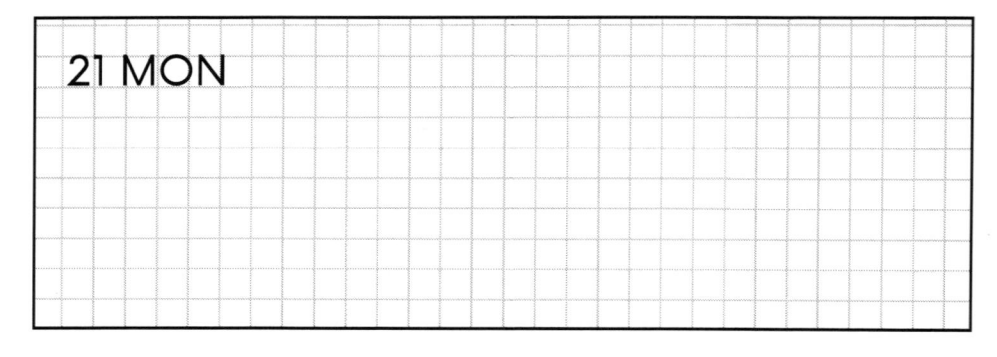

18 FRI

- **19 SAT**

- **20 SUN**

21 MON

DATE	START	BREAK	BREAK	FINISH	TOTAL HOURS

- VEHICLE INFORMATION
- START LOCATION
- END LOCATION
- PURPOSE

START	END	BUSINESS MILES	PERSONAL MILES

DATE	START	BREAK	BREAK	FINISH	TOTAL HOURS

- VEHICLE INFORMATION
- START LOCATION
- END LOCATION
- PURPOSE

START	END	BUSINESS MILES	PERSONAL MILES

DATE	START	BREAK	BREAK	FINISH	TOTAL HOURS

- VEHICLE INFORMATION
- START LOCATION
- END LOCATION
- PURPOSE

START	END	BUSINESS MILES	PERSONAL MILES

DATE	START	BREAK	BREAK	FINISH	TOTAL HOURS

- VEHICLE INFORMATION
- START LOCATION
- END LOCATION
- PURPOSE

START	END	BUSINESS MILES	PERSONAL MILES

MARCH 2022

22 TUE

23 WED

24 THU

25 FRI

DATE	START	BREAK	BREAK	FINISH	TOTAL HOURS

- VEHICLE INFORMATION
- START LOCATION
- END LOCATION
- PURPOSE

START	END	BUSINESS MILES	PERSONAL MILES

DATE	START	BREAK	BREAK	FINISH	TOTAL HOURS

- VEHICLE INFORMATION
- START LOCATION
- END LOCATION
- PURPOSE

START	END	BUSINESS MILES	PERSONAL MILES

DATE	START	BREAK	BREAK	FINISH	TOTAL HOURS

- VEHICLE INFORMATION
- START LOCATION
- END LOCATION
- PURPOSE

START	END	BUSINESS MILES	PERSONAL MILES

DATE	START	BREAK	BREAK	FINISH	TOTAL HOURS

- VEHICLE INFORMATION
- START LOCATION
- END LOCATION
- PURPOSE

START	END	BUSINESS MILES	PERSONAL MILES

MARCH 2022

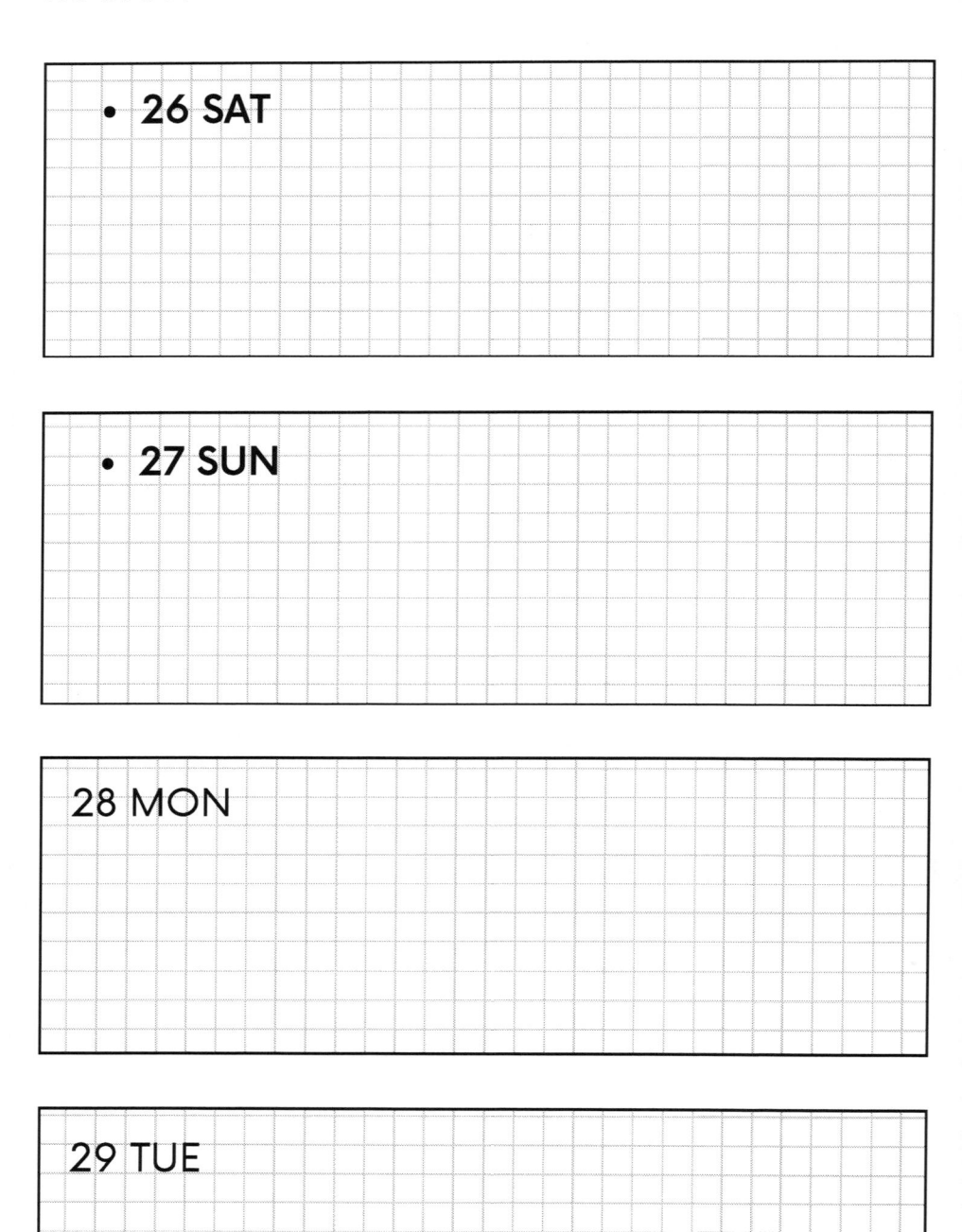

- **26 SAT**

- **27 SUN**

28 MON

29 TUE

DATE	START	BREAK	BREAK	FINISH	TOTAL HOURS

- VEHICLE INFORMATION
- START LOCATION
- END LOCATION
- PURPOSE

START	END	BUSINESS MILES	PERSONAL MILES

DATE	START	BREAK	BREAK	FINISH	TOTAL HOURS

- VEHICLE INFORMATION
- START LOCATION
- END LOCATION
- PURPOSE

START	END	BUSINESS MILES	PERSONAL MILES

DATE	START	BREAK	BREAK	FINISH	TOTAL HOURS

- VEHICLE INFORMATION
- START LOCATION
- END LOCATION
- PURPOSE

START	END	BUSINESS MILES	PERSONAL MILES

DATE	START	BREAK	BREAK	FINISH	TOTAL HOURS

- VEHICLE INFORMATION
- START LOCATION
- END LOCATION
- PURPOSE

START	END	BUSINESS MILES	PERSONAL MILES

MARCH/APRIL 2022

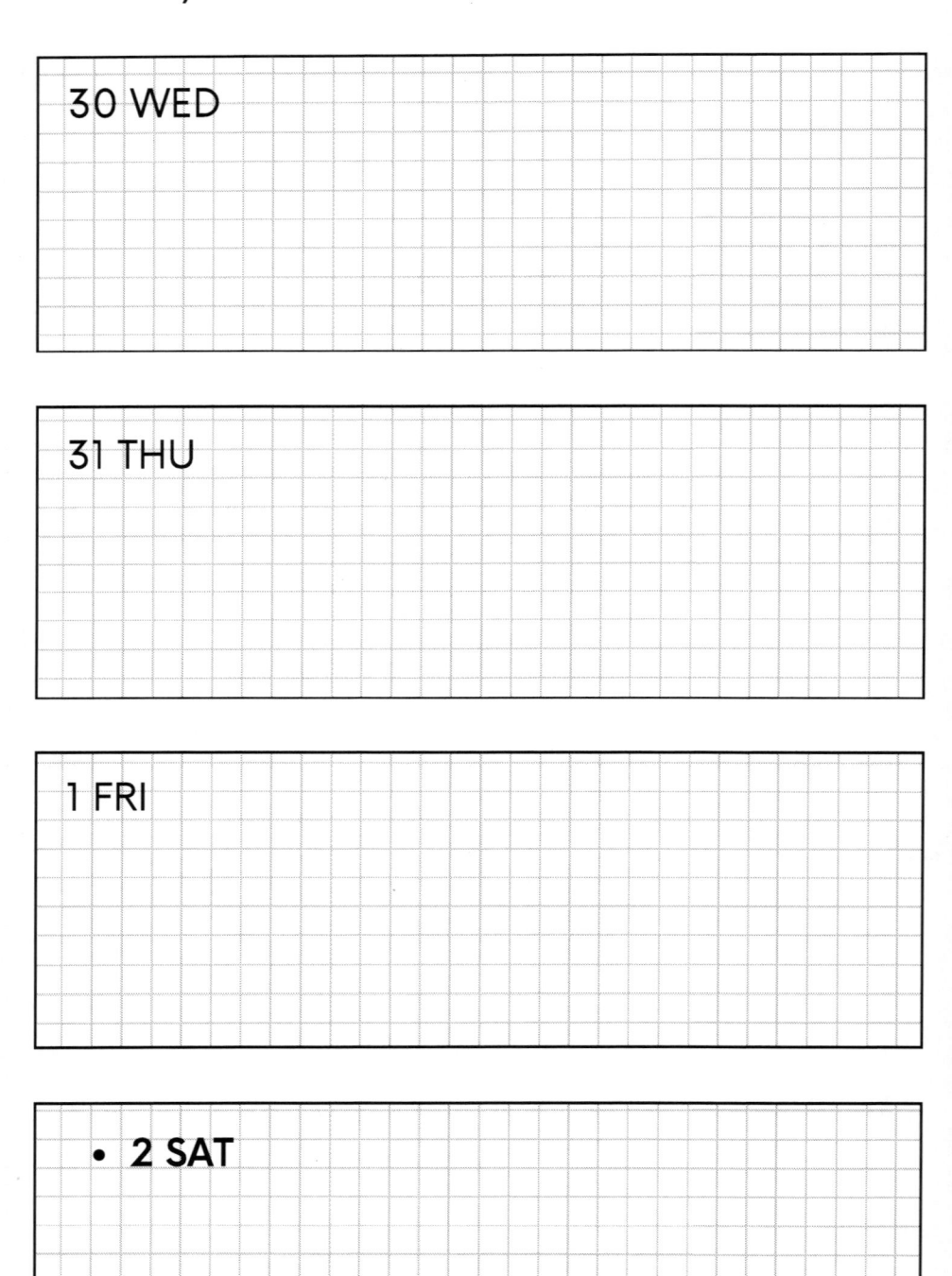

30 WED

31 THU

1 FRI

- **2 SAT**

DATE	START	BREAK	BREAK	FINISH	TOTAL HOURS

- VEHICLE INFORMATION
- START LOCATION
- END LOCATION
- PURPOSE

START	END	BUSINESS MILES	PERSONAL MILES

DATE	START	BREAK	BREAK	FINISH	TOTAL HOURS

- VEHICLE INFORMATION
- START LOCATION
- END LOCATION
- PURPOSE

START	END	BUSINESS MILES	PERSONAL MILES

DATE	START	BREAK	BREAK	FINISH	TOTAL HOURS

- VEHICLE INFORMATION
- START LOCATION
- END LOCATION
- PURPOSE

START	END	BUSINESS MILES	PERSONAL MILES

DATE	START	BREAK	BREAK	FINISH	TOTAL HOURS

- VEHICLE INFORMATION
- START LOCATION
- END LOCATION
- PURPOSE

START	END	BUSINESS MILES	PERSONAL MILES

APRIL 2022

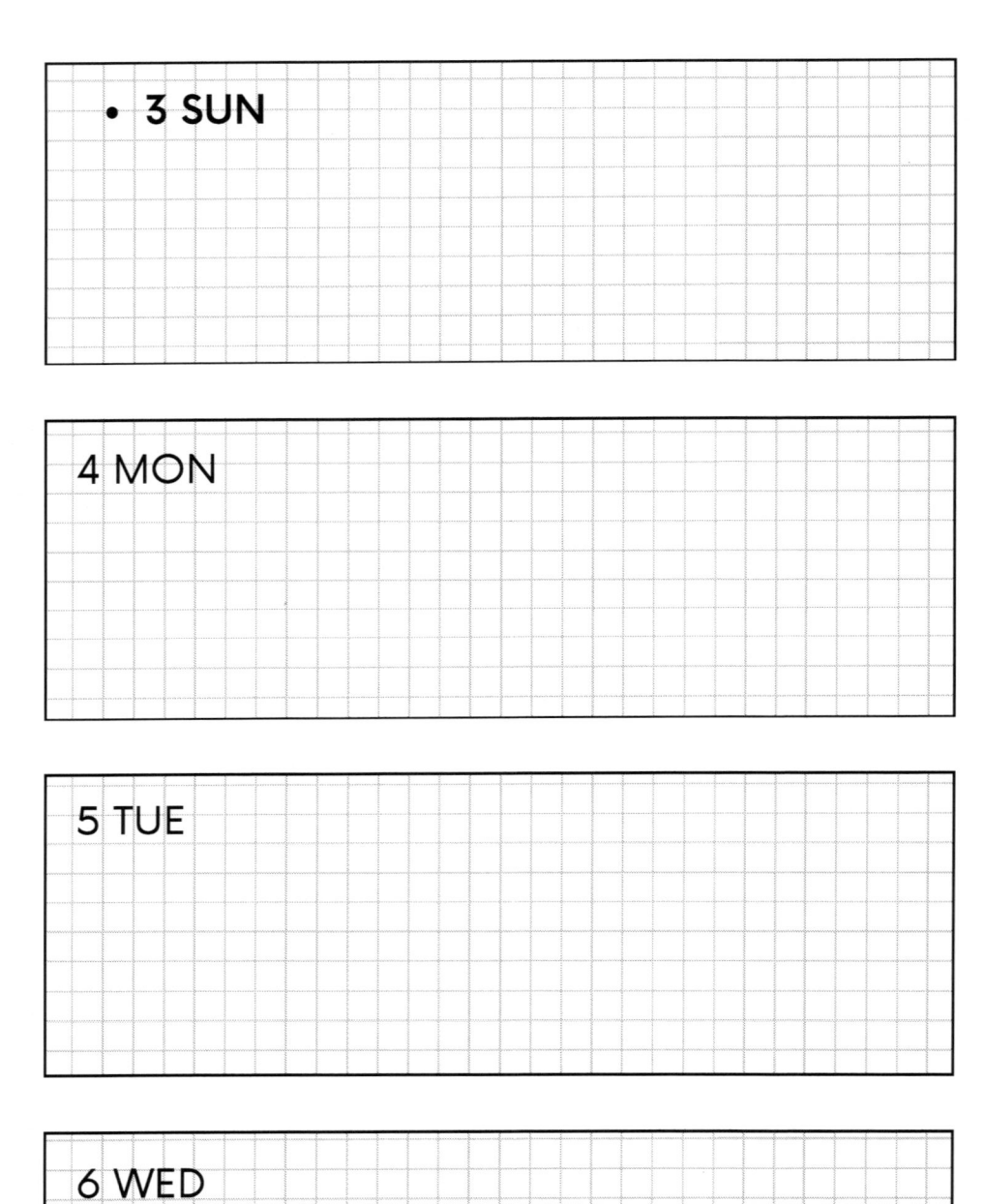

- **3 SUN**

4 MON

5 TUE

6 WED

DATE	START	BREAK	BREAK	FINISH	TOTAL HOURS

- VEHICLE INFORMATION
- START LOCATION
- END LOCATION
- PURPOSE

START	END	BUSINESS MILES	PERSONAL MILES

DATE	START	BREAK	BREAK	FINISH	TOTAL HOURS

- VEHICLE INFORMATION
- START LOCATION
- END LOCATION
- PURPOSE

START	END	BUSINESS MILES	PERSONAL MILES

DATE	START	BREAK	BREAK	FINISH	TOTAL HOURS

- VEHICLE INFORMATION
- START LOCATION
- END LOCATION
- PURPOSE

START	END	BUSINESS MILES	PERSONAL MILES

DATE	START	BREAK	BREAK	FINISH	TOTAL HOURS

- VEHICLE INFORMATION
- START LOCATION
- END LOCATION
- PURPOSE

START	END	BUSINESS MILES	PERSONAL MILES

APRIL 2022

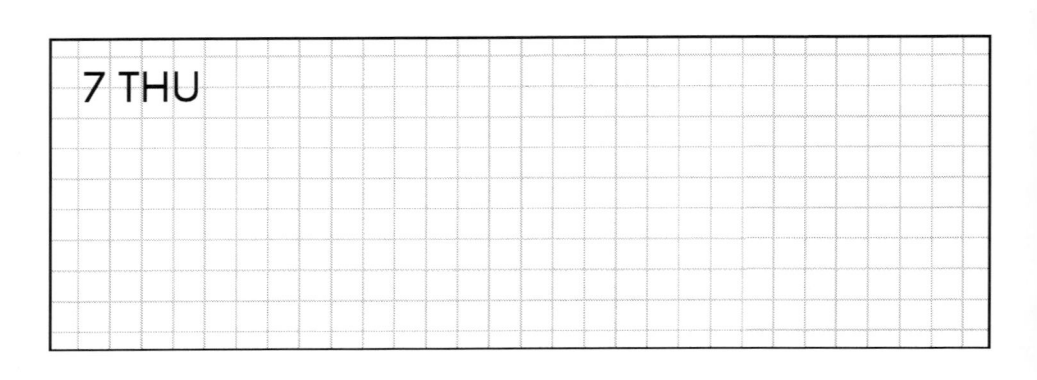

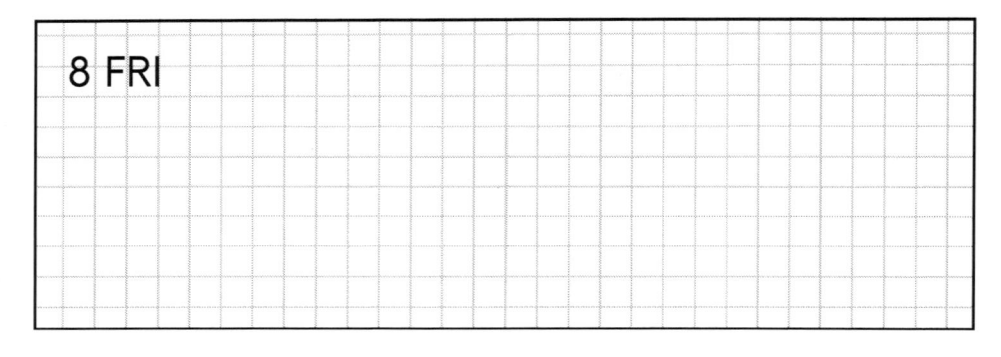

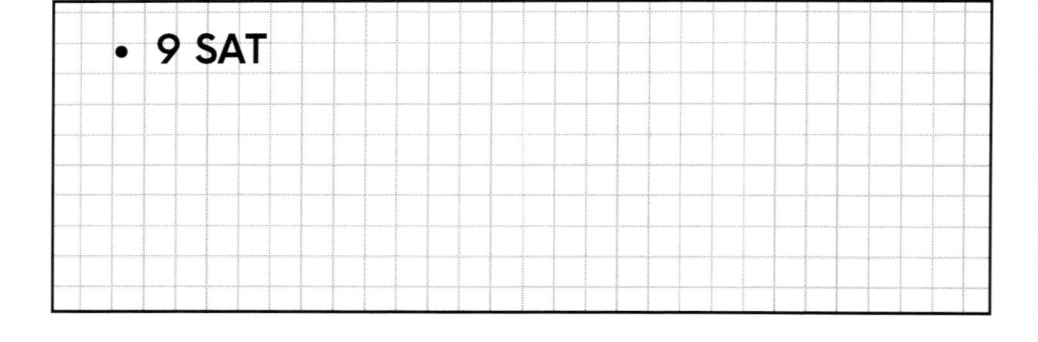

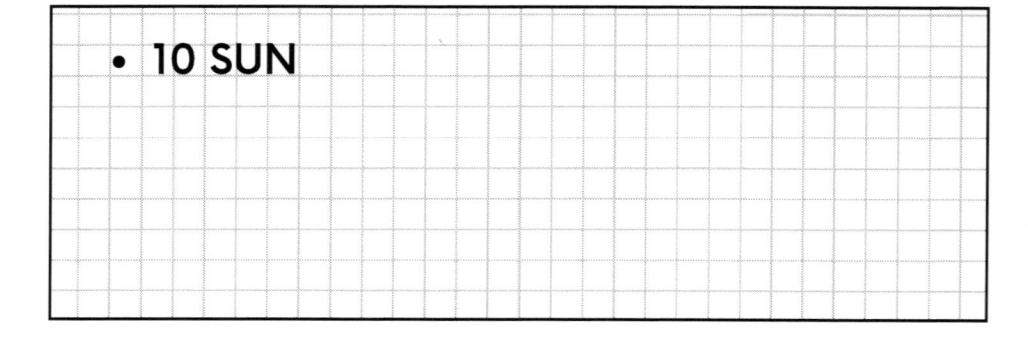

7 THU

8 FRI

- 9 SAT

- 10 SUN

DATE	START	BREAK	BREAK	FINISH	TOTAL HOURS

- VEHICLE INFORMATION
- START LOCATION
- END LOCATION
- PURPOSE

START	END	BUSINESS MILES	PERSONAL MILES

DATE	START	BREAK	BREAK	FINISH	TOTAL HOURS

- VEHICLE INFORMATION
- START LOCATION
- END LOCATION
- PURPOSE

START	END	BUSINESS MILES	PERSONAL MILES

DATE	START	BREAK	BREAK	FINISH	TOTAL HOURS

- VEHICLE INFORMATION
- START LOCATION
- END LOCATION
- PURPOSE

START	END	BUSINESS MILES	PERSONAL MILES

DATE	START	BREAK	BREAK	FINISH	TOTAL HOURS

- VEHICLE INFORMATION
- START LOCATION
- END LOCATION
- PURPOSE

START	END	BUSINESS MILES	PERSONAL MILES

APRIL 2022

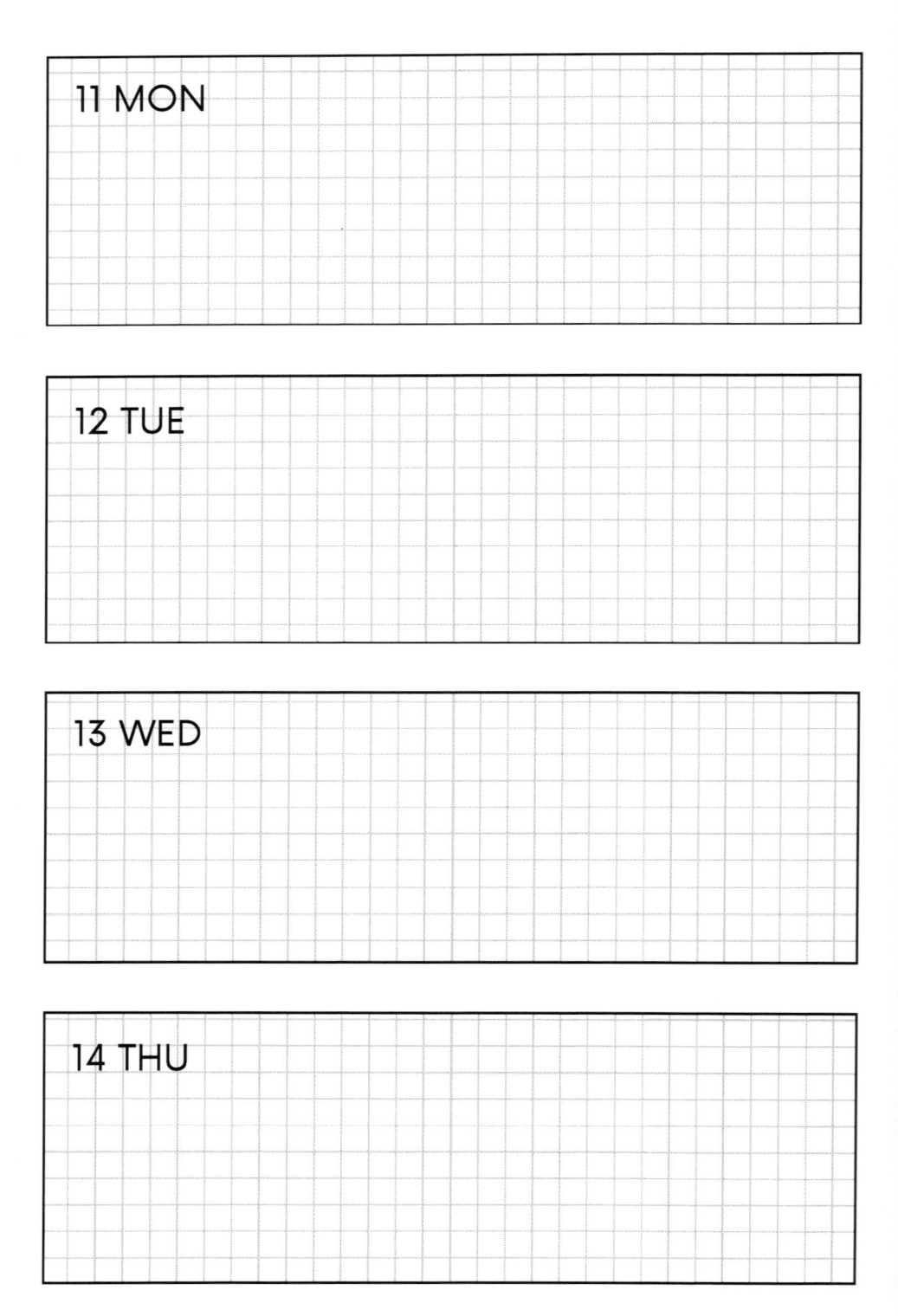

11 MON

12 TUE

13 WED

14 THU

DATE	START	BREAK	BREAK	FINISH	TOTAL HOURS

- VEHICLE INFORMATION
- START LOCATION
- END LOCATION
- PURPOSE

START	END	BUSINESS MILES	PERSONAL MILES

DATE	START	BREAK	BREAK	FINISH	TOTAL HOURS

- VEHICLE INFORMATION
- START LOCATION
- END LOCATION
- PURPOSE

START	END	BUSINESS MILES	PERSONAL MILES

DATE	START	BREAK	BREAK	FINISH	TOTAL HOURS

- VEHICLE INFORMATION
- START LOCATION
- END LOCATION
- PURPOSE

START	END	BUSINESS MILES	PERSONAL MILES

DATE	START	BREAK	BREAK	FINISH	TOTAL HOURS

- VEHICLE INFORMATION
- START LOCATION
- END LOCATION
- PURPOSE

START	END	BUSINESS MILES	PERSONAL MILES

APRIL 2022

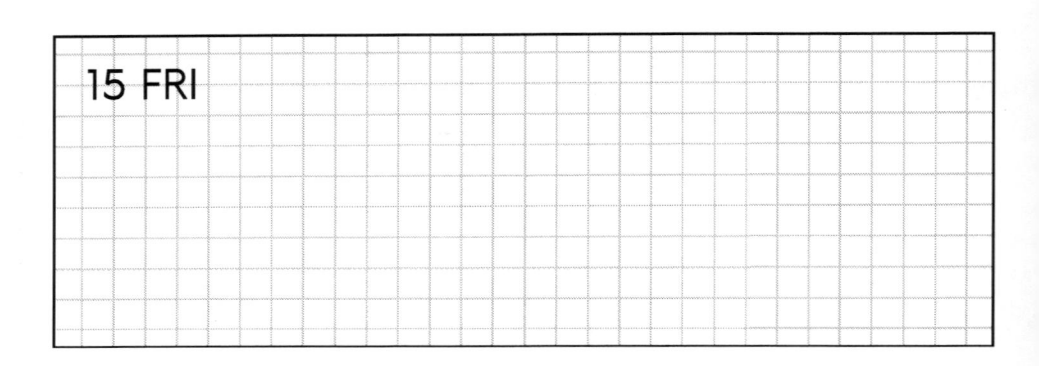

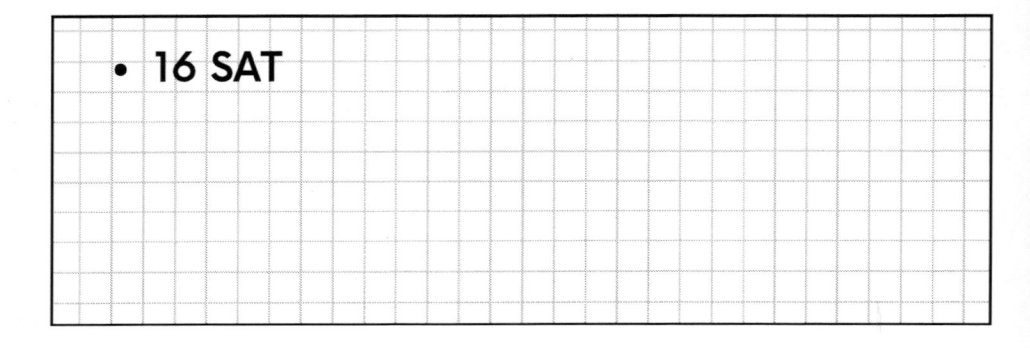

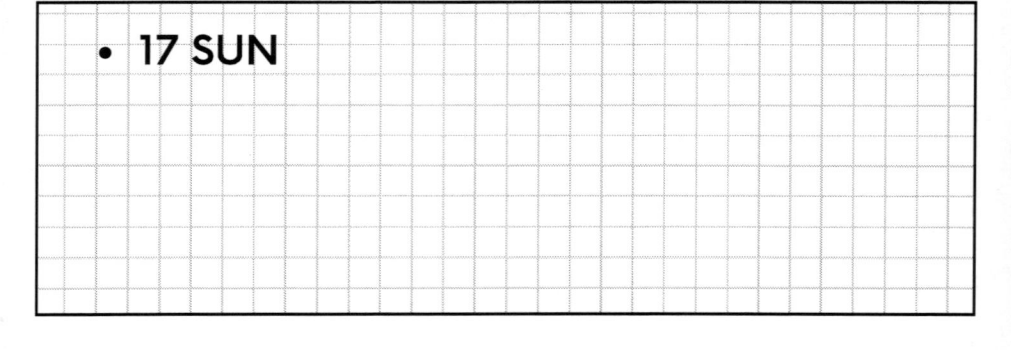

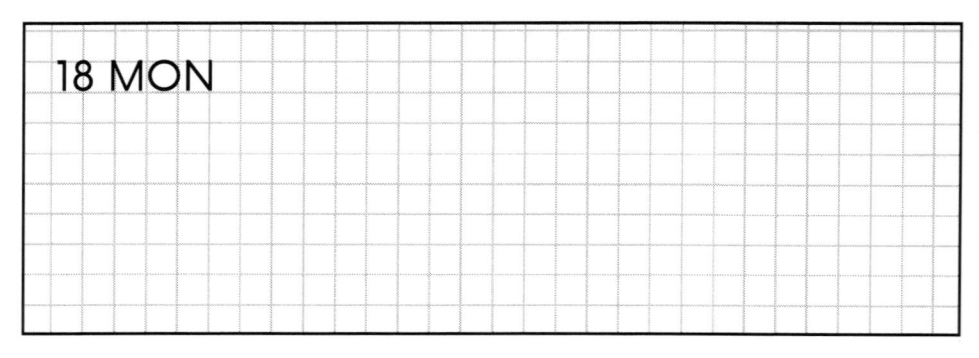

15 FRI

- **16 SAT**

- **17 SUN**

18 MON

DATE	START	BREAK	BREAK	FINISH	TOTAL HOURS

- VEHICLE INFORMATION
- START LOCATION
- END LOCATION
- PURPOSE

START	END	BUSINESS MILES	PERSONAL MILES

DATE	START	BREAK	BREAK	FINISH	TOTAL HOURS

- VEHICLE INFORMATION
- START LOCATION
- END LOCATION
- PURPOSE

START	END	BUSINESS MILES	PERSONAL MILES

DATE	START	BREAK	BREAK	FINISH	TOTAL HOURS

- VEHICLE INFORMATION
- START LOCATION
- END LOCATION
- PURPOSE

START	END	BUSINESS MILES	PERSONAL MILES

DATE	START	BREAK	BREAK	FINISH	TOTAL HOURS

- VEHICLE INFORMATION
- START LOCATION
- END LOCATION
- PURPOSE

START	END	BUSINESS MILES	PERSONAL MILES

APRIL   2022

19 TUE

20 WED

21 THU

22 FRI

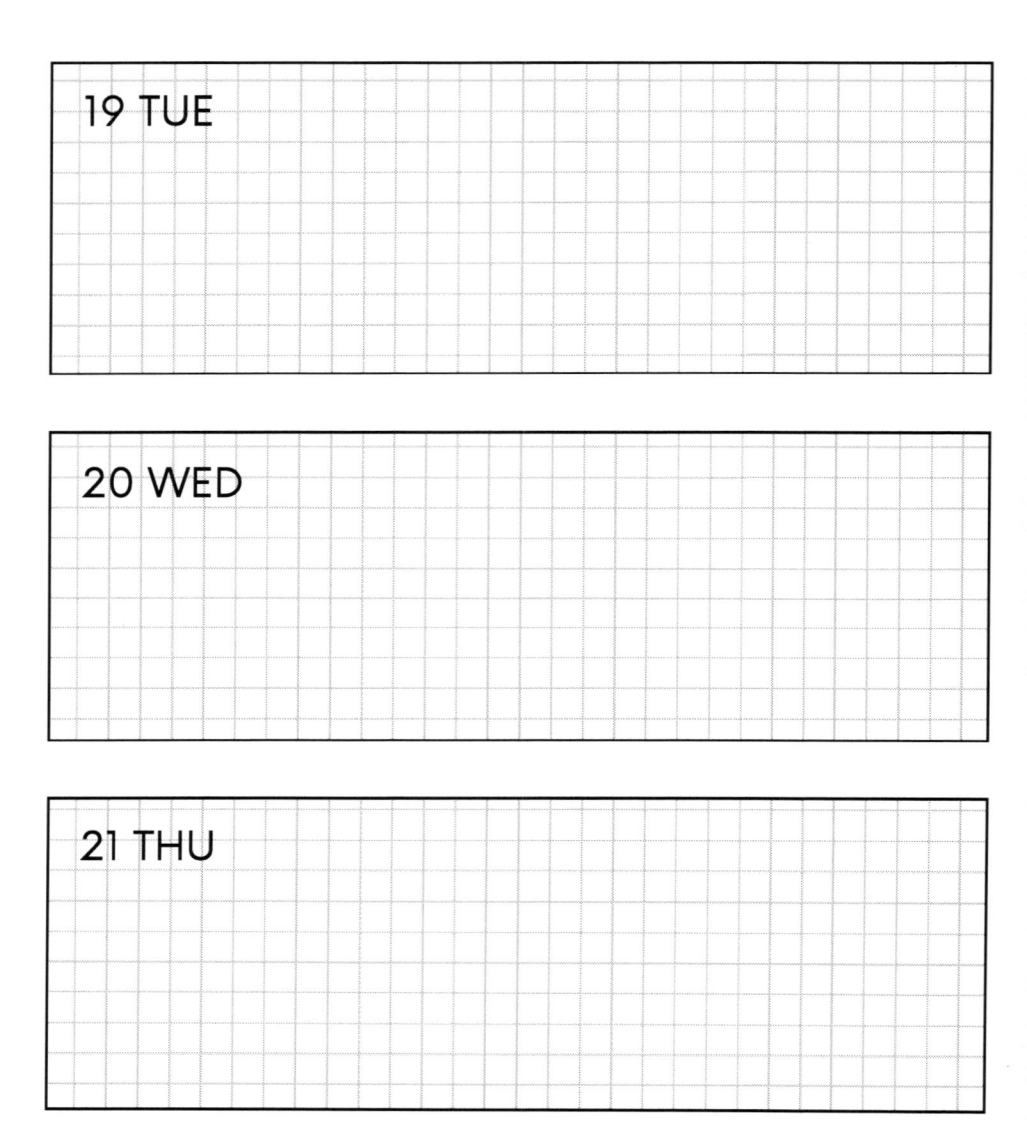

DATE	START	BREAK	BREAK	FINISH	TOTAL HOURS

- VEHICLE INFORMATION
- START LOCATION
- END LOCATION
- PURPOSE

START	END	BUSINESS MILES	PERSONAL MILES

DATE	START	BREAK	BREAK	FINISH	TOTAL HOURS

- VEHICLE INFORMATION
- START LOCATION
- END LOCATION
- PURPOSE

START	END	BUSINESS MILES	PERSONAL MILES

DATE	START	BREAK	BREAK	FINISH	TOTAL HOURS

- VEHICLE INFORMATION
- START LOCATION
- END LOCATION
- PURPOSE

START	END	BUSINESS MILES	PERSONAL MILES

DATE	START	BREAK	BREAK	FINISH	TOTAL HOURS

- VEHICLE INFORMATION
- START LOCATION
- END LOCATION
- PURPOSE

START	END	BUSINESS MILES	PERSONAL MILES

APRIL 2022

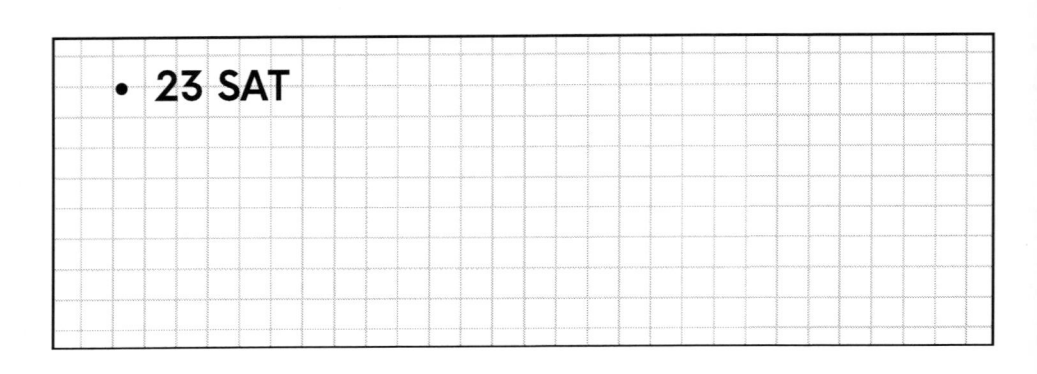

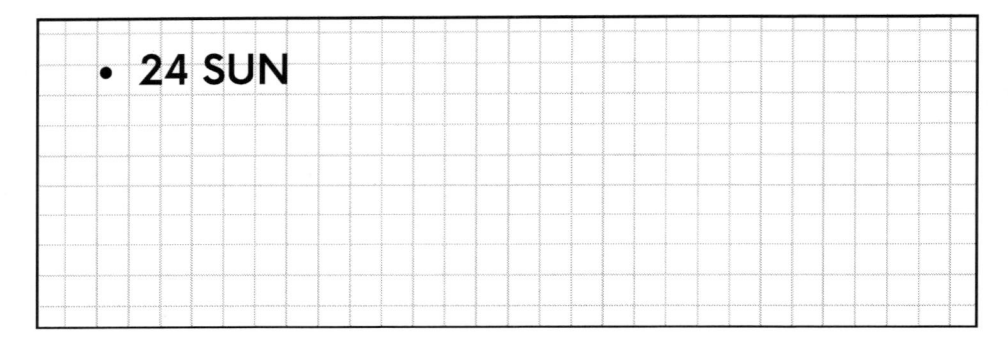

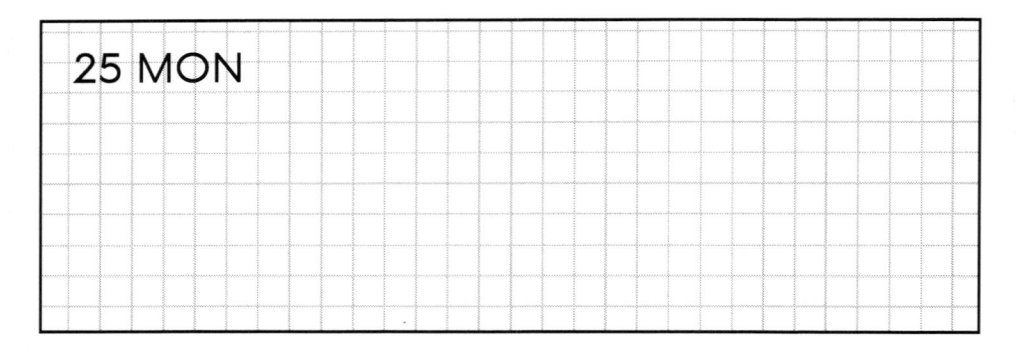

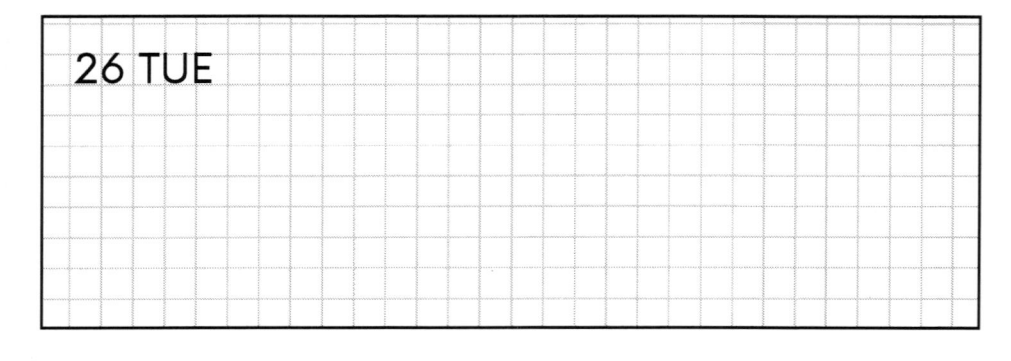

- **23 SAT**

- **24 SUN**

25 MON

26 TUE

DATE	START	BREAK	BREAK	FINISH	TOTAL HOURS

- VEHICLE INFORMATION
- START LOCATION
- END LOCATION
- PURPOSE

START	END	BUSINESS MILES	PERSONAL MILES

DATE	START	BREAK	BREAK	FINISH	TOTAL HOURS

- VEHICLE INFORMATION
- START LOCATION
- END LOCATION
- PURPOSE

START	END	BUSINESS MILES	PERSONAL MILES

DATE	START	BREAK	BREAK	FINISH	TOTAL HOURS

- VEHICLE INFORMATION
- START LOCATION
- END LOCATION
- PURPOSE

START	END	BUSINESS MILES	PERSONAL MILES

DATE	START	BREAK	BREAK	FINISH	TOTAL HOURS

- VEHICLE INFORMATION
- START LOCATION
- END LOCATION
- PURPOSE

START	END	BUSINESS MILES	PERSONAL MILES

APRIL 2022

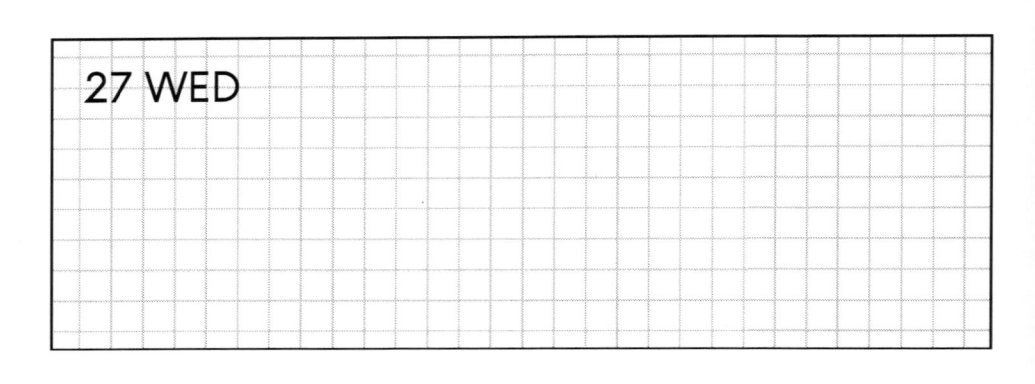

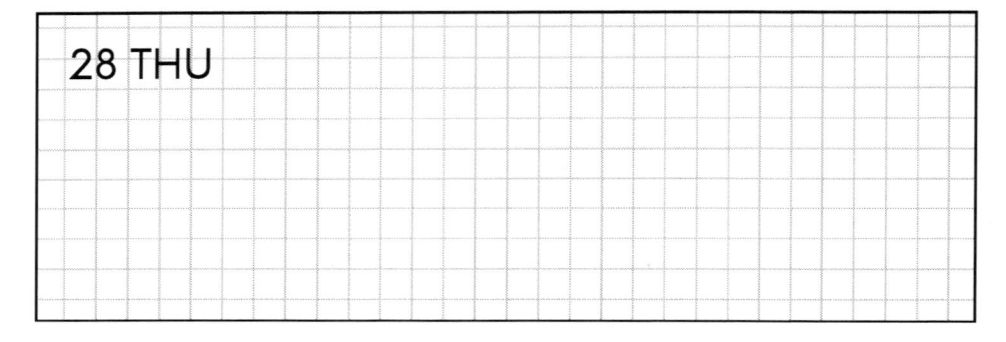

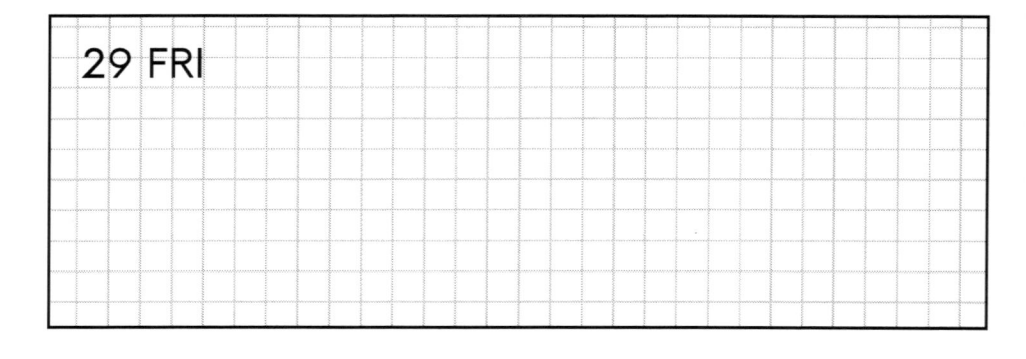

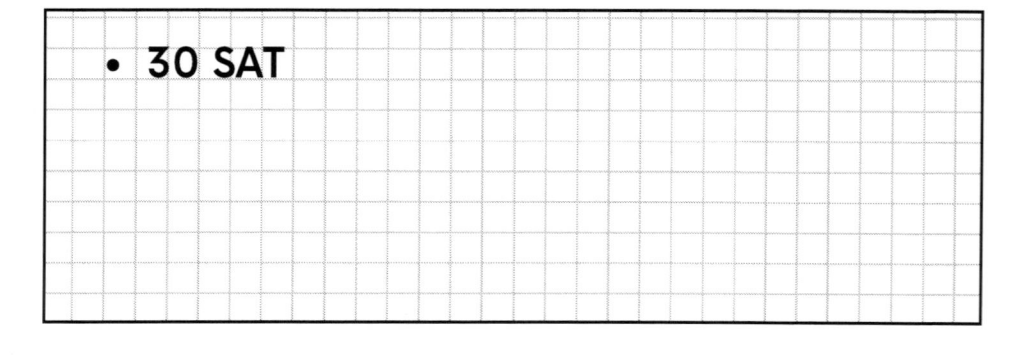

27 WED

28 THU

29 FRI

- **30 SAT**

DATE	START	BREAK	BREAK	FINISH	TOTAL HOURS

- VEHICLE INFORMATION
- START LOCATION
- END LOCATION
- PURPOSE

START	END	BUSINESS MILES	PERSONAL MILES

DATE	START	BREAK	BREAK	FINISH	TOTAL HOURS

- VEHICLE INFORMATION
- START LOCATION
- END LOCATION
- PURPOSE

START	END	BUSINESS MILES	PERSONAL MILES

DATE	START	BREAK	BREAK	FINISH	TOTAL HOURS

- VEHICLE INFORMATION
- START LOCATION
- END LOCATION
- PURPOSE

START	END	BUSINESS MILES	PERSONAL MILES

DATE	START	BREAK	BREAK	FINISH	TOTAL HOURS

- VEHICLE INFORMATION
- START LOCATION
- END LOCATION
- PURPOSE

START	END	BUSINESS MILES	PERSONAL MILES

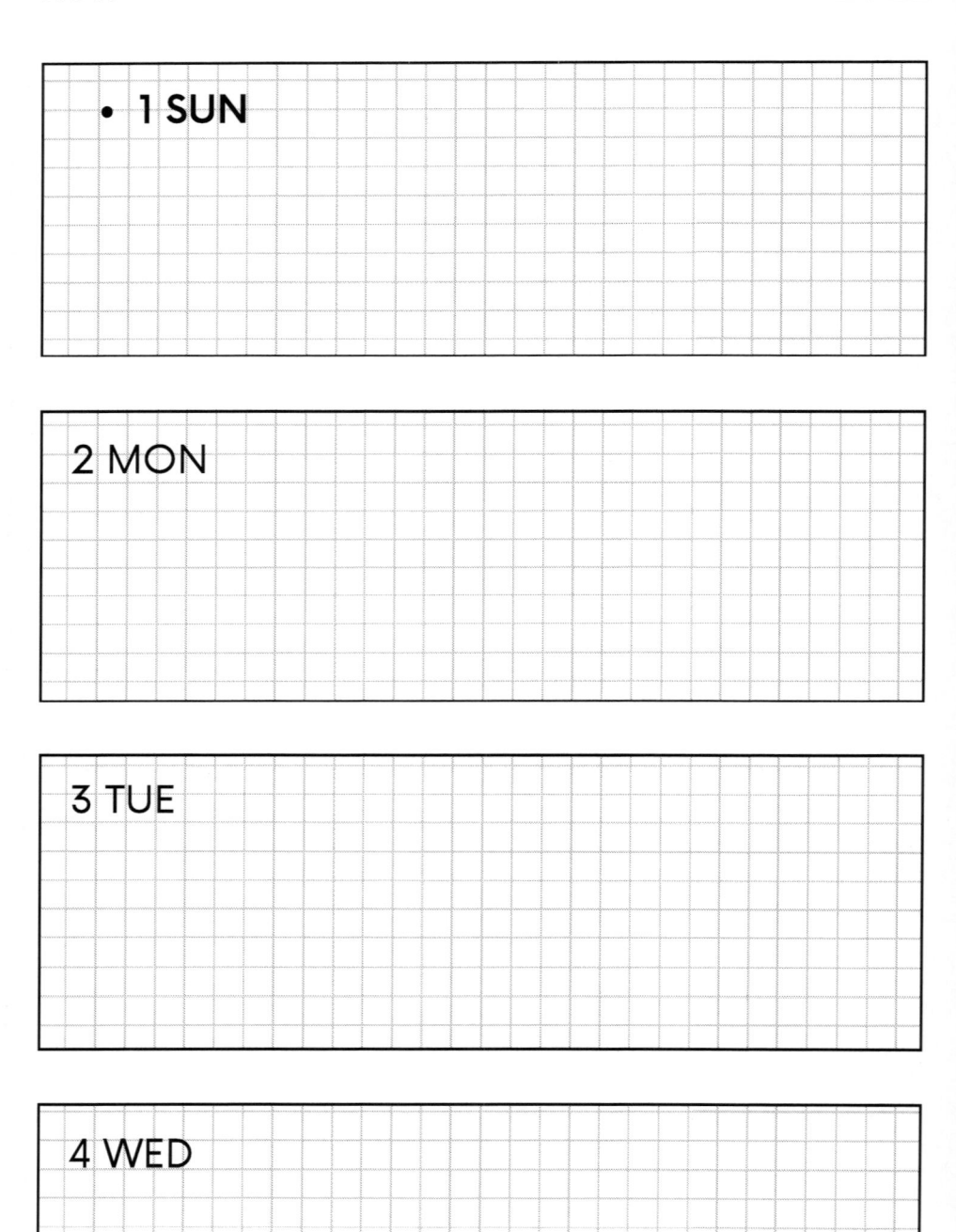

MAY 2022

- 1 SUN

2 MON

3 TUE

4 WED

DATE	START	BREAK	BREAK	FINISH	TOTAL HOURS

- VEHICLE INFORMATION
- START LOCATION
- END LOCATION
- PURPOSE

START	END	BUSINESS MILES	PERSONAL MILES

DATE	START	BREAK	BREAK	FINISH	TOTAL HOURS

- VEHICLE INFORMATION
- START LOCATION
- END LOCATION
- PURPOSE

START	END	BUSINESS MILES	PERSONAL MILES

DATE	START	BREAK	BREAK	FINISH	TOTAL HOURS

- VEHICLE INFORMATION
- START LOCATION
- END LOCATION
- PURPOSE

START	END	BUSINESS MILES	PERSONAL MILES

DATE	START	BREAK	BREAK	FINISH	TOTAL HOURS

- VEHICLE INFORMATION
- START LOCATION
- END LOCATION
- PURPOSE

START	END	BUSINESS MILES	PERSONAL MILES

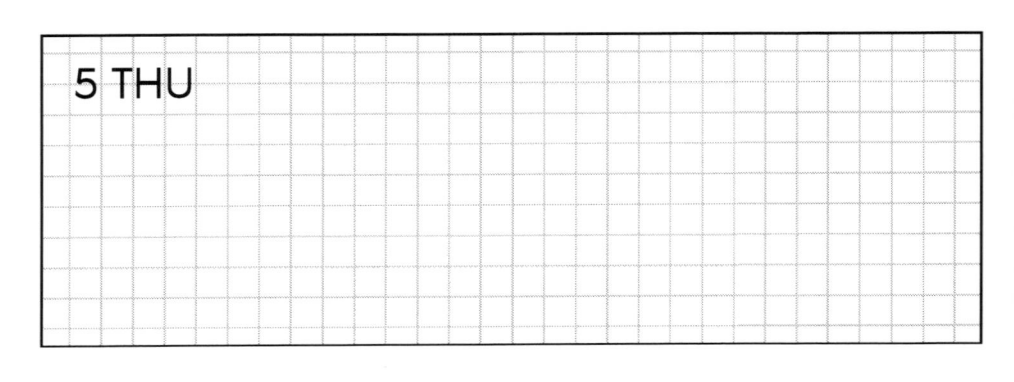

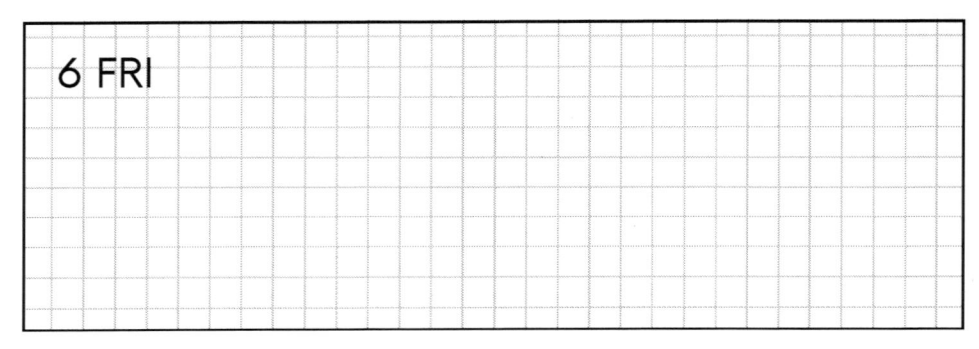

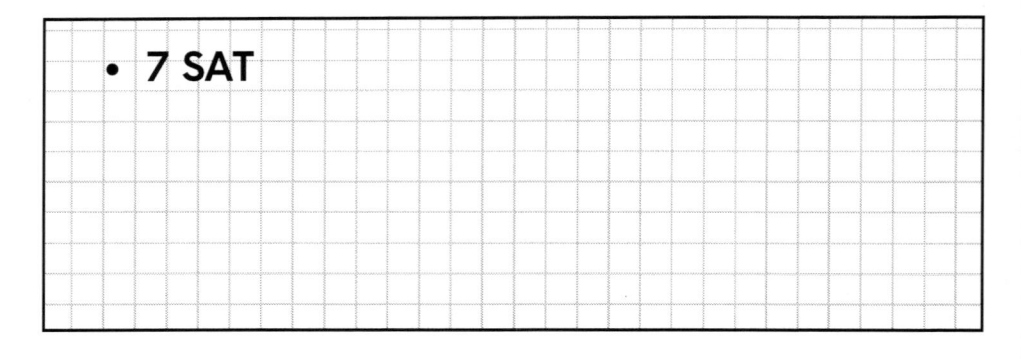

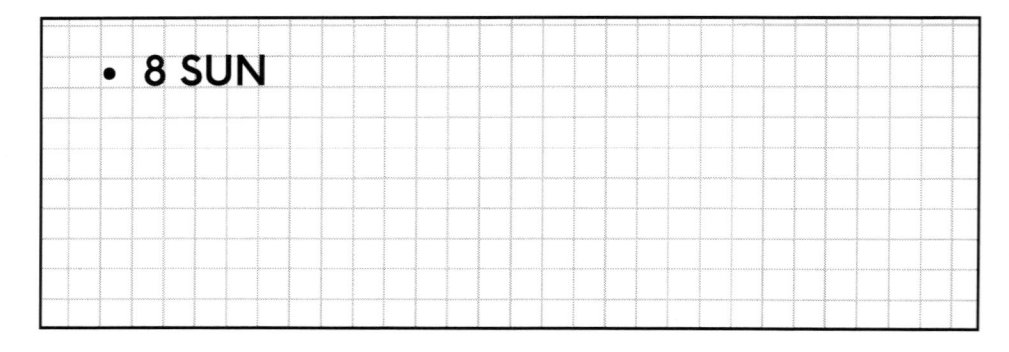

MAY 2022

5 THU

6 FRI

- 7 SAT

- 8 SUN

DATE	START	BREAK	BREAK	FINISH	TOTAL HOURS

- VEHICLE INFORMATION
- START LOCATION
- END LOCATION
- PURPOSE

START	END	BUSINESS MILES	PERSONAL MILES

DATE	START	BREAK	BREAK	FINISH	TOTAL HOURS

- VEHICLE INFORMATION
- START LOCATION
- END LOCATION
- PURPOSE

START	END	BUSINESS MILES	PERSONAL MILES

DATE	START	BREAK	BREAK	FINISH	TOTAL HOURS

- VEHICLE INFORMATION
- START LOCATION
- END LOCATION
- PURPOSE

START	END	BUSINESS MILES	PERSONAL MILES

DATE	START	BREAK	BREAK	FINISH	TOTAL HOURS

- VEHICLE INFORMATION
- START LOCATION
- END LOCATION
- PURPOSE

START	END	BUSINESS MILES	PERSONAL MILES

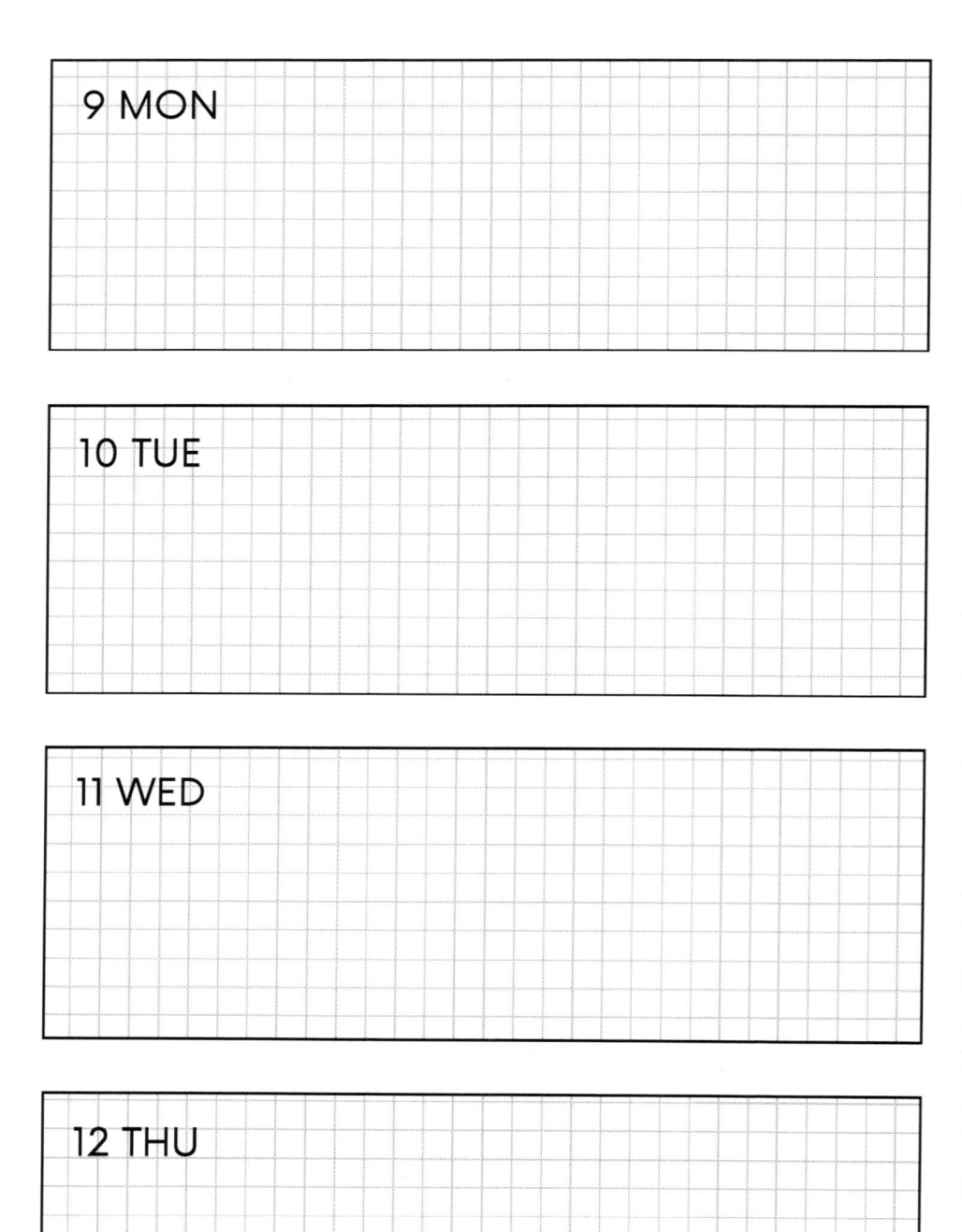

MAY   2022

9 MON

10 TUE

11 WED

12 THU

DATE	START	BREAK	BREAK	FINISH	TOTAL HOURS

- VEHICLE INFORMATION
- START LOCATION
- END LOCATION
- PURPOSE

START	END	BUSINESS MILES	PERSONAL MILES

DATE	START	BREAK	BREAK	FINISH	TOTAL HOURS

- VEHICLE INFORMATION
- START LOCATION
- END LOCATION
- PURPOSE

START	END	BUSINESS MILES	PERSONAL MILES

DATE	START	BREAK	BREAK	FINISH	TOTAL HOURS

- VEHICLE INFORMATION
- START LOCATION
- END LOCATION
- PURPOSE

START	END	BUSINESS MILES	PERSONAL MILES

DATE	START	BREAK	BREAK	FINISH	TOTAL HOURS

- VEHICLE INFORMATION
- START LOCATION
- END LOCATION
- PURPOSE

START	END	BUSINESS MILES	PERSONAL MILES

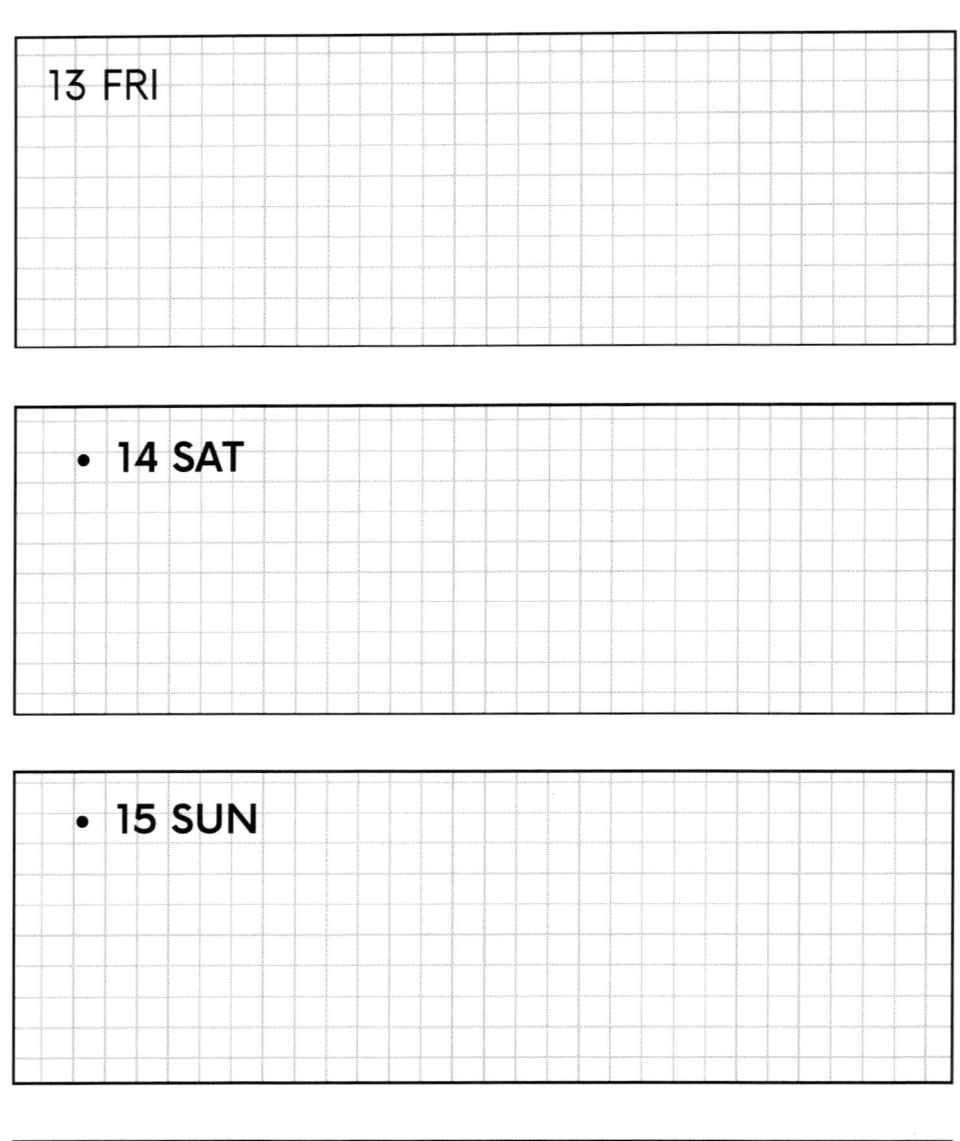

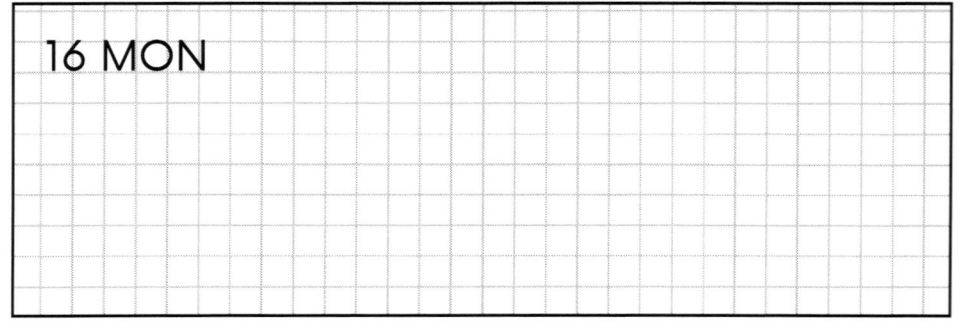

MAY 2022

13 FRI

- **14 SAT**

- **15 SUN**

16 MON

DATE	START	BREAK	BREAK	FINISH	TOTAL HOURS

- VEHICLE INFORMATION
- START LOCATION
- END LOCATION
- PURPOSE

START	END	BUSINESS MILES	PERSONAL MILES

DATE	START	BREAK	BREAK	FINISH	TOTAL HOURS

- VEHICLE INFORMATION
- START LOCATION
- END LOCATION
- PURPOSE

START	END	BUSINESS MILES	PERSONAL MILES

DATE	START	BREAK	BREAK	FINISH	TOTAL HOURS

- VEHICLE INFORMATION
- START LOCATION
- END LOCATION
- PURPOSE

START	END	BUSINESS MILES	PERSONAL MILES

DATE	START	BREAK	BREAK	FINISH	TOTAL HOURS

- VEHICLE INFORMATION
- START LOCATION
- END LOCATION
- PURPOSE

START	END	BUSINESS MILES	PERSONAL MILES

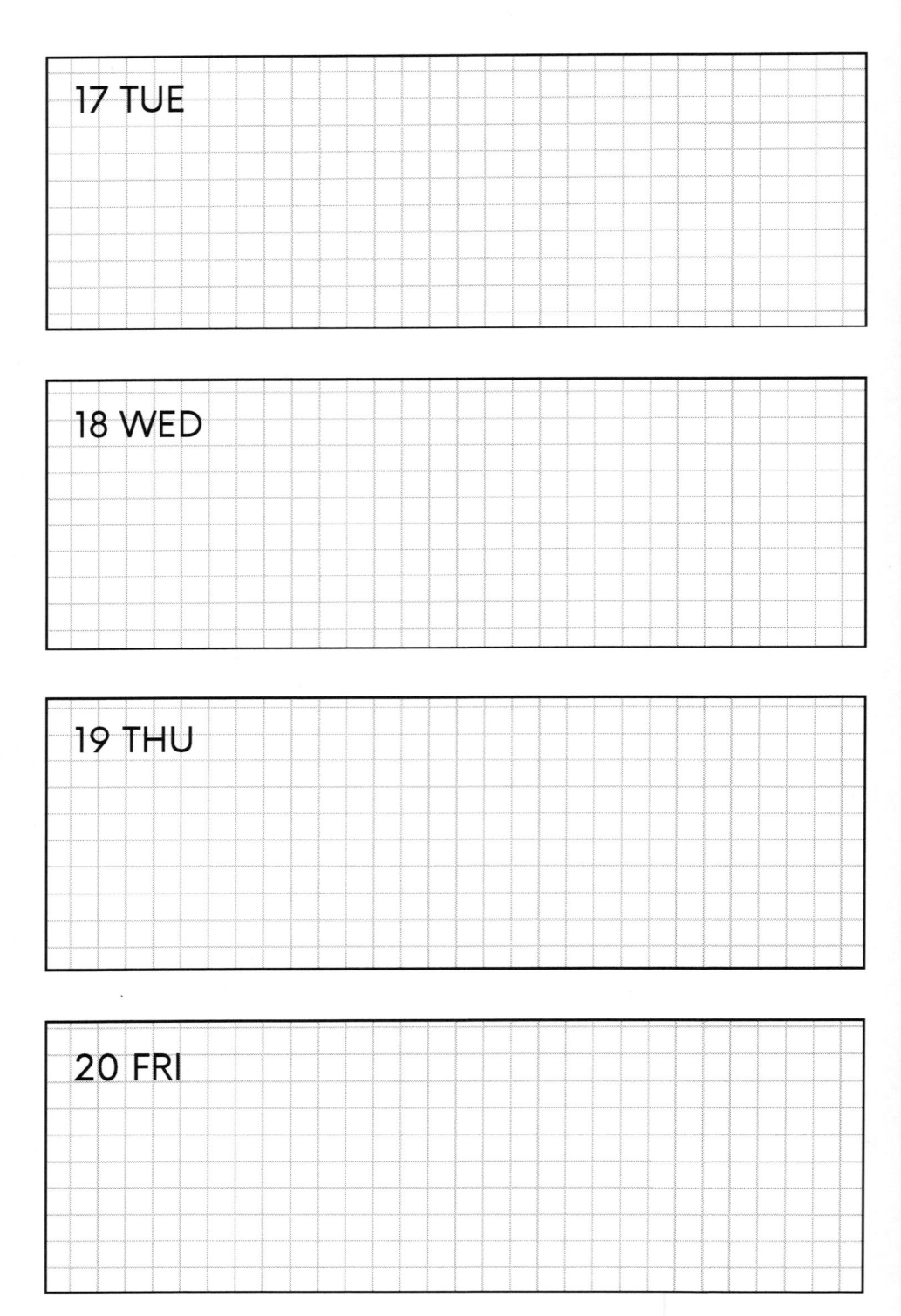

MAY 2022

17 TUE

18 WED

19 THU

20 FRI

DATE	START	BREAK	BREAK	FINISH	TOTAL HOURS

- VEHICLE INFORMATION
- START LOCATION
- END LOCATION
- PURPOSE

START	END	BUSINESS MILES	PERSONAL MILES

DATE	START	BREAK	BREAK	FINISH	TOTAL HOURS

- VEHICLE INFORMATION
- START LOCATION
- END LOCATION
- PURPOSE

START	END	BUSINESS MILES	PERSONAL MILES

DATE	START	BREAK	BREAK	FINISH	TOTAL HOURS

- VEHICLE INFORMATION
- START LOCATION
- END LOCATION
- PURPOSE

START	END	BUSINESS MILES	PERSONAL MILES

DATE	START	BREAK	BREAK	FINISH	TOTAL HOURS

- VEHICLE INFORMATION
- START LOCATION
- END LOCATION
- PURPOSE

START	END	BUSINESS MILES	PERSONAL MILES

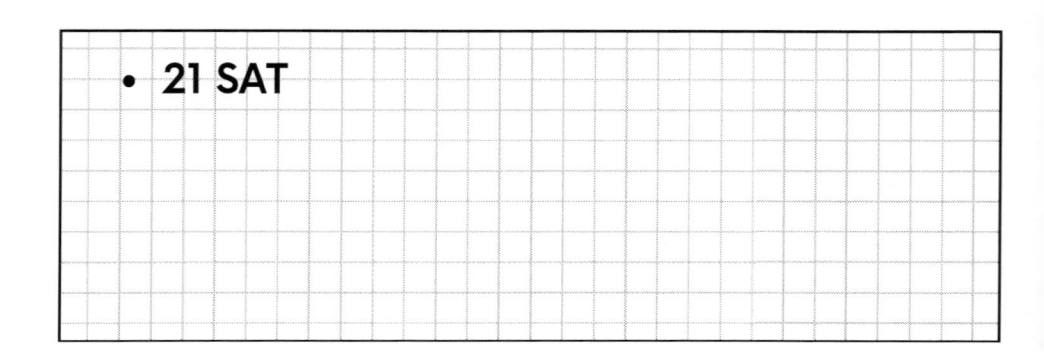

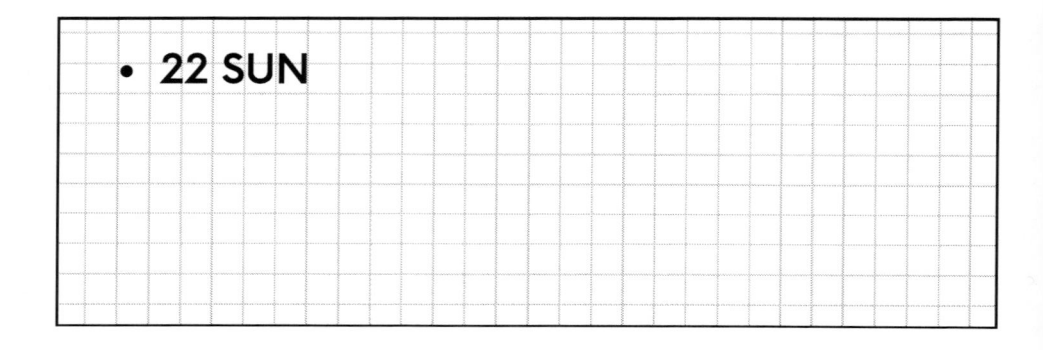

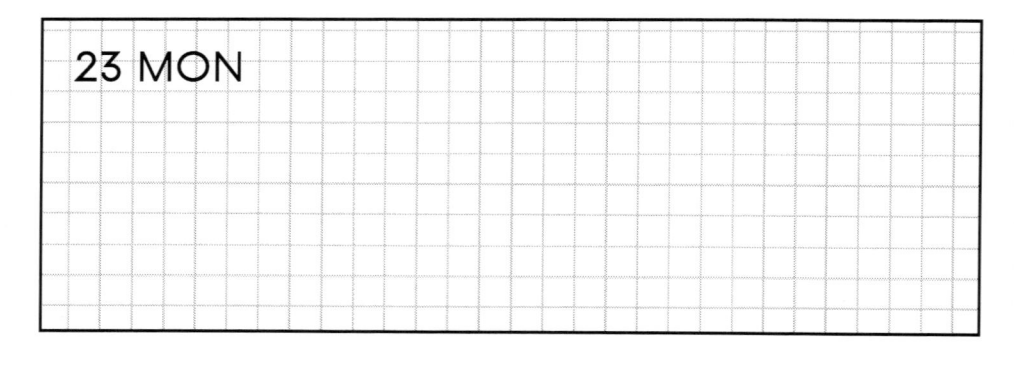

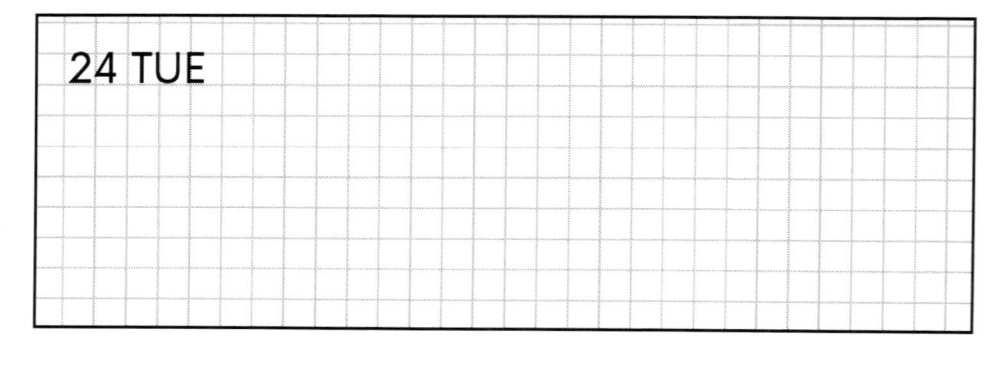

MAY   2022

- **21 SAT**

- **22 SUN**

23 MON

24 TUE

DATE	START	BREAK	BREAK	FINISH	TOTAL HOURS

- VEHICLE INFORMATION
- START LOCATION
- END LOCATION
- PURPOSE

START	END	BUSINESS MILES	PERSONAL MILES

DATE	START	BREAK	BREAK	FINISH	TOTAL HOURS

- VEHICLE INFORMATION
- START LOCATION
- END LOCATION
- PURPOSE

START	END	BUSINESS MILES	PERSONAL MILES

DATE	START	BREAK	BREAK	FINISH	TOTAL HOURS

- VEHICLE INFORMATION
- START LOCATION
- END LOCATION
- PURPOSE

START	END	BUSINESS MILES	PERSONAL MILES

DATE	START	BREAK	BREAK	FINISH	TOTAL HOURS

- VEHICLE INFORMATION
- START LOCATION
- END LOCATION
- PURPOSE

START	END	BUSINESS MILES	PERSONAL MILES

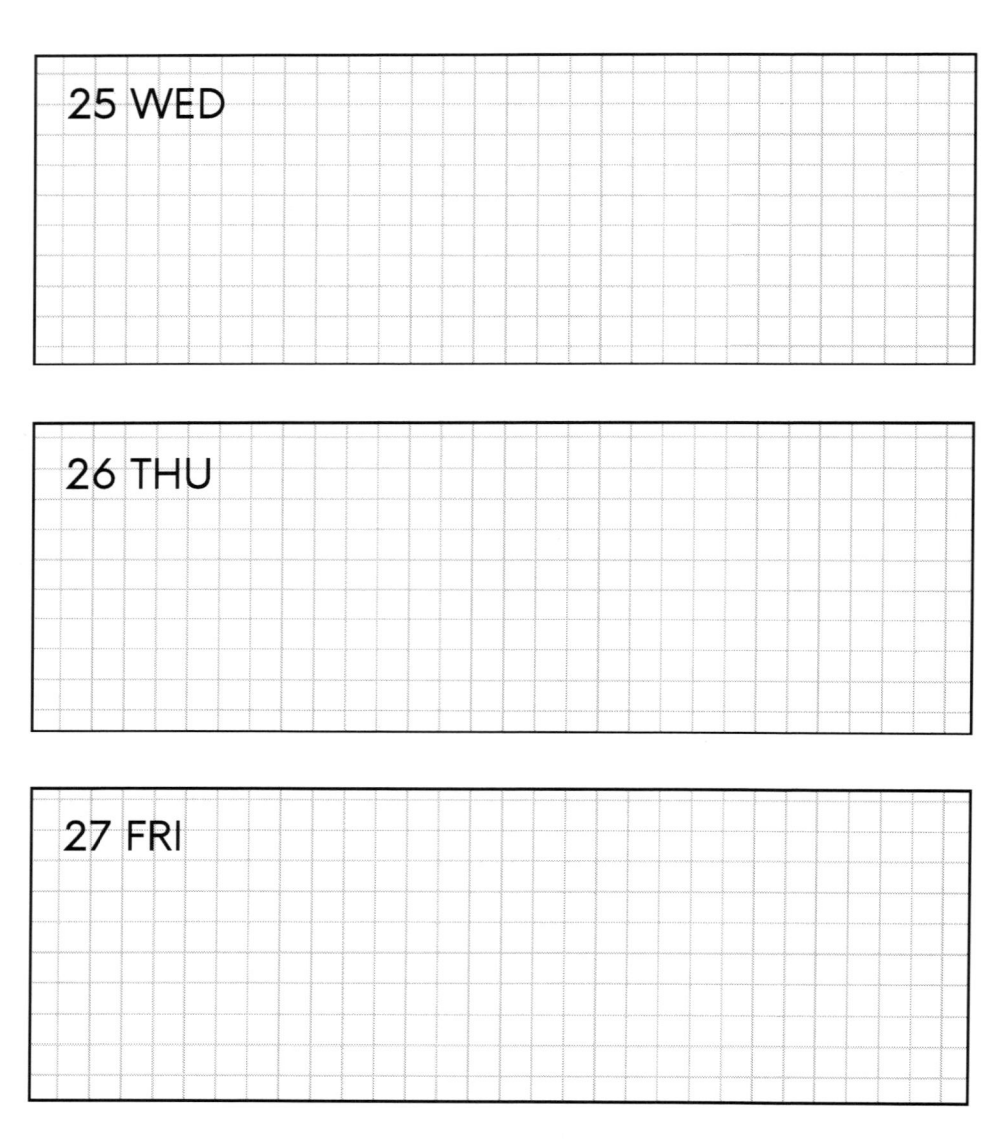

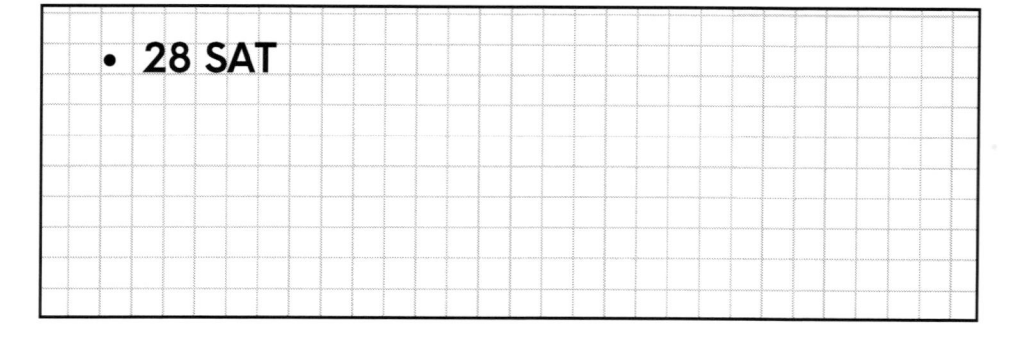

MAY 2022

25 WED

26 THU

27 FRI

- **28 SAT**

DATE	START	BREAK	BREAK	FINISH	TOTAL HOURS

- VEHICLE INFORMATION
- START LOCATION
- END LOCATION
- PURPOSE

START	END	BUSINESS MILES	PERSONAL MILES

DATE	START	BREAK	BREAK	FINISH	TOTAL HOURS

- VEHICLE INFORMATION
- START LOCATION
- END LOCATION
- PURPOSE

START	END	BUSINESS MILES	PERSONAL MILES

DATE	START	BREAK	BREAK	FINISH	TOTAL HOURS

- VEHICLE INFORMATION
- START LOCATION
- END LOCATION
- PURPOSE

START	END	BUSINESS MILES	PERSONAL MILES

DATE	START	BREAK	BREAK	FINISH	TOTAL HOURS

- VEHICLE INFORMATION
- START LOCATION
- END LOCATION
- PURPOSE

START	END	BUSINESS MILES	PERSONAL MILES

MAY/JUNE   2022

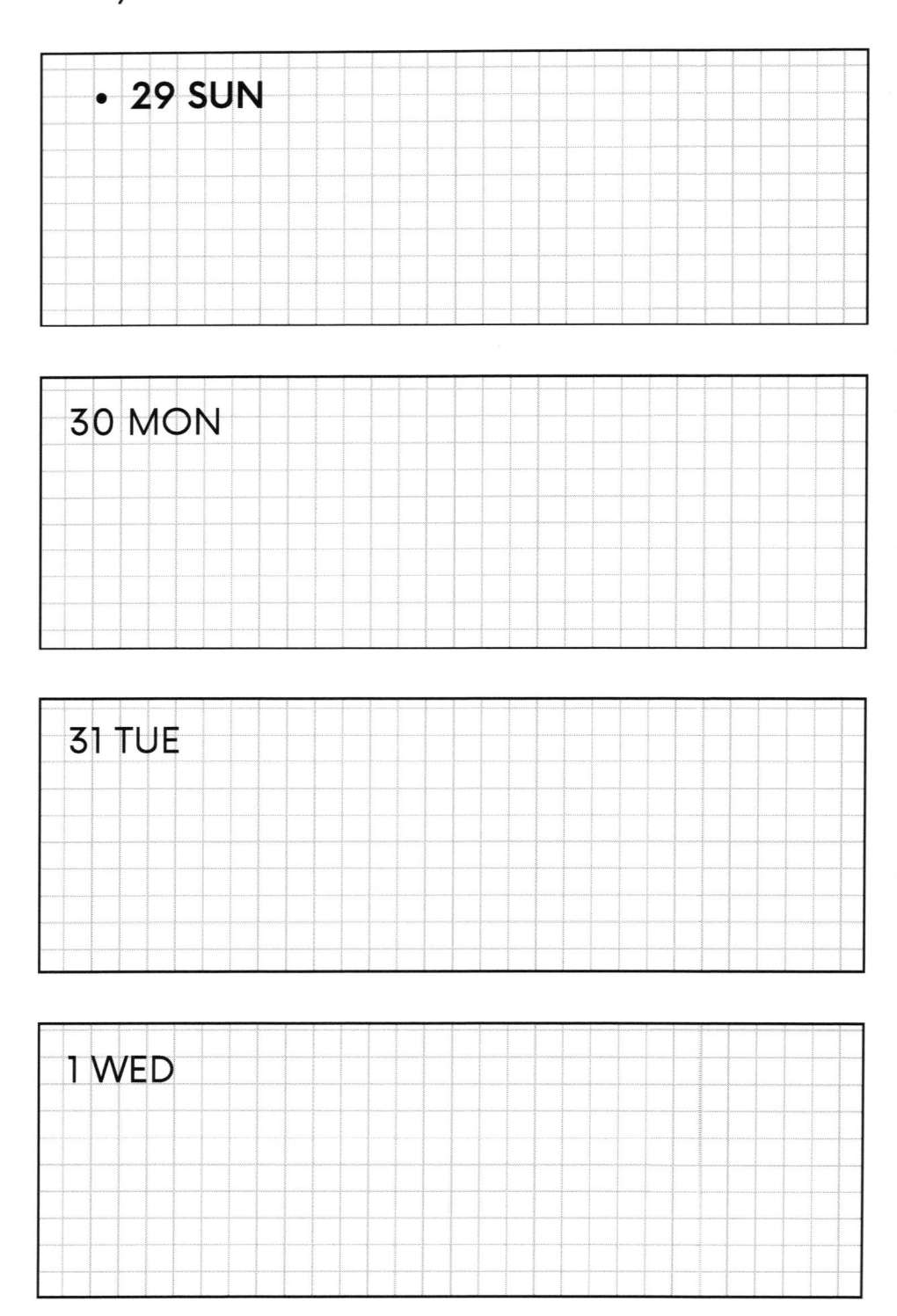

- **29 SUN**

30 MON

31 TUE

1 WED

DATE	START	BREAK	BREAK	FINISH	TOTAL HOURS

- VEHICLE INFORMATION
- START LOCATION
- END LOCATION
- PURPOSE

START	END	BUSINESS MILES	PERSONAL MILES

DATE	START	BREAK	BREAK	FINISH	TOTAL HOURS

- VEHICLE INFORMATION
- START LOCATION
- END LOCATION
- PURPOSE

START	END	BUSINESS MILES	PERSONAL MILES

DATE	START	BREAK	BREAK	FINISH	TOTAL HOURS

- VEHICLE INFORMATION
- START LOCATION
- END LOCATION
- PURPOSE

START	END	BUSINESS MILES	PERSONAL MILES

DATE	START	BREAK	BREAK	FINISH	TOTAL HOURS

- VEHICLE INFORMATION
- START LOCATION
- END LOCATION
- PURPOSE

START	END	BUSINESS MILES	PERSONAL MILES

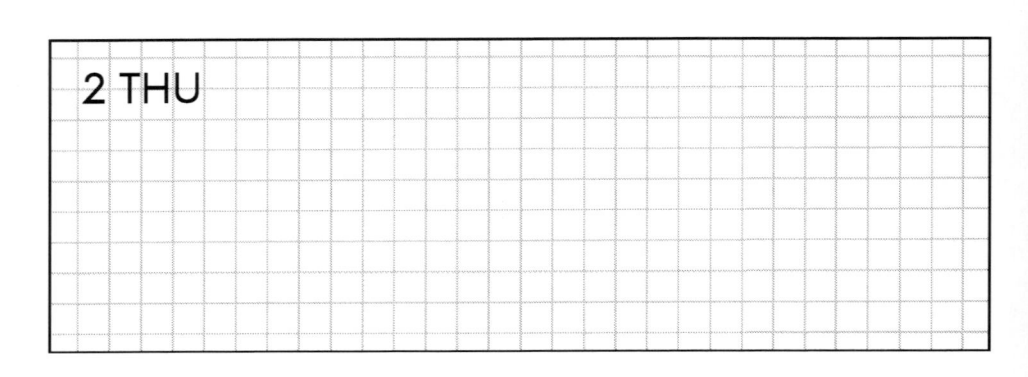

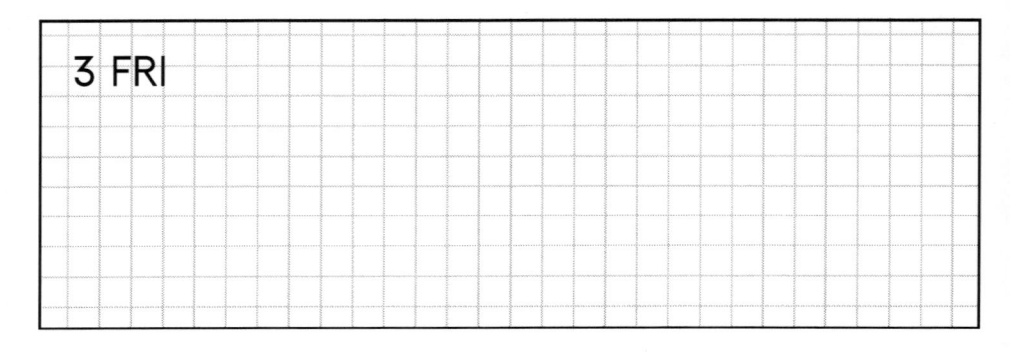

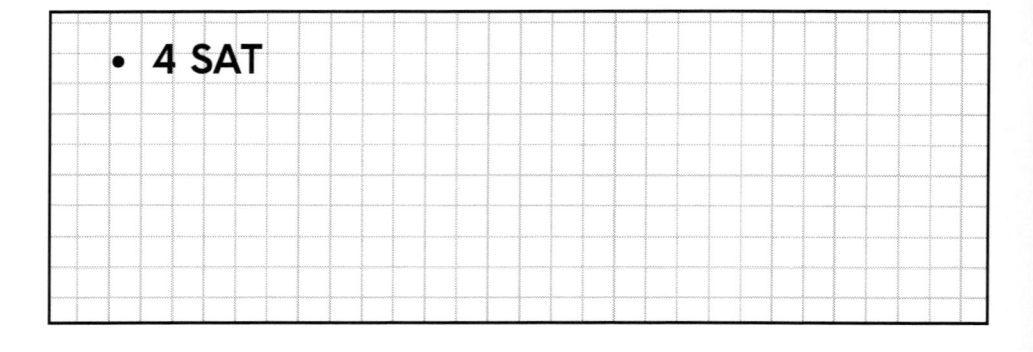

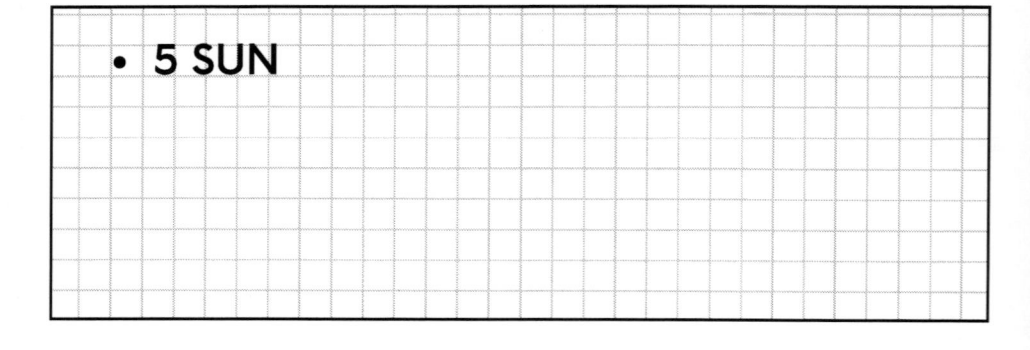

JUNE 2022

2 THU

3 FRI

- 4 SAT

- 5 SUN

DATE	START	BREAK	BREAK	FINISH	TOTAL HOURS

- VEHICLE INFORMATION
- START LOCATION
- END LOCATION
- PURPOSE

START	END	BUSINESS MILES	PERSONAL MILES

DATE	START	BREAK	BREAK	FINISH	TOTAL HOURS

- VEHICLE INFORMATION
- START LOCATION
- END LOCATION
- PURPOSE

START	END	BUSINESS MILES	PERSONAL MILES

DATE	START	BREAK	BREAK	FINISH	TOTAL HOURS

- VEHICLE INFORMATION
- START LOCATION
- END LOCATION
- PURPOSE

START	END	BUSINESS MILES	PERSONAL MILES

DATE	START	BREAK	BREAK	FINISH	TOTAL HOURS

- VEHICLE INFORMATION
- START LOCATION
- END LOCATION
- PURPOSE

START	END	BUSINESS MILES	PERSONAL MILES

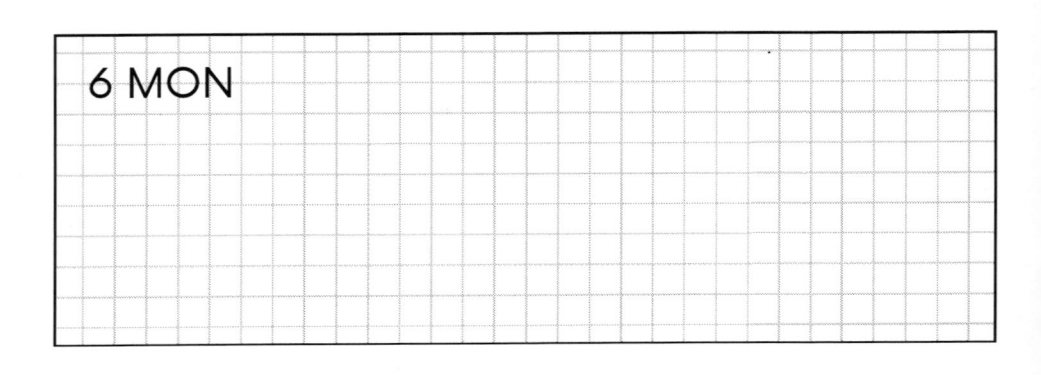

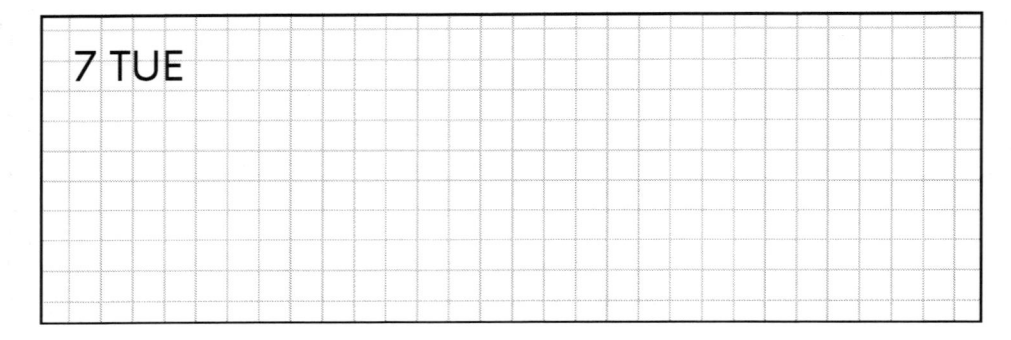

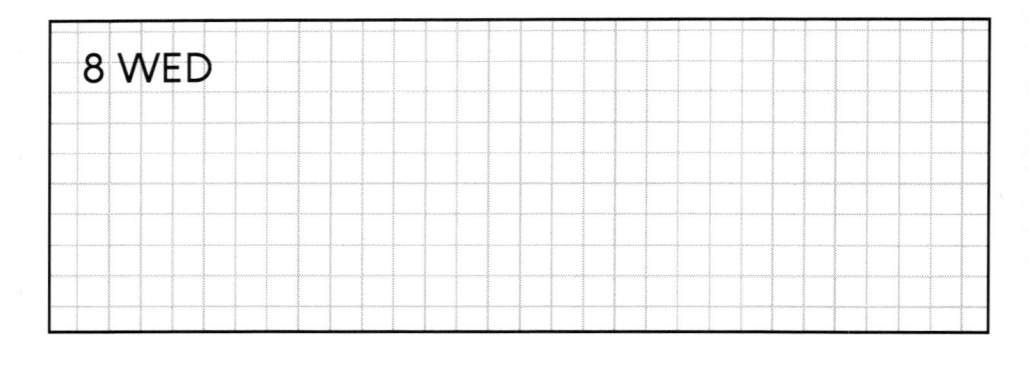

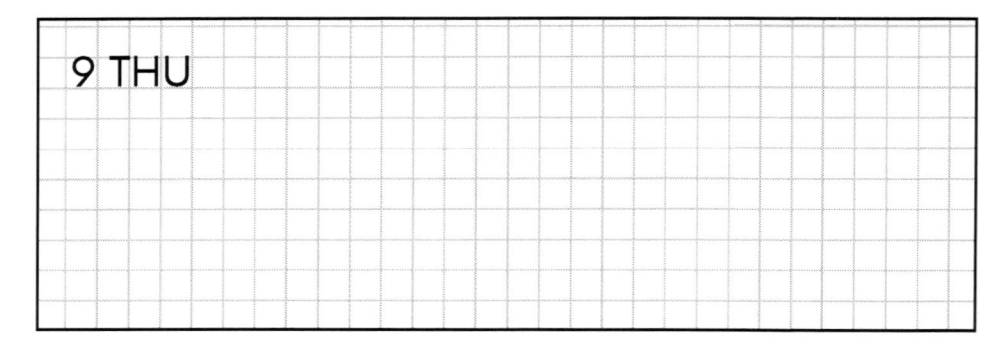

JUNE 2022

6 MON

7 TUE

8 WED

9 THU

DATE	START	BREAK	BREAK	FINISH	TOTAL HOURS

- VEHICLE INFORMATION
- START LOCATION
- END LOCATION
- PURPOSE

START	END	BUSINESS MILES	PERSONAL MILES

DATE	START	BREAK	BREAK	FINISH	TOTAL HOURS

- VEHICLE INFORMATION
- START LOCATION
- END LOCATION
- PURPOSE

START	END	BUSINESS MILES	PERSONAL MILES

DATE	START	BREAK	BREAK	FINISH	TOTAL HOURS

- VEHICLE INFORMATION
- START LOCATION
- END LOCATION
- PURPOSE

START	END	BUSINESS MILES	PERSONAL MILES

DATE	START	BREAK	BREAK	FINISH	TOTAL HOURS

- VEHICLE INFORMATION
- START LOCATION
- END LOCATION
- PURPOSE

START	END	BUSINESS MILES	PERSONAL MILES

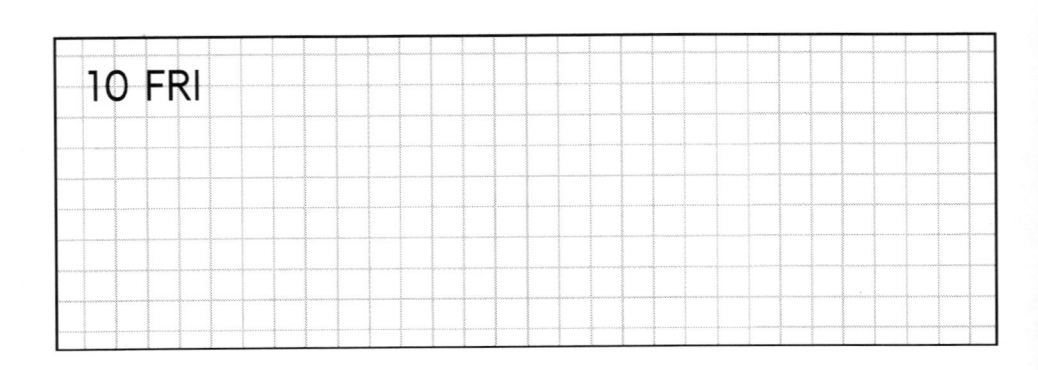

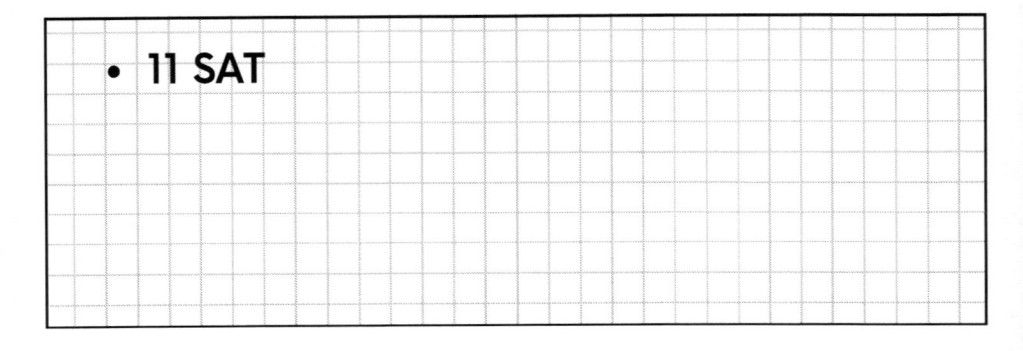

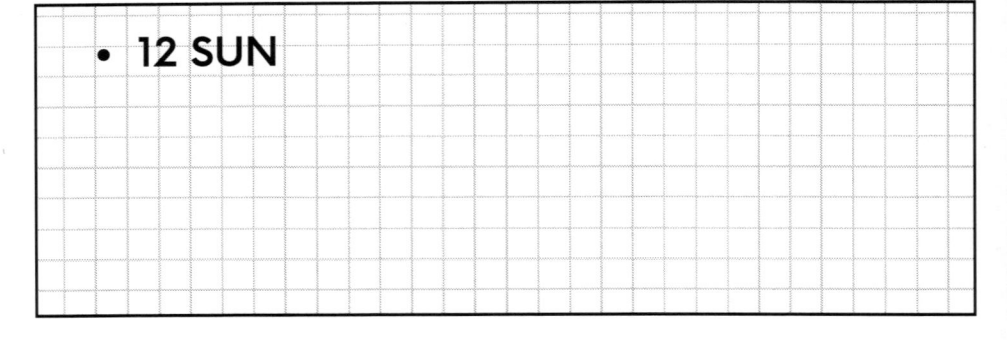

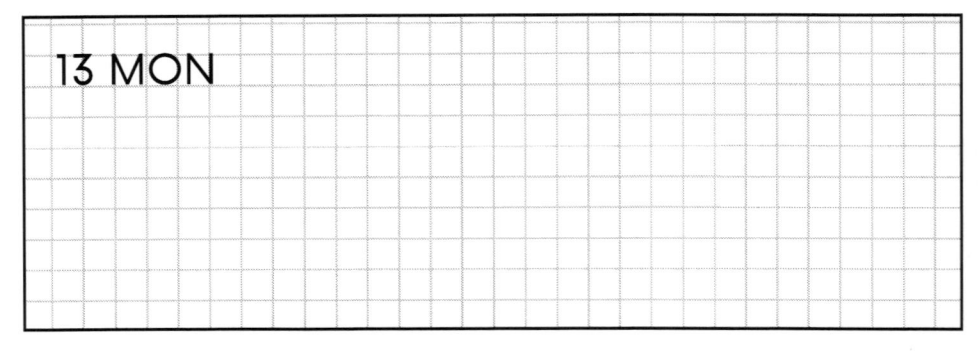

JUNE 2022

10 FRI

- 11 SAT

- 12 SUN

13 MON

DATE	START	BREAK	BREAK	FINISH	TOTAL HOURS

- **VEHICLE INFORMATION**
- **START LOCATION**
- **END LOCATION**
- **PURPOSE**

START	END	BUSINESS MILES	PERSONAL MILES

DATE	START	BREAK	BREAK	FINISH	TOTAL HOURS

- **VEHICLE INFORMATION**
- **START LOCATION**
- **END LOCATION**
- **PURPOSE**

START	END	BUSINESS MILES	PERSONAL MILES

DATE	START	BREAK	BREAK	FINISH	TOTAL HOURS

- **VEHICLE INFORMATION**
- **START LOCATION**
- **END LOCATION**
- **PURPOSE**

START	END	BUSINESS MILES	PERSONAL MILES

DATE	START	BREAK	BREAK	FINISH	TOTAL HOURS

- **VEHICLE INFORMATION**
- **START LOCATION**
- **END LOCATION**
- **PURPOSE**

START	END	BUSINESS MILES	PERSONAL MILES

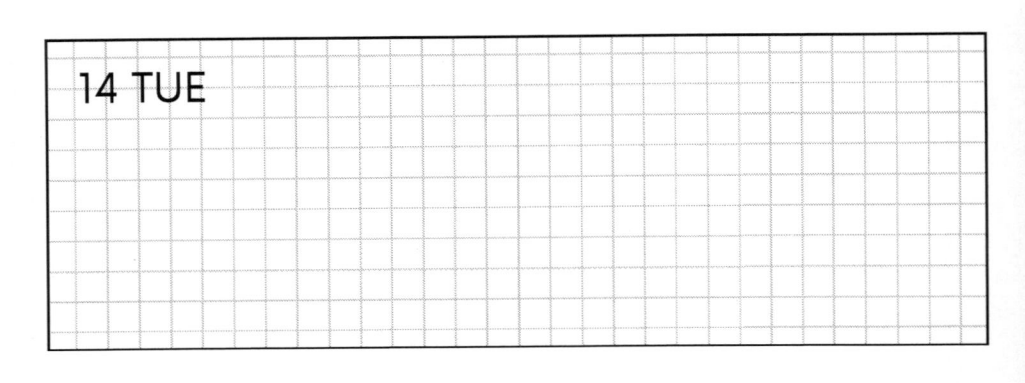

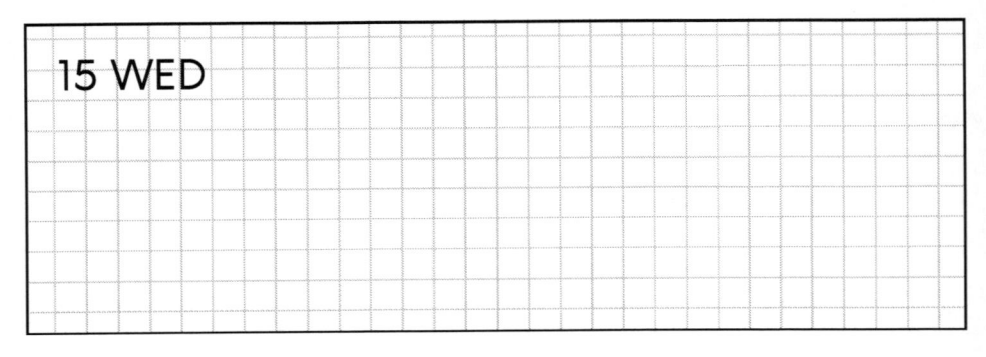

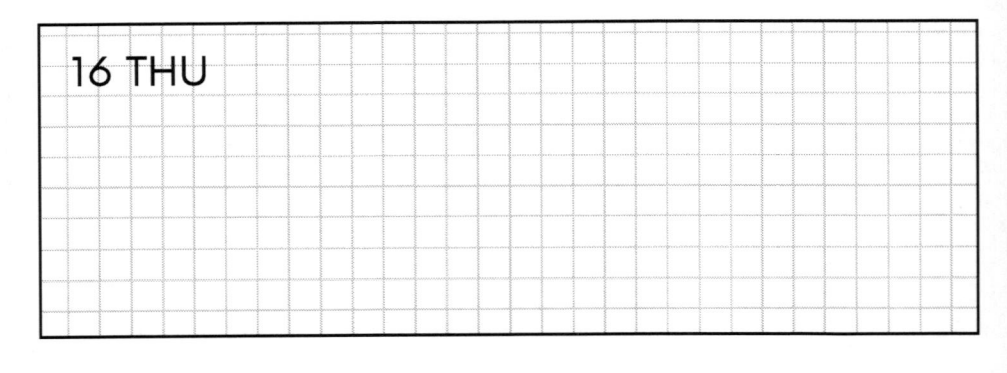

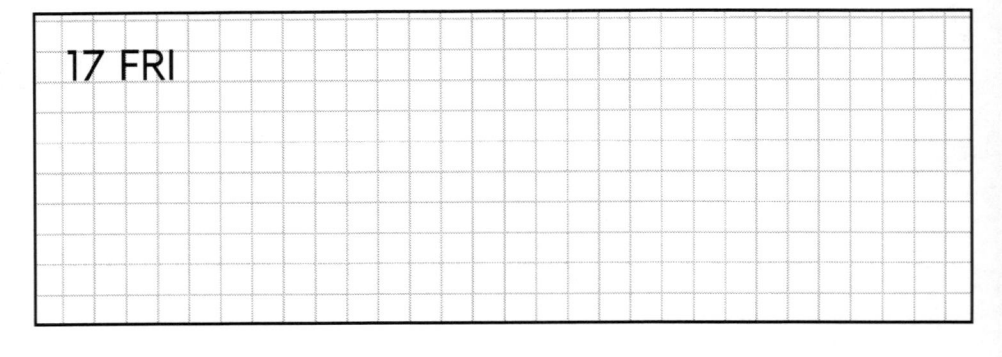

JUNE 2022

14 TUE

15 WED

16 THU

17 FRI

DATE	START	BREAK	BREAK	FINISH	TOTAL HOURS

- VEHICLE INFORMATION
- START LOCATION
- END LOCATION
- PURPOSE

START	END	BUSINESS MILES	PERSONAL MILES

DATE	START	BREAK	BREAK	FINISH	TOTAL HOURS

- VEHICLE INFORMATION
- START LOCATION
- END LOCATION
- PURPOSE

START	END	BUSINESS MILES	PERSONAL MILES

DATE	START	BREAK	BREAK	FINISH	TOTAL HOURS

- VEHICLE INFORMATION
- START LOCATION
- END LOCATION
- PURPOSE

START	END	BUSINESS MILES	PERSONAL MILES

DATE	START	BREAK	BREAK	FINISH	TOTAL HOURS

- VEHICLE INFORMATION
- START LOCATION
- END LOCATION
- PURPOSE

START	END	BUSINESS MILES	PERSONAL MILES

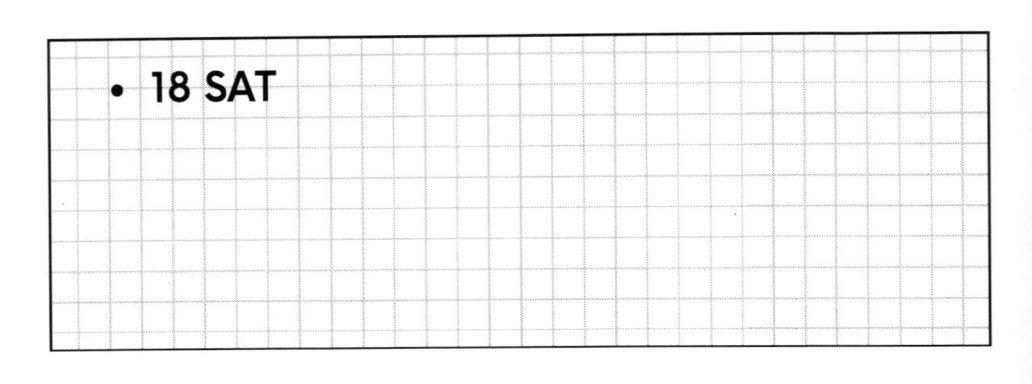

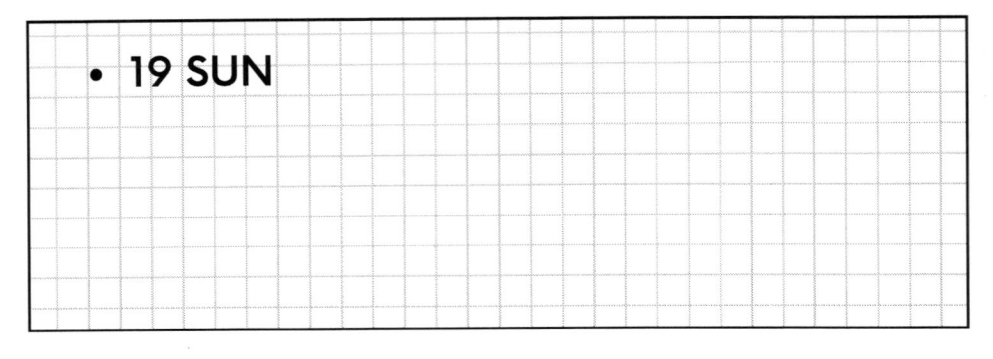

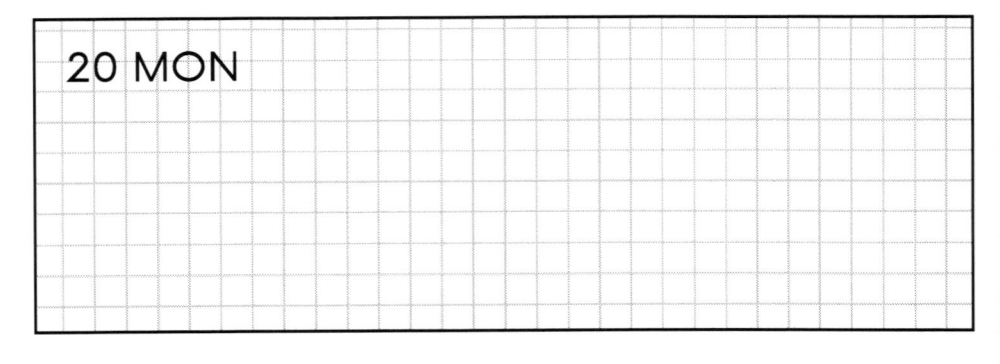

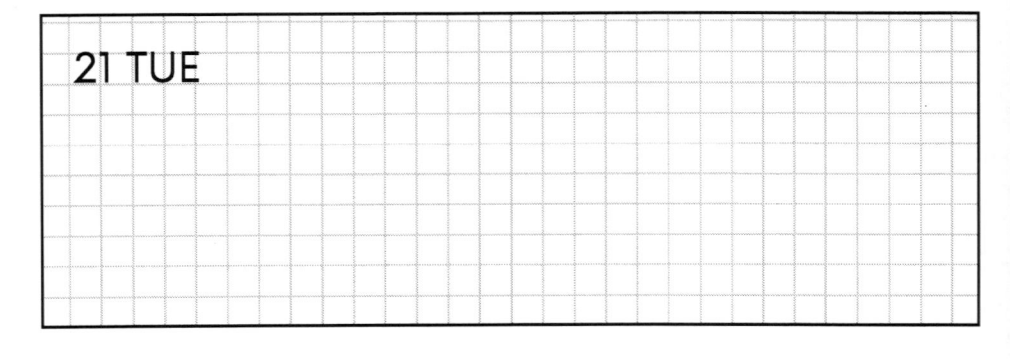

JUNE 2022

- **18 SAT**

- **19 SUN**

20 MON

21 TUE

DATE	START	BREAK	BREAK	FINISH	TOTAL HOURS

- VEHICLE INFORMATION
- START LOCATION
- END LOCATION
- PURPOSE

START	END	BUSINESS MILES	PERSONAL MILES

DATE	START	BREAK	BREAK	FINISH	TOTAL HOURS

- VEHICLE INFORMATION
- START LOCATION
- END LOCATION
- PURPOSE

START	END	BUSINESS MILES	PERSONAL MILES

DATE	START	BREAK	BREAK	FINISH	TOTAL HOURS

- VEHICLE INFORMATION
- START LOCATION
- END LOCATION
- PURPOSE

START	END	BUSINESS MILES	PERSONAL MILES

DATE	START	BREAK	BREAK	FINISH	TOTAL HOURS

- VEHICLE INFORMATION
- START LOCATION
- END LOCATION
- PURPOSE

START	END	BUSINESS MILES	PERSONAL MILES

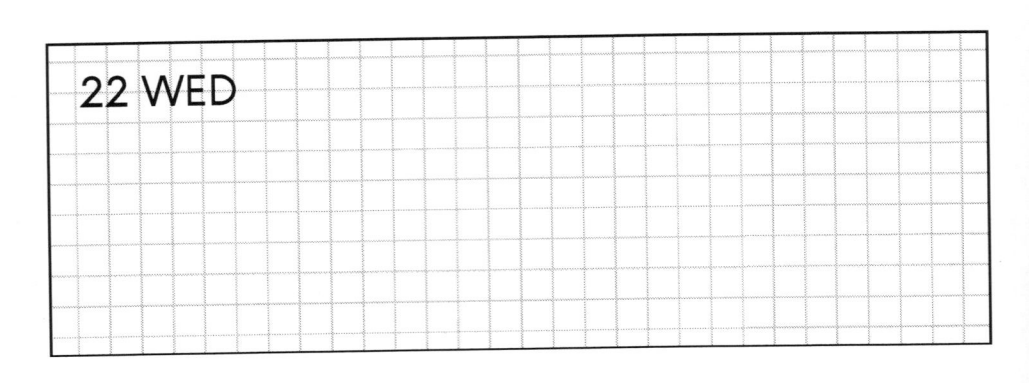

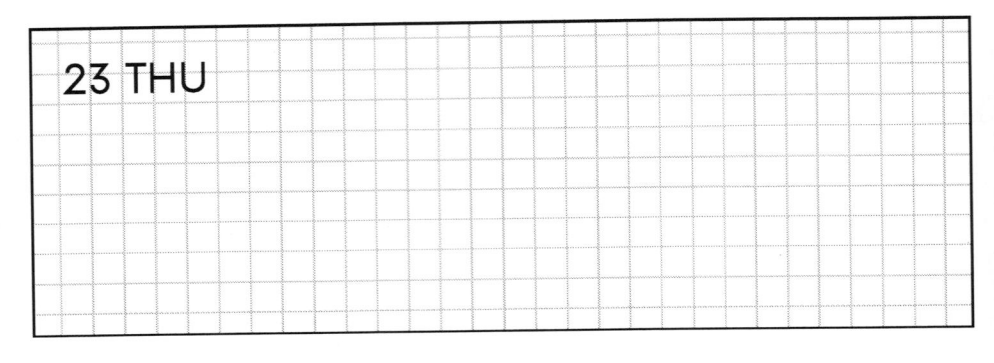

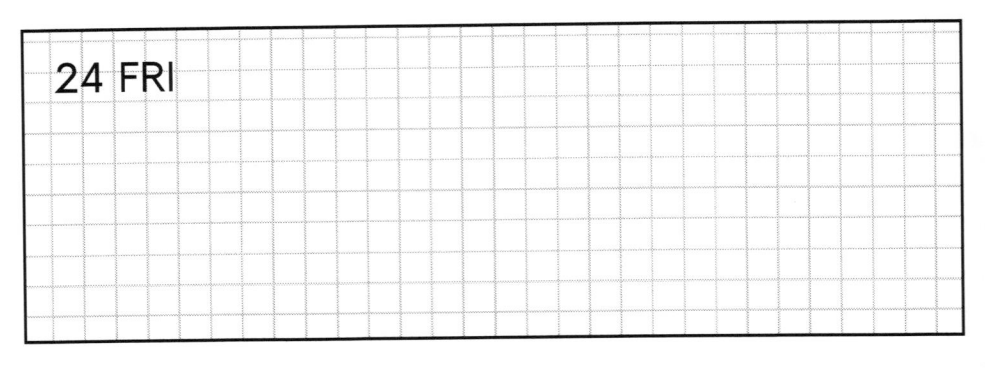

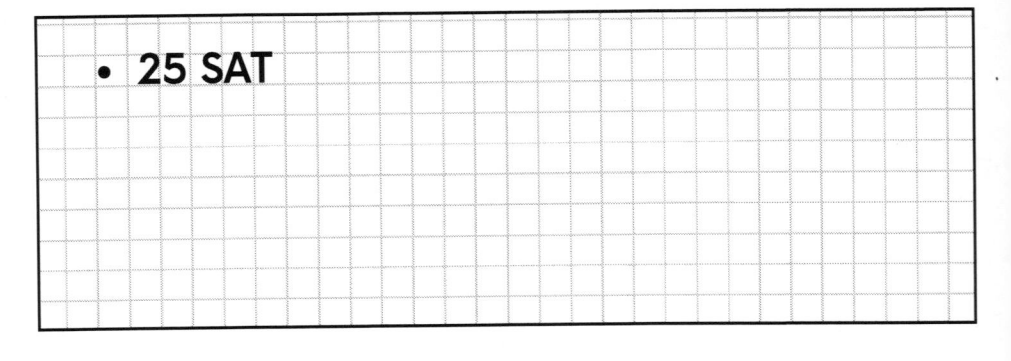

JUNE   2022

22 WED

23 THU

24 FRI

- **25 SAT**

DATE	START	BREAK	BREAK	FINISH	TOTAL HOURS

- VEHICLE INFORMATION
- START LOCATION
- END LOCATION
- PURPOSE

START	END	BUSINESS MILES	PERSONAL MILES

DATE	START	BREAK	BREAK	FINISH	TOTAL HOURS

- VEHICLE INFORMATION
- START LOCATION
- END LOCATION
- PURPOSE

START	END	BUSINESS MILES	PERSONAL MILES

DATE	START	BREAK	BREAK	FINISH	TOTAL HOURS

- VEHICLE INFORMATION
- START LOCATION
- END LOCATION
- PURPOSE

START	END	BUSINESS MILES	PERSONAL MILES

DATE	START	BREAK	BREAK	FINISH	TOTAL HOURS

- VEHICLE INFORMATION
- START LOCATION
- END LOCATION
- PURPOSE

START	END	BUSINESS MILES	PERSONAL MILES

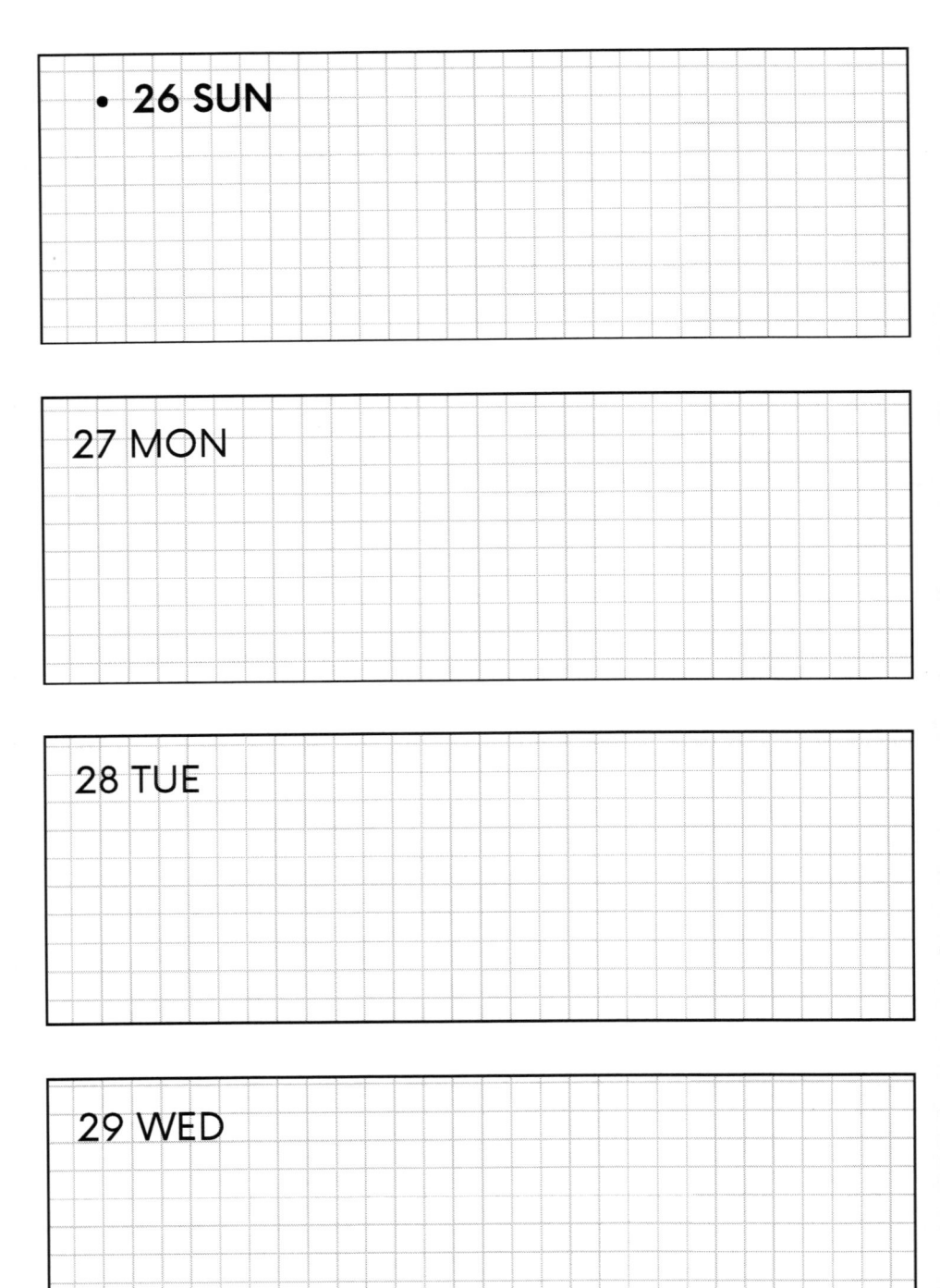

JUNE   2022

- **26 SUN**

27 MON

28 TUE

29 WED

DATE	START	BREAK	BREAK	FINISH	TOTAL HOURS

- **VEHICLE INFORMATION**
- **START LOCATION**
- **END LOCATION**
- **PURPOSE**

START	END	BUSINESS MILES	PERSONAL MILES

DATE	START	BREAK	BREAK	FINISH	TOTAL HOURS

- **VEHICLE INFORMATION**
- **START LOCATION**
- **END LOCATION**
- **PURPOSE**

START	END	BUSINESS MILES	PERSONAL MILES

DATE	START	BREAK	BREAK	FINISH	TOTAL HOURS

- **VEHICLE INFORMATION**
- **START LOCATION**
- **END LOCATION**
- **PURPOSE**

START	END	BUSINESS MILES	PERSONAL MILES

DATE	START	BREAK	BREAK	FINISH	TOTAL HOURS

- **VEHICLE INFORMATION**
- **START LOCATION**
- **END LOCATION**
- **PURPOSE**

START	END	BUSINESS MILES	PERSONAL MILES

JUNE/JULY 2022

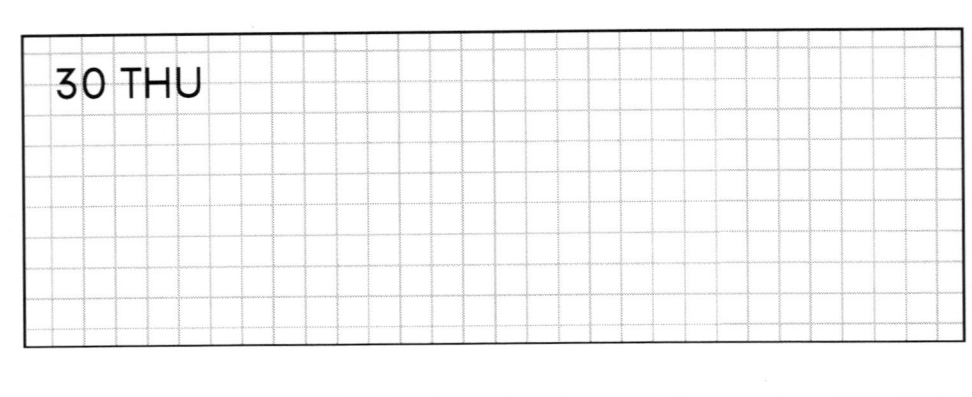

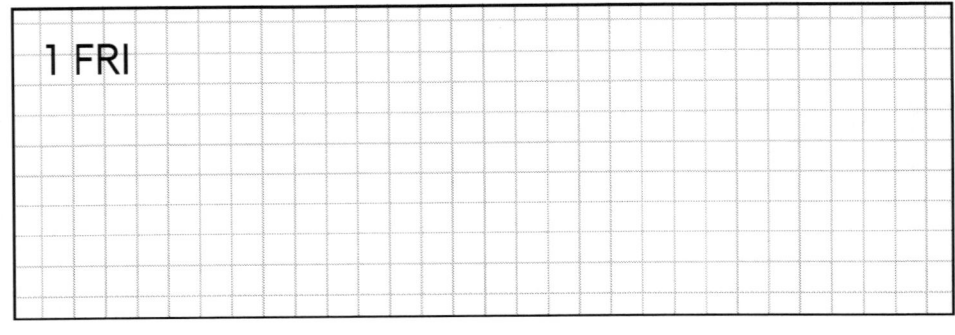

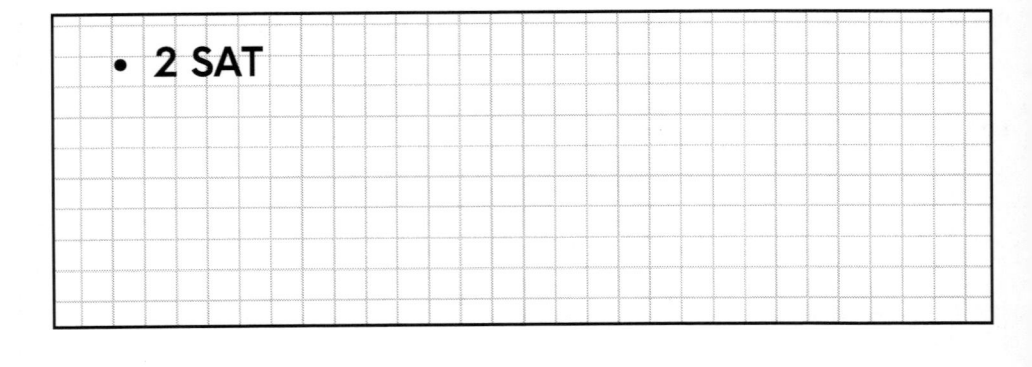

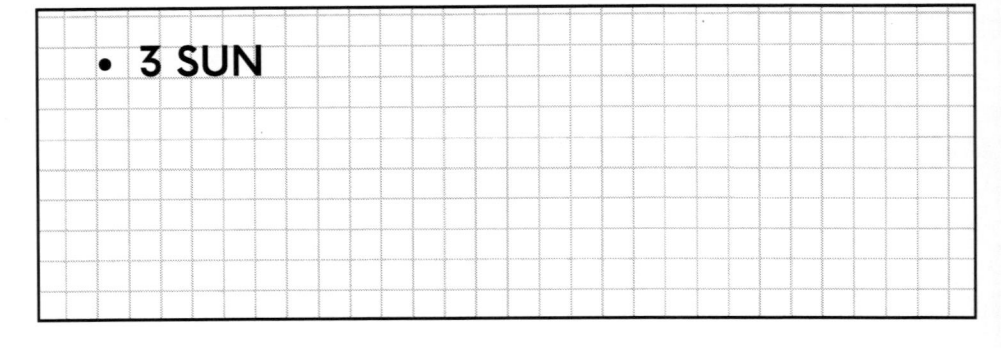

30 THU

1 FRI

- **2 SAT**

- **3 SUN**

DATE	START	BREAK	BREAK	FINISH	TOTAL HOURS

- VEHICLE INFORMATION
- START LOCATION
- END LOCATION
- PURPOSE

START	END	BUSINESS MILES	PERSONAL MILES

DATE	START	BREAK	BREAK	FINISH	TOTAL HOURS

- VEHICLE INFORMATION
- START LOCATION
- END LOCATION
- PURPOSE

START	END	BUSINESS MILES	PERSONAL MILES

DATE	START	BREAK	BREAK	FINISH	TOTAL HOURS

- VEHICLE INFORMATION
- START LOCATION
- END LOCATION
- PURPOSE

START	END	BUSINESS MILES	PERSONAL MILES

DATE	START	BREAK	BREAK	FINISH	TOTAL HOURS

- VEHICLE INFORMATION
- START LOCATION
- END LOCATION
- PURPOSE

START	END	BUSINESS MILES	PERSONAL MILES

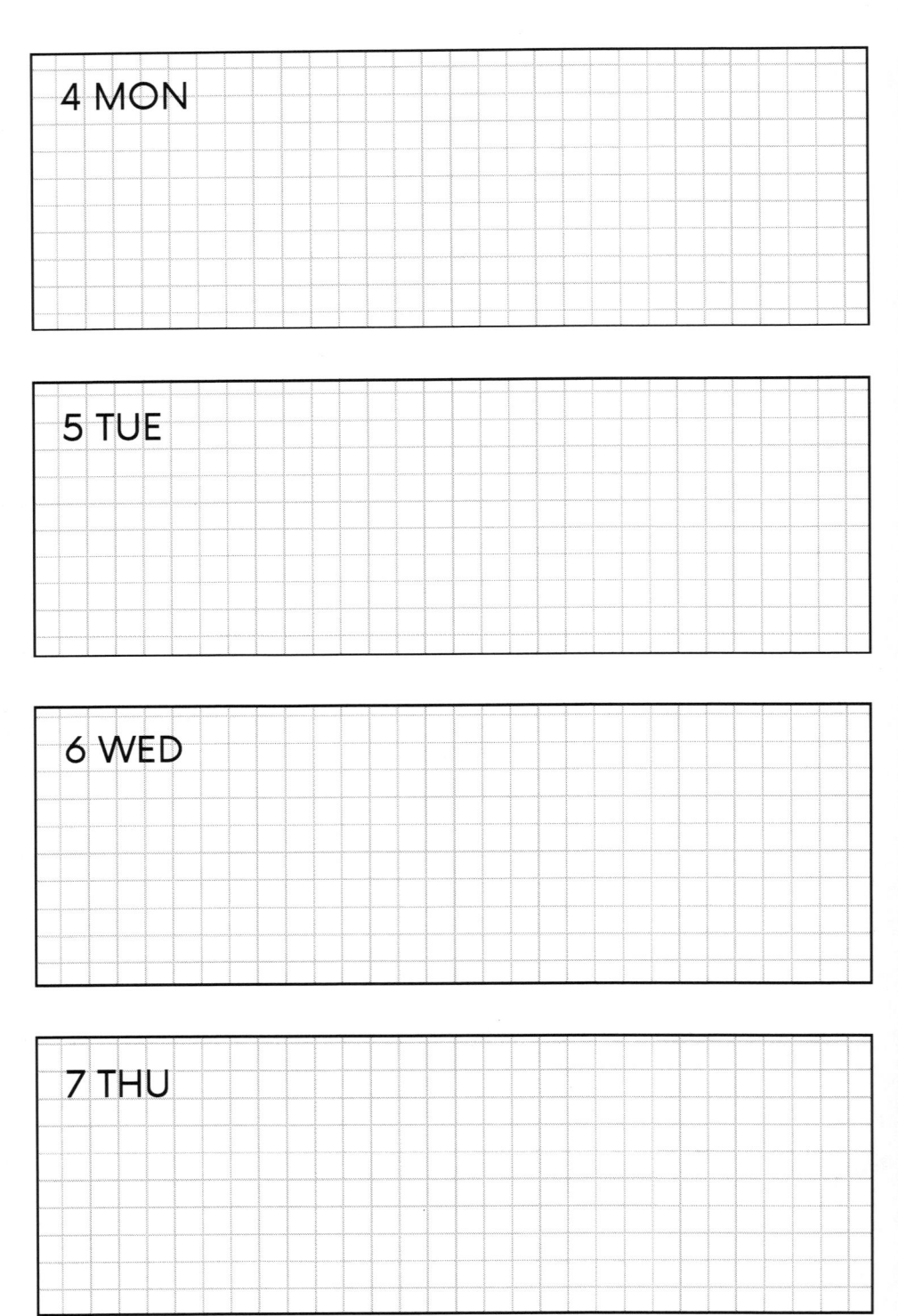

JULY   2022

4 MON

5 TUE

6 WED

7 THU

DATE	START	BREAK	BREAK	FINISH	TOTAL HOURS

- VEHICLE INFORMATION
- START LOCATION
- END LOCATION
- PURPOSE

START	END	BUSINESS MILES	PERSONAL MILES

DATE	START	BREAK	BREAK	FINISH	TOTAL HOURS

- VEHICLE INFORMATION
- START LOCATION
- END LOCATION
- PURPOSE

START	END	BUSINESS MILES	PERSONAL MILES

DATE	START	BREAK	BREAK	FINISH	TOTAL HOURS

- VEHICLE INFORMATION
- START LOCATION
- END LOCATION
- PURPOSE

START	END	BUSINESS MILES	PERSONAL MILES

DATE	START	BREAK	BREAK	FINISH	TOTAL HOURS

- VEHICLE INFORMATION
- START LOCATION
- END LOCATION
- PURPOSE

START	END	BUSINESS MILES	PERSONAL MILES

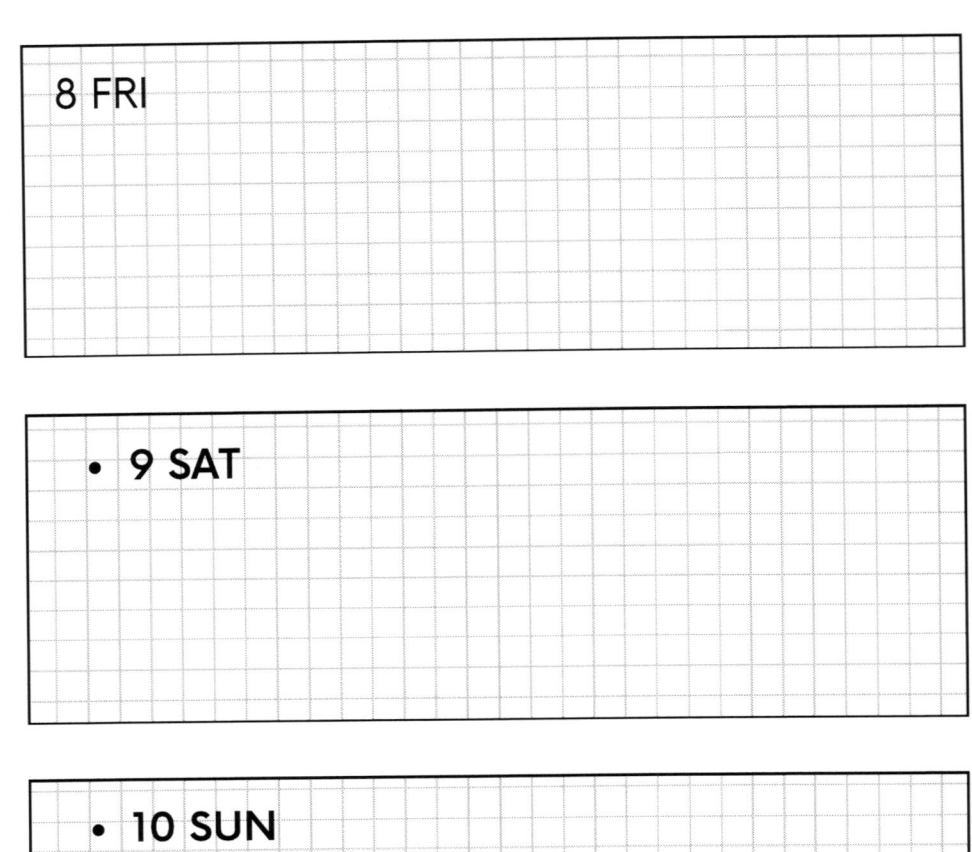

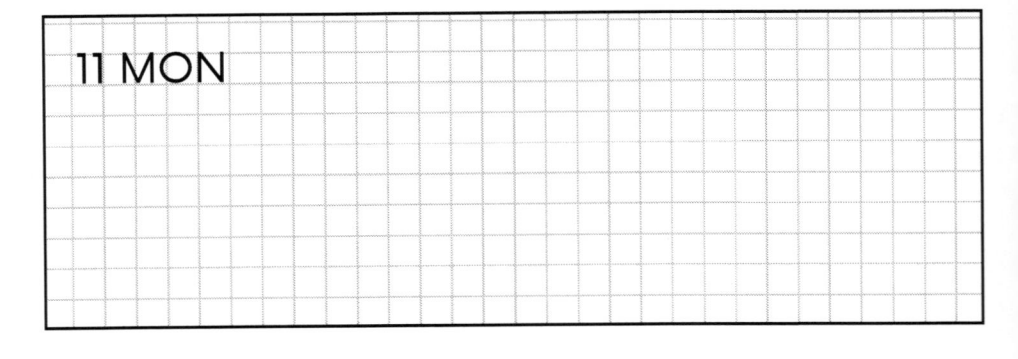

JULY 2022

8 FRI

- 9 SAT

- 10 SUN

11 MON

DATE	START	BREAK	BREAK	FINISH	TOTAL HOURS

- VEHICLE INFORMATION
- START LOCATION
- END LOCATION
- PURPOSE

START	END	BUSINESS MILES	PERSONAL MILES

DATE	START	BREAK	BREAK	FINISH	TOTAL HOURS

- VEHICLE INFORMATION
- START LOCATION
- END LOCATION
- PURPOSE

START	END	BUSINESS MILES	PERSONAL MILES

DATE	START	BREAK	BREAK	FINISH	TOTAL HOURS

- VEHICLE INFORMATION
- START LOCATION
- END LOCATION
- PURPOSE

START	END	BUSINESS MILES	PERSONAL MILES

DATE	START	BREAK	BREAK	FINISH	TOTAL HOURS

- VEHICLE INFORMATION
- START LOCATION
- END LOCATION
- PURPOSE

START	END	BUSINESS MILES	PERSONAL MILES

JULY 2022

12 TUE

13 WED

14 THU

15 FRI

DATE	START	BREAK	BREAK	FINISH	TOTAL HOURS

- **VEHICLE INFORMATION**
- **START LOCATION**
- **END LOCATION**
- **PURPOSE**

START	END	BUSINESS MILES	PERSONAL MILES

DATE	START	BREAK	BREAK	FINISH	TOTAL HOURS

- **VEHICLE INFORMATION**
- **START LOCATION**
- **END LOCATION**
- **PURPOSE**

START	END	BUSINESS MILES	PERSONAL MILES

DATE	START	BREAK	BREAK	FINISH	TOTAL HOURS

- **VEHICLE INFORMATION**
- **START LOCATION**
- **END LOCATION**
- **PURPOSE**

START	END	BUSINESS MILES	PERSONAL MILES

DATE	START	BREAK	BREAK	FINISH	TOTAL HOURS

- **VEHICLE INFORMATION**
- **START LOCATION**
- **END LOCATION**
- **PURPOSE**

START	END	BUSINESS MILES	PERSONAL MILES

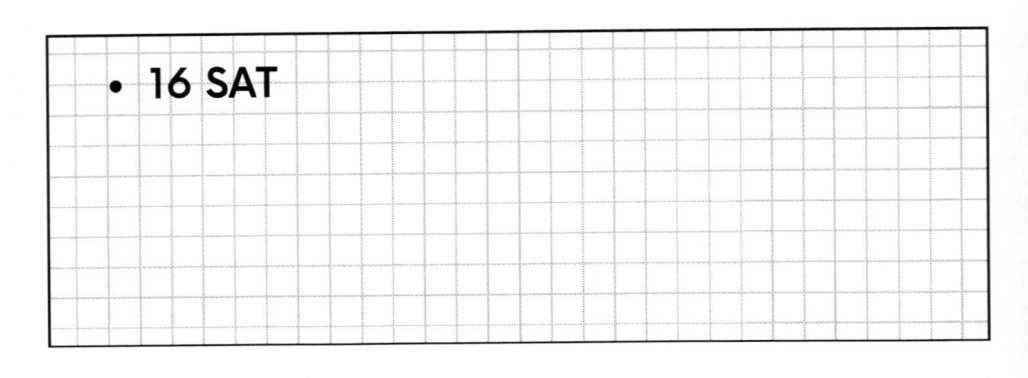

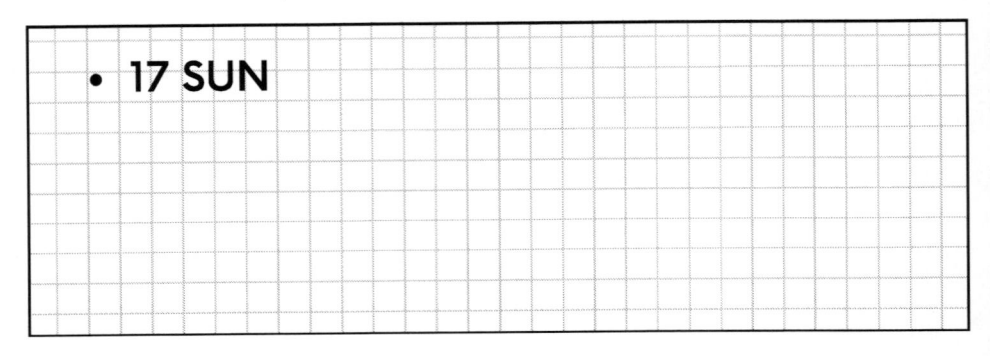

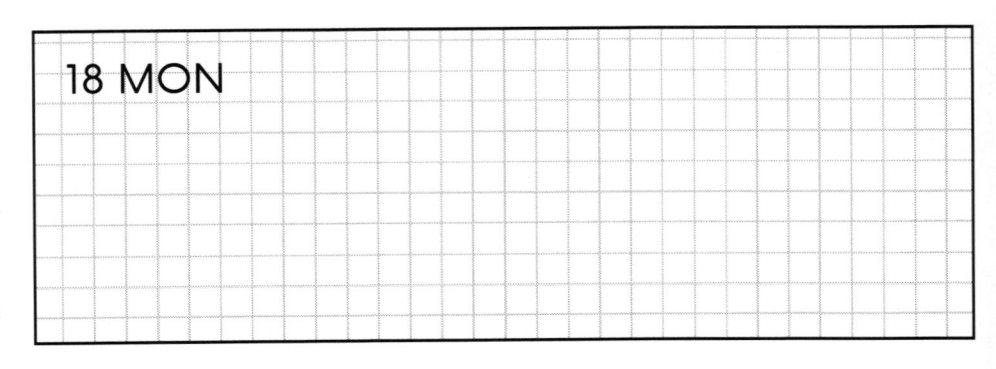

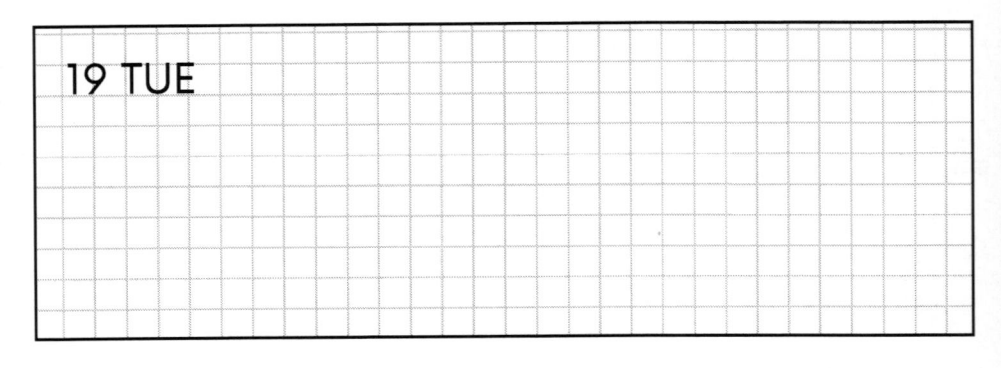

JULY 2022

- **16 SAT**

- **17 SUN**

18 MON

19 TUE

DATE	START	BREAK	BREAK	FINISH	TOTAL HOURS

- VEHICLE INFORMATION
- START LOCATION
- END LOCATION
- PURPOSE

START	END	BUSINESS MILES	PERSONAL MILES

DATE	START	BREAK	BREAK	FINISH	TOTAL HOURS

- VEHICLE INFORMATION
- START LOCATION
- END LOCATION
- PURPOSE

START	END	BUSINESS MILES	PERSONAL MILES

DATE	START	BREAK	BREAK	FINISH	TOTAL HOURS

- VEHICLE INFORMATION
- START LOCATION
- END LOCATION
- PURPOSE

START	END	BUSINESS MILES	PERSONAL MILES

DATE	START	BREAK	BREAK	FINISH	TOTAL HOURS

- VEHICLE INFORMATION
- START LOCATION
- END LOCATION
- PURPOSE

START	END	BUSINESS MILES	PERSONAL MILES

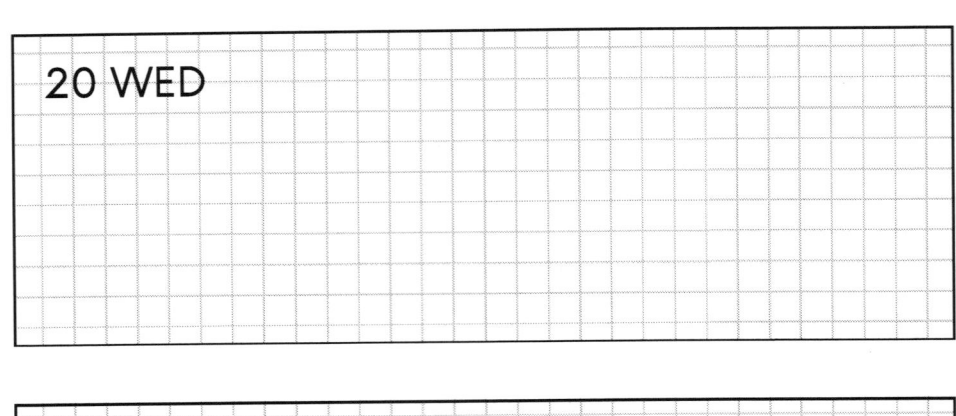

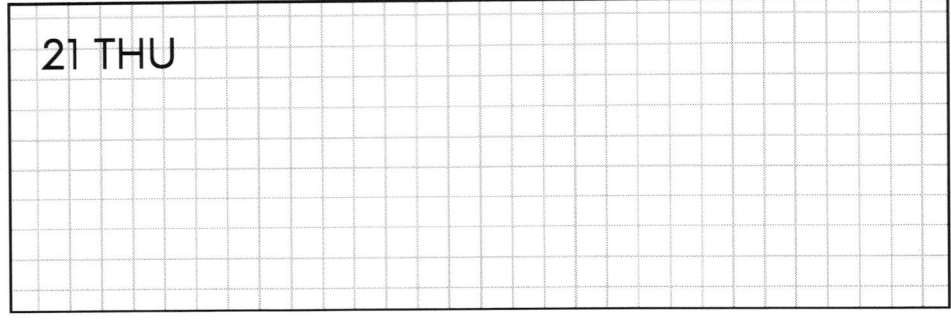

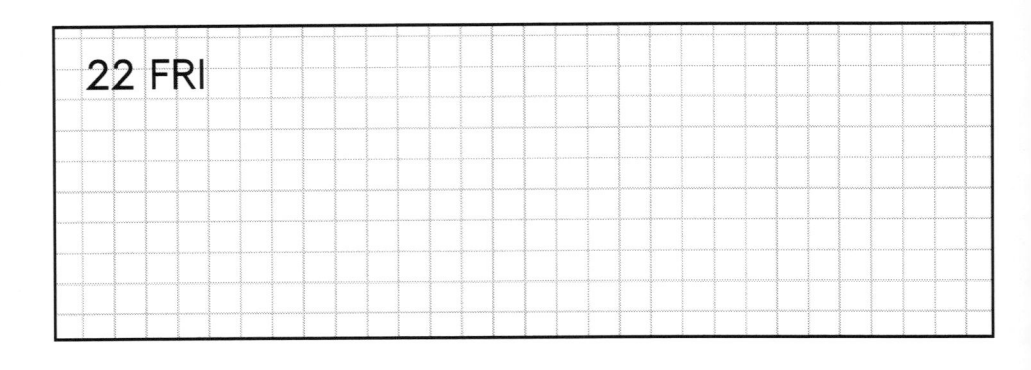

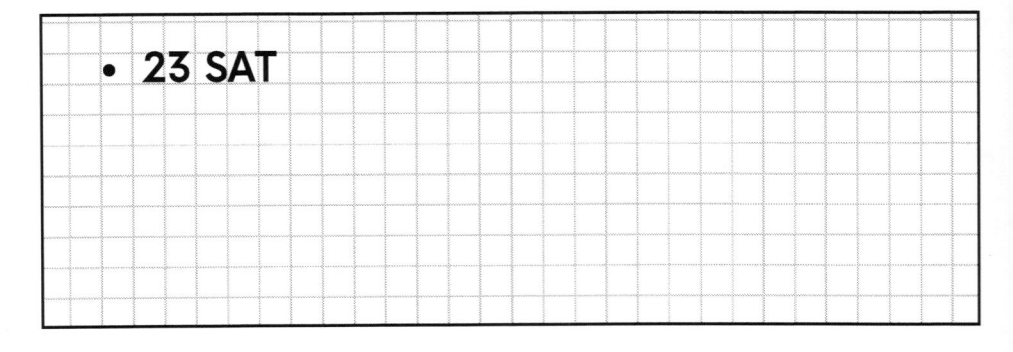

JULY 2022

20 WED

21 THU

22 FRI

- **23 SAT**

DATE	START	BREAK	BREAK	FINISH	TOTAL HOURS

- VEHICLE INFORMATION
- START LOCATION
- END LOCATION
- PURPOSE

START	END	BUSINESS MILES	PERSONAL MILES

DATE	START	BREAK	BREAK	FINISH	TOTAL HOURS

- VEHICLE INFORMATION
- START LOCATION
- END LOCATION
- PURPOSE

START	END	BUSINESS MILES	PERSONAL MILES

DATE	START	BREAK	BREAK	FINISH	TOTAL HOURS

- VEHICLE INFORMATION
- START LOCATION
- END LOCATION
- PURPOSE

START	END	BUSINESS MILES	PERSONAL MILES

DATE	START	BREAK	BREAK	FINISH	TOTAL HOURS

- VEHICLE INFORMATION
- START LOCATION
- END LOCATION
- PURPOSE

START	END	BUSINESS MILES	PERSONAL MILES

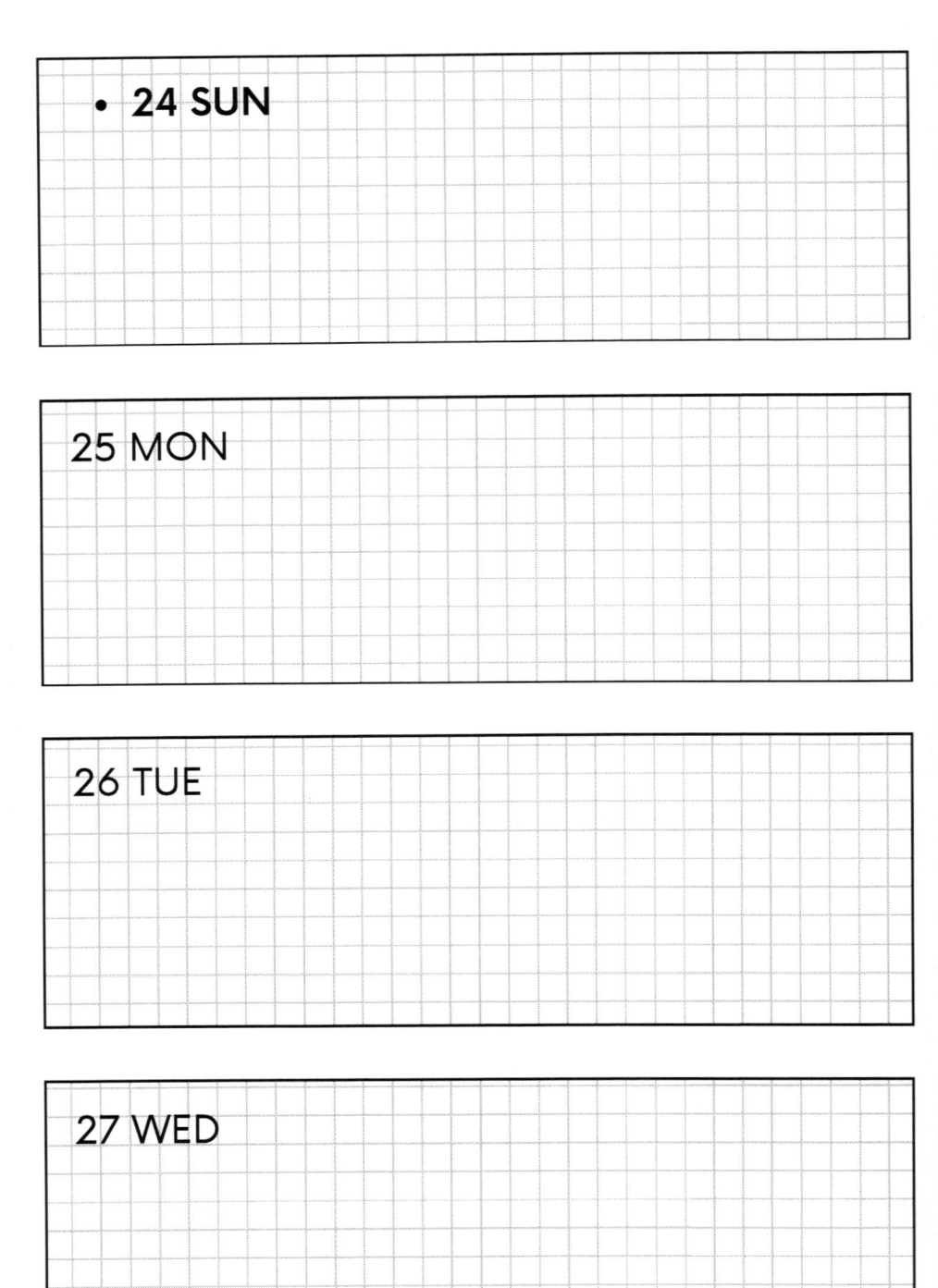

JULY 2022

- **24 SUN**

25 MON

26 TUE

27 WED

DATE	START	BREAK	BREAK	FINISH	TOTAL HOURS

- VEHICLE INFORMATION
- START LOCATION
- END LOCATION
- PURPOSE

START	END	BUSINESS MILES	PERSONAL MILES

DATE	START	BREAK	BREAK	FINISH	TOTAL HOURS

- VEHICLE INFORMATION
- START LOCATION
- END LOCATION
- PURPOSE

START	END	BUSINESS MILES	PERSONAL MILES

DATE	START	BREAK	BREAK	FINISH	TOTAL HOURS

- VEHICLE INFORMATION
- START LOCATION
- END LOCATION
- PURPOSE

START	END	BUSINESS MILES	PERSONAL MILES

DATE	START	BREAK	BREAK	FINISH	TOTAL HOURS

- VEHICLE INFORMATION
- START LOCATION
- END LOCATION
- PURPOSE

START	END	BUSINESS MILES	PERSONAL MILES

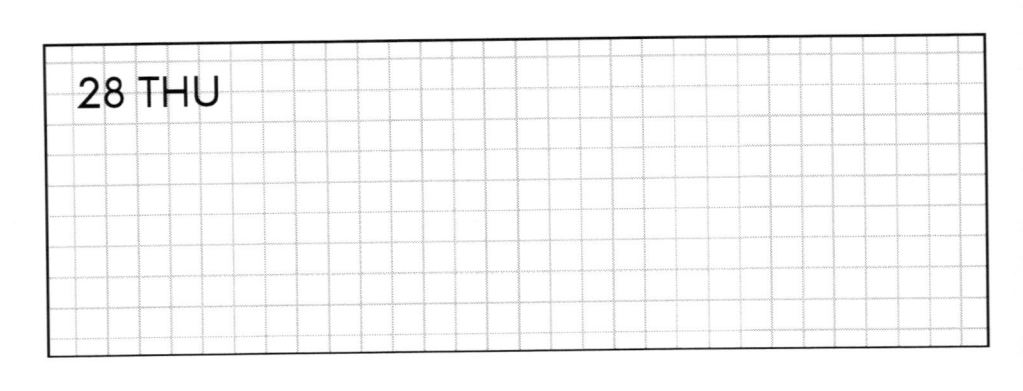

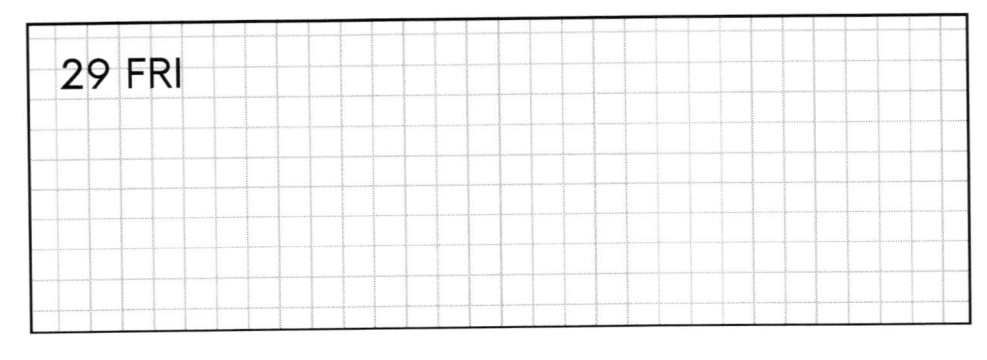

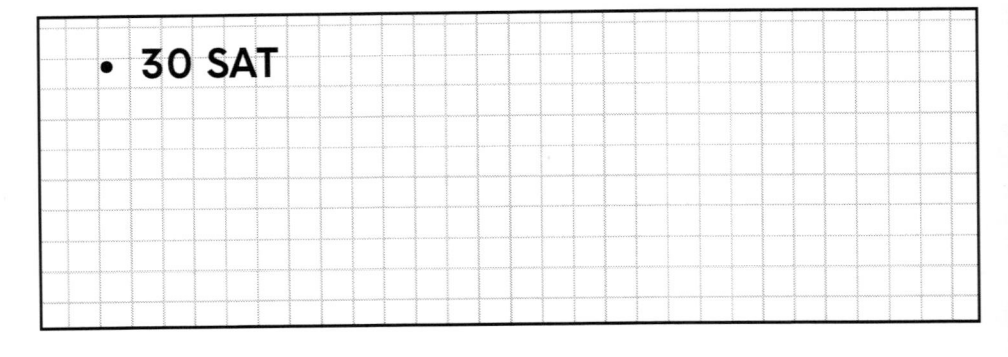

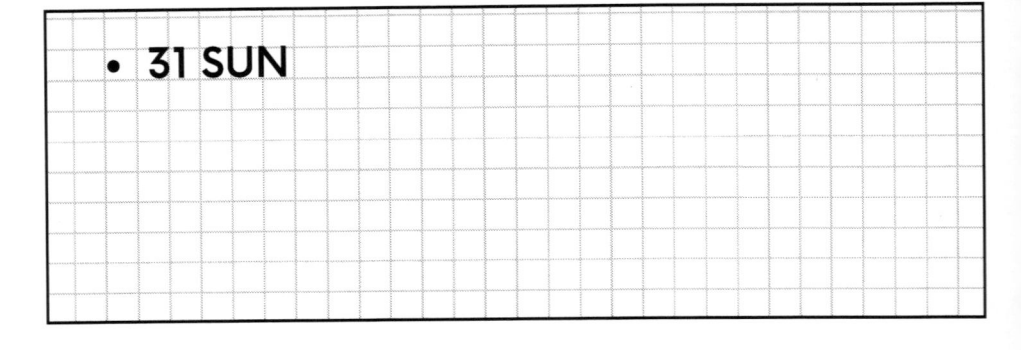

JULY 2022

28 THU

29 FRI

- ### 30 SAT

- ### 31 SUN

DATE	START	BREAK	BREAK	FINISH	TOTAL HOURS

- VEHICLE INFORMATION
- START LOCATION
- END LOCATION
- PURPOSE

START	END	BUSINESS MILES	PERSONAL MILES

DATE	START	BREAK	BREAK	FINISH	TOTAL HOURS

- VEHICLE INFORMATION
- START LOCATION
- END LOCATION
- PURPOSE

START	END	BUSINESS MILES	PERSONAL MILES

DATE	START	BREAK	BREAK	FINISH	TOTAL HOURS

- VEHICLE INFORMATION
- START LOCATION
- END LOCATION
- PURPOSE

START	END	BUSINESS MILES	PERSONAL MILES

DATE	START	BREAK	BREAK	FINISH	TOTAL HOURS

- VEHICLE INFORMATION
- START LOCATION
- END LOCATION
- PURPOSE

START	END	BUSINESS MILES	PERSONAL MILES

AUGUST 2022

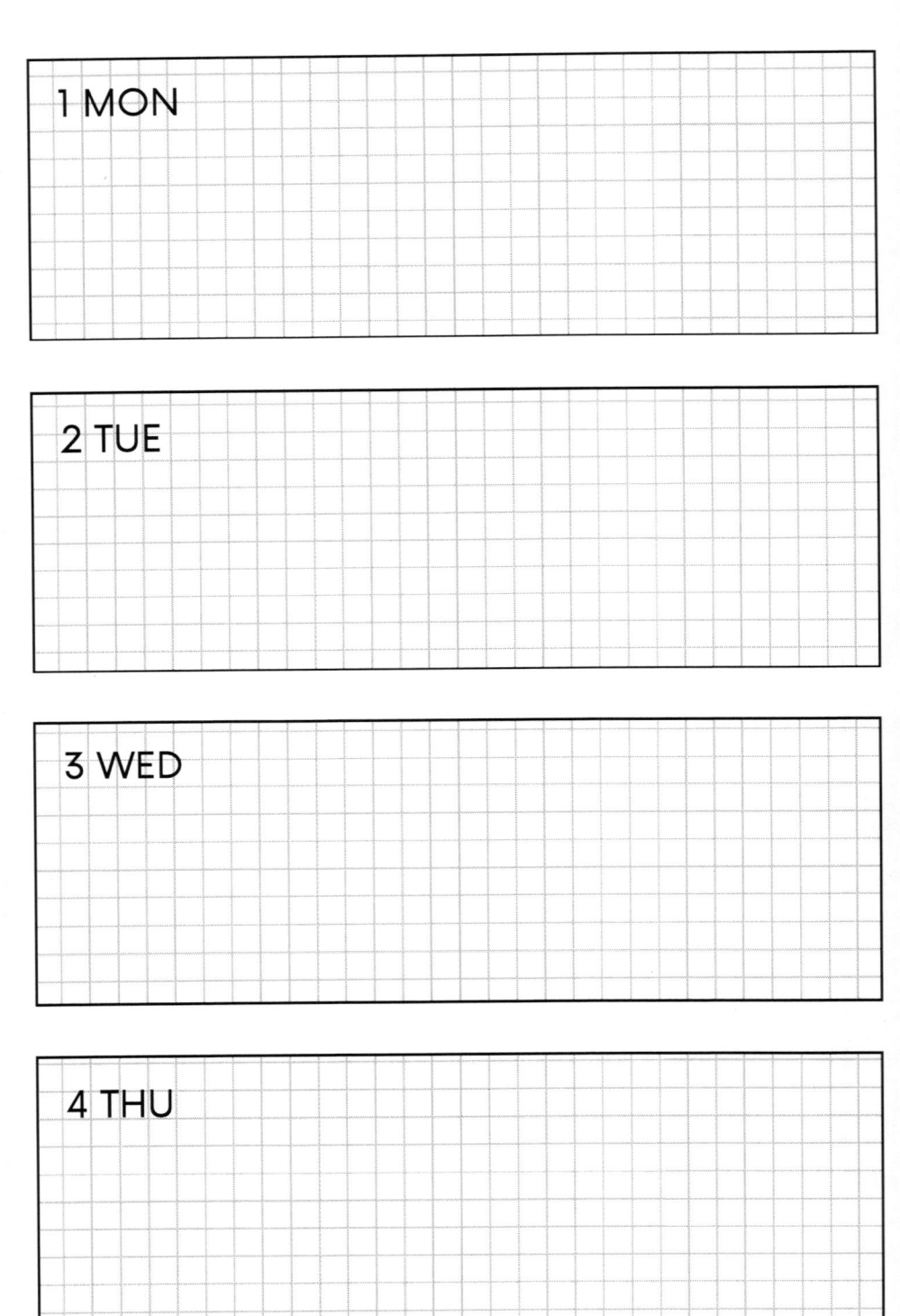

1 MON

2 TUE

3 WED

4 THU

DATE	START	BREAK	BREAK	FINISH	TOTAL HOURS

- VEHICLE INFORMATION
- START LOCATION
- END LOCATION
- PURPOSE

START	END	BUSINESS MILES	PERSONAL MILES

DATE	START	BREAK	BREAK	FINISH	TOTAL HOURS

- VEHICLE INFORMATION
- START LOCATION
- END LOCATION
- PURPOSE

START	END	BUSINESS MILES	PERSONAL MILES

DATE	START	BREAK	BREAK	FINISH	TOTAL HOURS

- VEHICLE INFORMATION
- START LOCATION
- END LOCATION
- PURPOSE

START	END	BUSINESS MILES	PERSONAL MILES

DATE	START	BREAK	BREAK	FINISH	TOTAL HOURS

- VEHICLE INFORMATION
- START LOCATION
- END LOCATION
- PURPOSE

START	END	BUSINESS MILES	PERSONAL MILES

AUGUST 2022

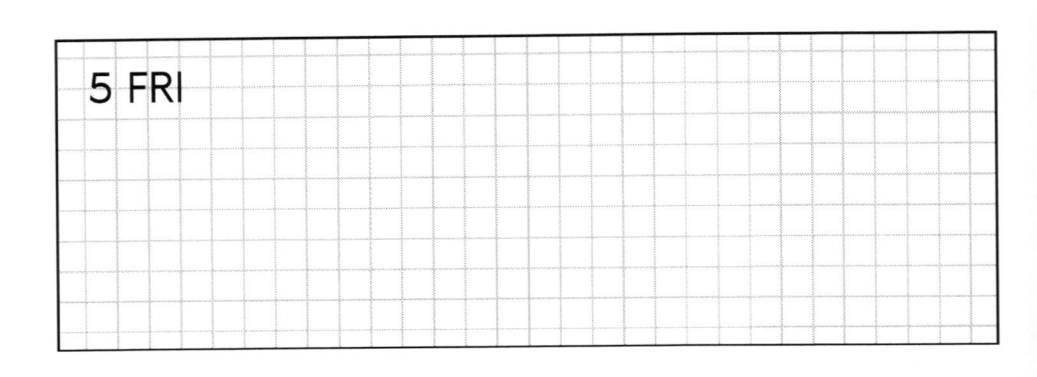

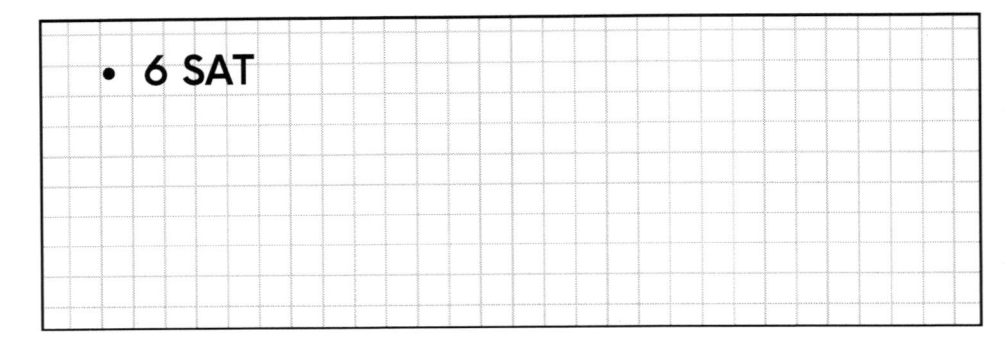

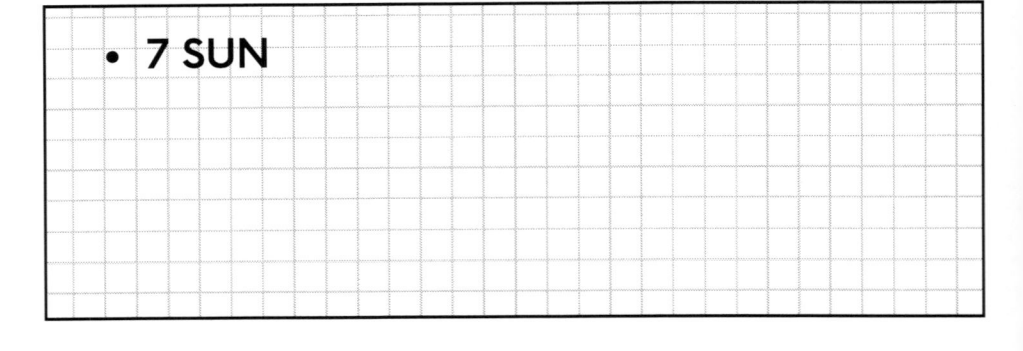

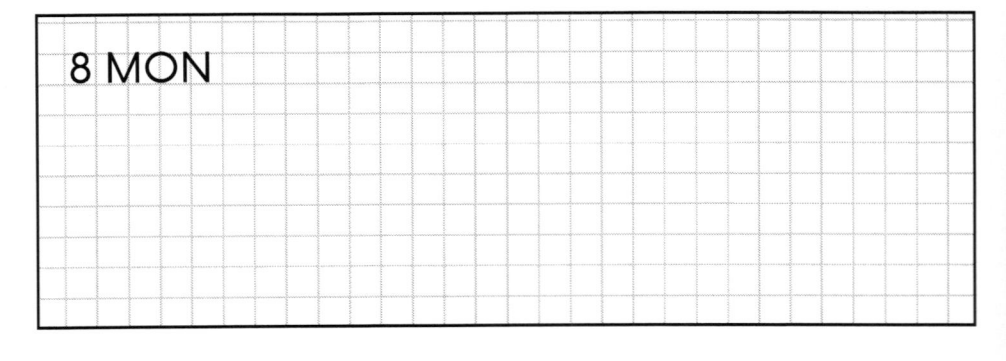

5 FRI

- **6 SAT**

- **7 SUN**

8 MON

DATE	START	BREAK	BREAK	FINISH	TOTAL HOURS

- VEHICLE INFORMATION
- START LOCATION
- END LOCATION
- PURPOSE

START	END	BUSINESS MILES	PERSONAL MILES

DATE	START	BREAK	BREAK	FINISH	TOTAL HOURS

- VEHICLE INFORMATION
- START LOCATION
- END LOCATION
- PURPOSE

START	END	BUSINESS MILES	PERSONAL MILES

DATE	START	BREAK	BREAK	FINISH	TOTAL HOURS

- VEHICLE INFORMATION
- START LOCATION
- END LOCATION
- PURPOSE

START	END	BUSINESS MILES	PERSONAL MILES

DATE	START	BREAK	BREAK	FINISH	TOTAL HOURS

- VEHICLE INFORMATION
- START LOCATION
- END LOCATION
- PURPOSE

START	END	BUSINESS MILES	PERSONAL MILES

AUGUST 2022

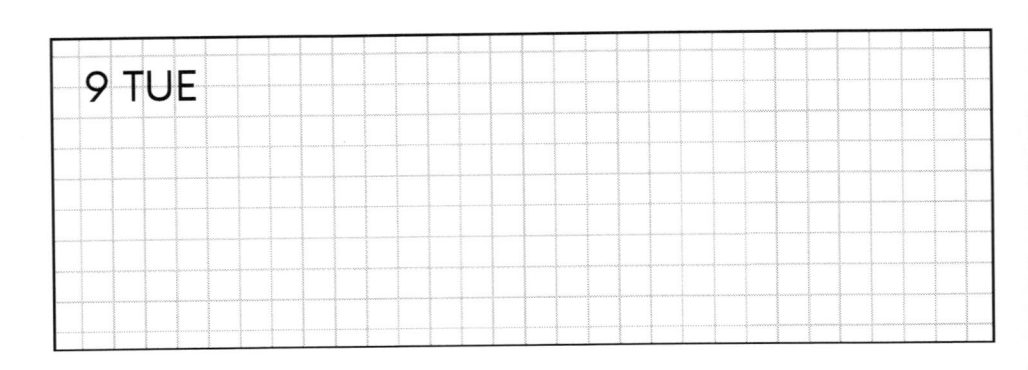

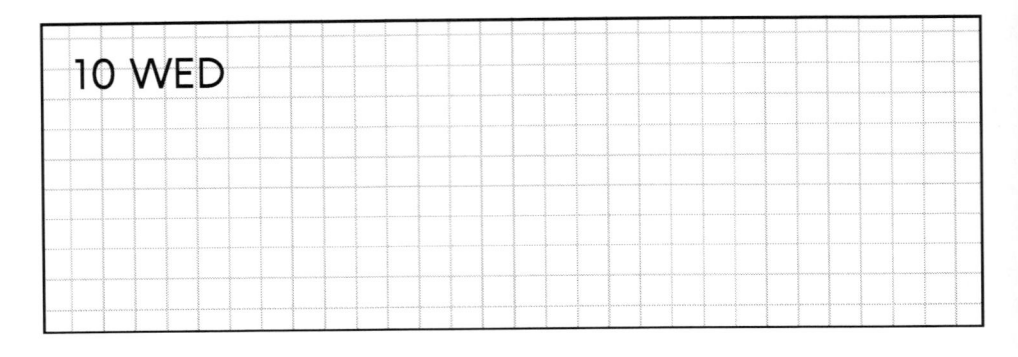

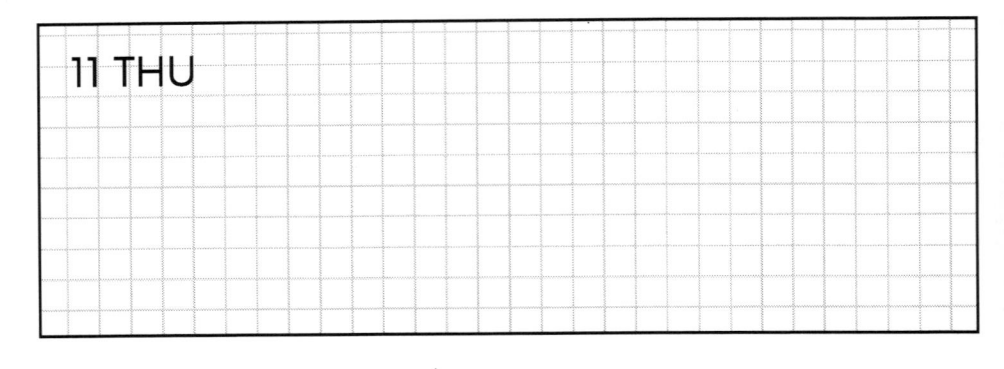

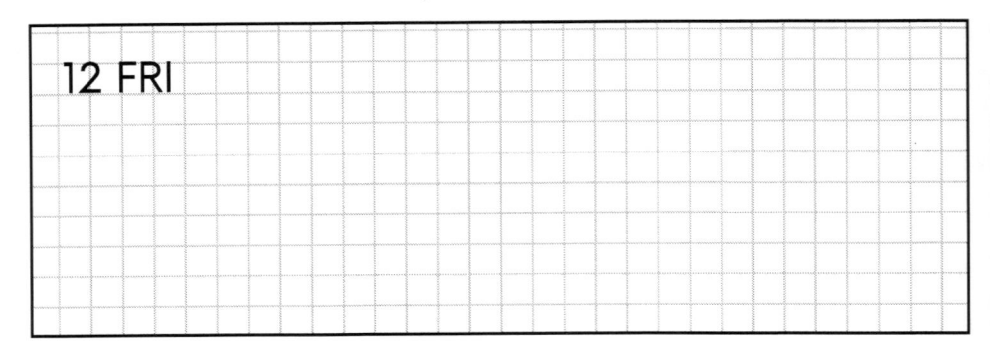

9 TUE

10 WED

11 THU

12 FRI

DATE	START	BREAK	BREAK	FINISH	TOTAL HOURS

- VEHICLE INFORMATION
- START LOCATION
- END LOCATION
- PURPOSE

START	END	BUSINESS MILES	PERSONAL MILES

DATE	START	BREAK	BREAK	FINISH	TOTAL HOURS

- VEHICLE INFORMATION
- START LOCATION
- END LOCATION
- PURPOSE

START	END	BUSINESS MILES	PERSONAL MILES

DATE	START	BREAK	BREAK	FINISH	TOTAL HOURS

- VEHICLE INFORMATION
- START LOCATION
- END LOCATION
- PURPOSE

START	END	BUSINESS MILES	PERSONAL MILES

DATE	START	BREAK	BREAK	FINISH	TOTAL HOURS

- VEHICLE INFORMATION
- START LOCATION
- END LOCATION
- PURPOSE

START	END	BUSINESS MILES	PERSONAL MILES

AUGUST 2022

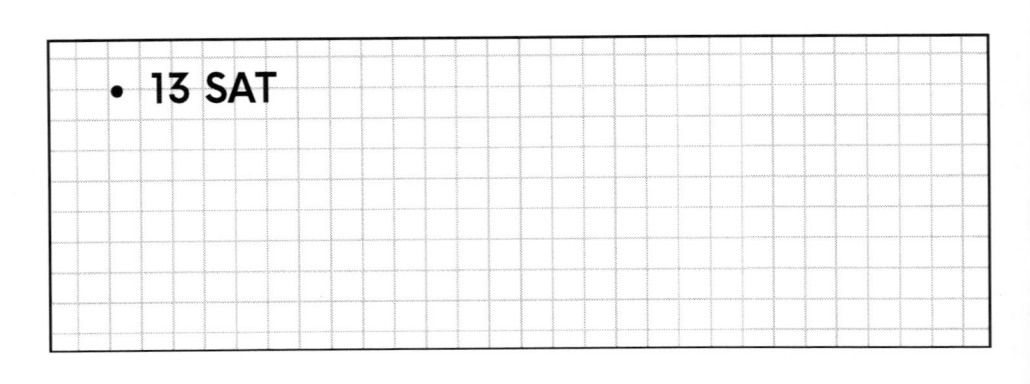

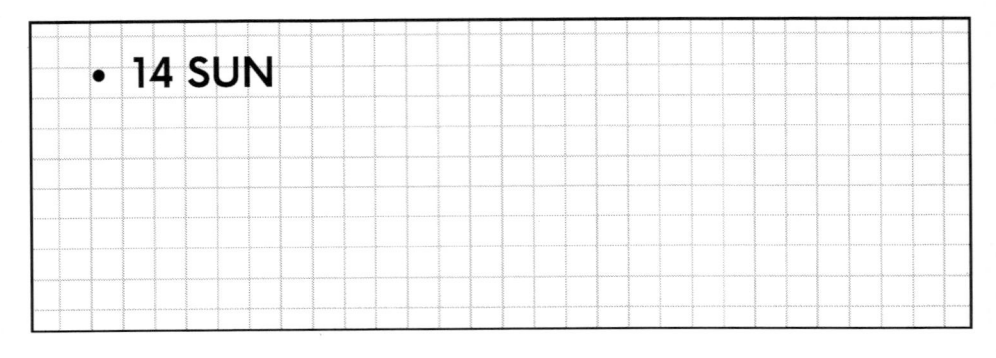

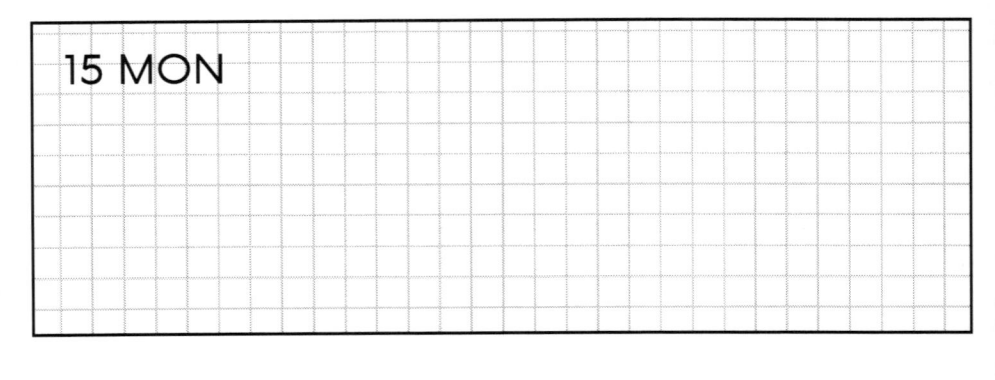

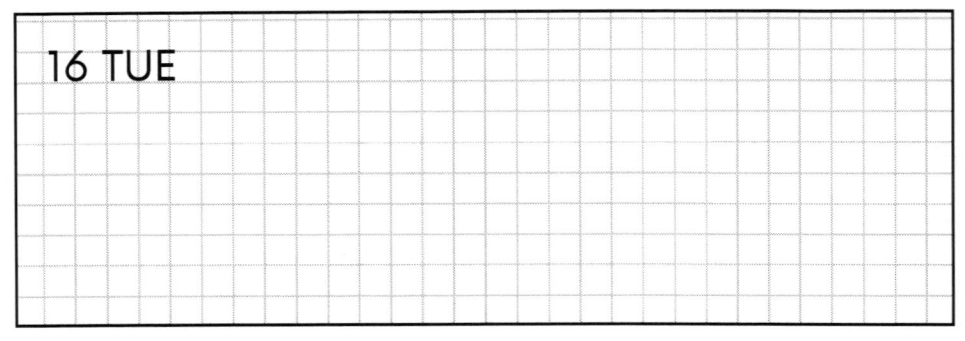

- **13 SAT**

- **14 SUN**

15 MON

16 TUE

DATE	START	BREAK	BREAK	FINISH	TOTAL HOURS

- VEHICLE INFORMATION
- START LOCATION
- END LOCATION
- PURPOSE

START	END	BUSINESS MILES	PERSONAL MILES

DATE	START	BREAK	BREAK	FINISH	TOTAL HOURS

- VEHICLE INFORMATION
- START LOCATION
- END LOCATION
- PURPOSE

START	END	BUSINESS MILES	PERSONAL MILES

DATE	START	BREAK	BREAK	FINISH	TOTAL HOURS

- VEHICLE INFORMATION
- START LOCATION
- END LOCATION
- PURPOSE

START	END	BUSINESS MILES	PERSONAL MILES

DATE	START	BREAK	BREAK	FINISH	TOTAL HOURS

- VEHICLE INFORMATION
- START LOCATION
- END LOCATION
- PURPOSE

START	END	BUSINESS MILES	PERSONAL MILES

AUGUST 2022

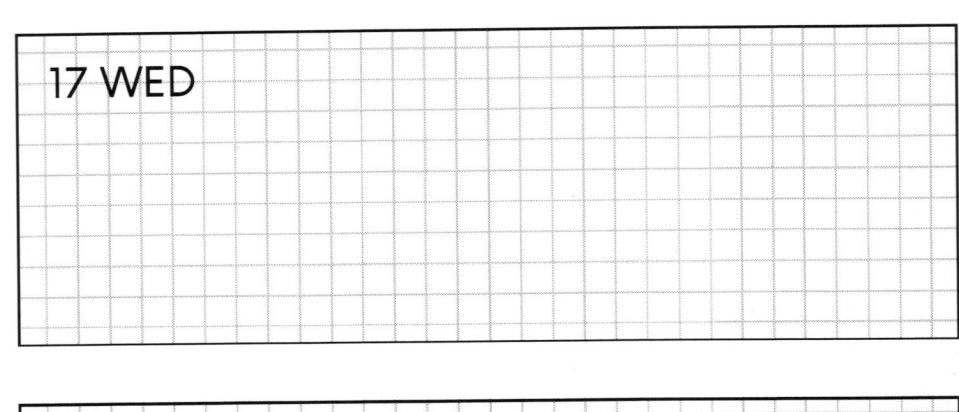

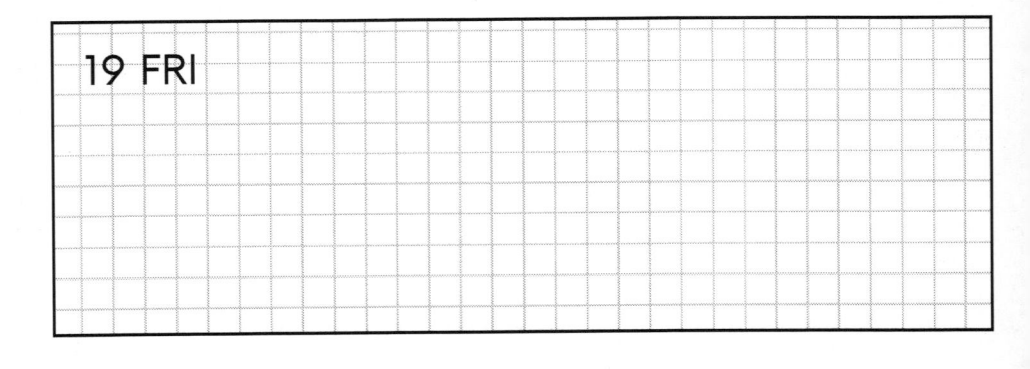

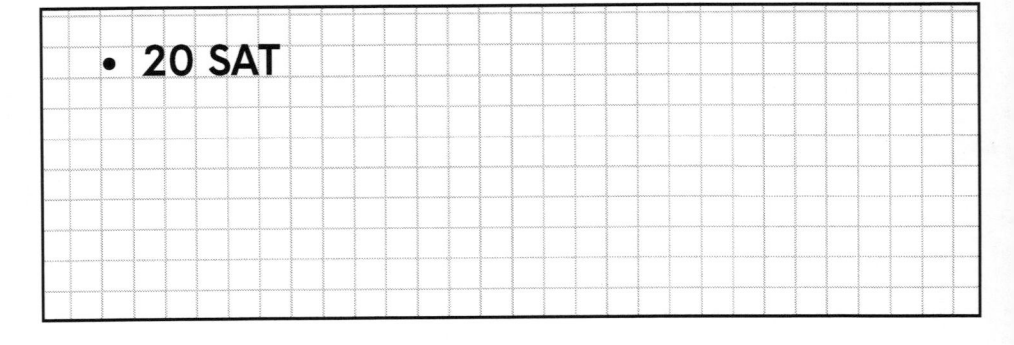

17 WED

18 THU

19 FRI

- **20 SAT**

DATE	START	BREAK	BREAK	FINISH	TOTAL HOURS

- VEHICLE INFORMATION
- START LOCATION
- END LOCATION
- PURPOSE

START	END	BUSINESS MILES	PERSONAL MILES

DATE	START	BREAK	BREAK	FINISH	TOTAL HOURS

- VEHICLE INFORMATION
- START LOCATION
- END LOCATION
- PURPOSE

START	END	BUSINESS MILES	PERSONAL MILES

DATE	START	BREAK	BREAK	FINISH	TOTAL HOURS

- VEHICLE INFORMATION
- START LOCATION
- END LOCATION
- PURPOSE

START	END	BUSINESS MILES	PERSONAL MILES

DATE	START	BREAK	BREAK	FINISH	TOTAL HOURS

- VEHICLE INFORMATION
- START LOCATION
- END LOCATION
- PURPOSE

START	END	BUSINESS MILES	PERSONAL MILES

AUGUST 2022

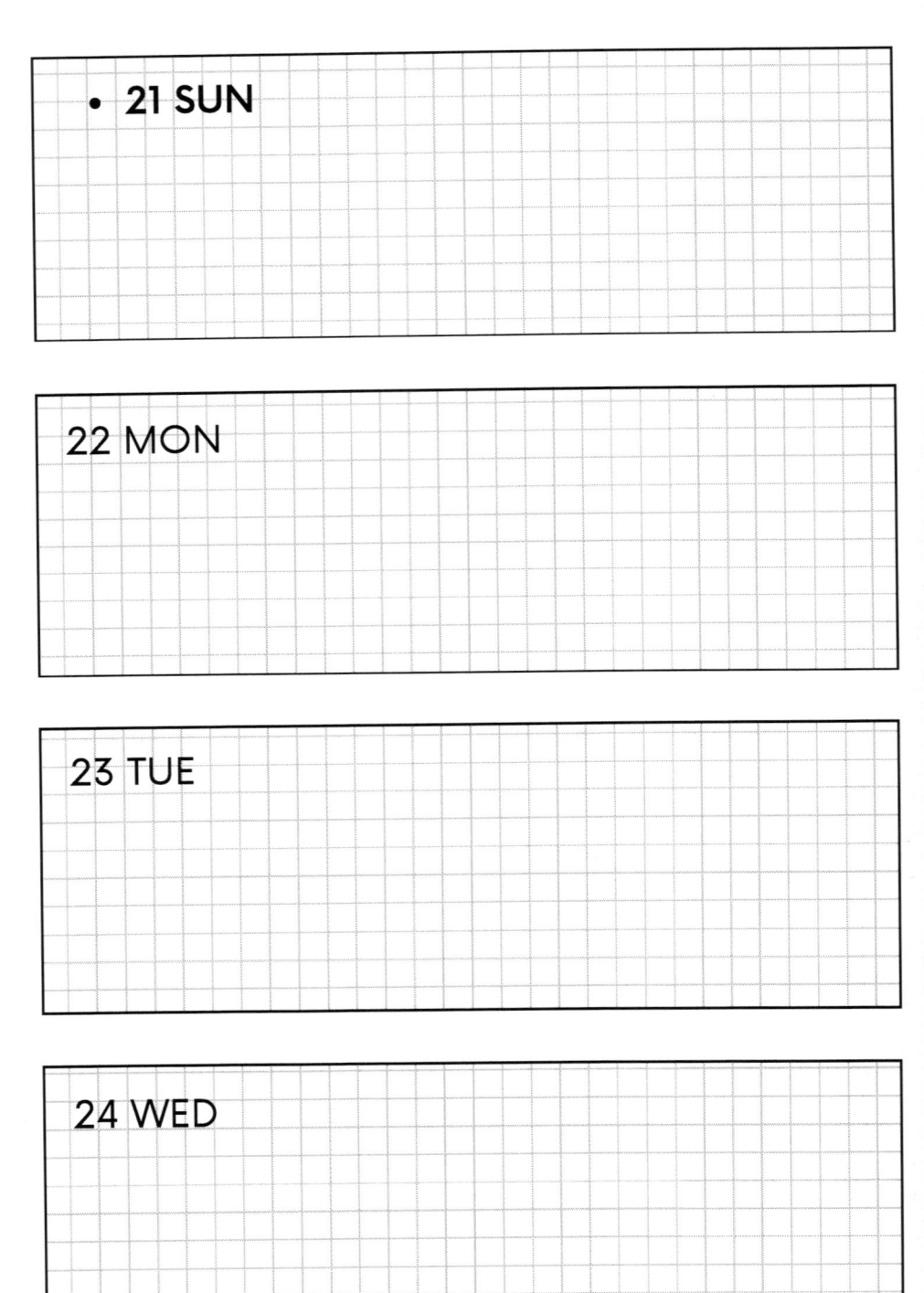

- **21 SUN**

22 MON

23 TUE

24 WED

DATE	START	BREAK	BREAK	FINISH	TOTAL HOURS

- VEHICLE INFORMATION
- START LOCATION
- END LOCATION
- PURPOSE

START	END	BUSINESS MILES	PERSONAL MILES

DATE	START	BREAK	BREAK	FINISH	TOTAL HOURS

- VEHICLE INFORMATION
- START LOCATION
- END LOCATION
- PURPOSE

START	END	BUSINESS MILES	PERSONAL MILES

DATE	START	BREAK	BREAK	FINISH	TOTAL HOURS

- VEHICLE INFORMATION
- START LOCATION
- END LOCATION
- PURPOSE

START	END	BUSINESS MILES	PERSONAL MILES

DATE	START	BREAK	BREAK	FINISH	TOTAL HOURS

- VEHICLE INFORMATION
- START LOCATION
- END LOCATION
- PURPOSE

START	END	BUSINESS MILES	PERSONAL MILES

AUGUST 2022

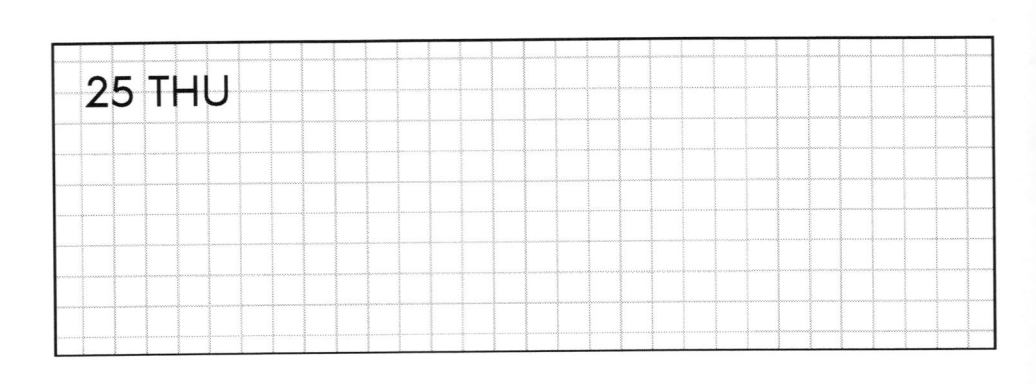

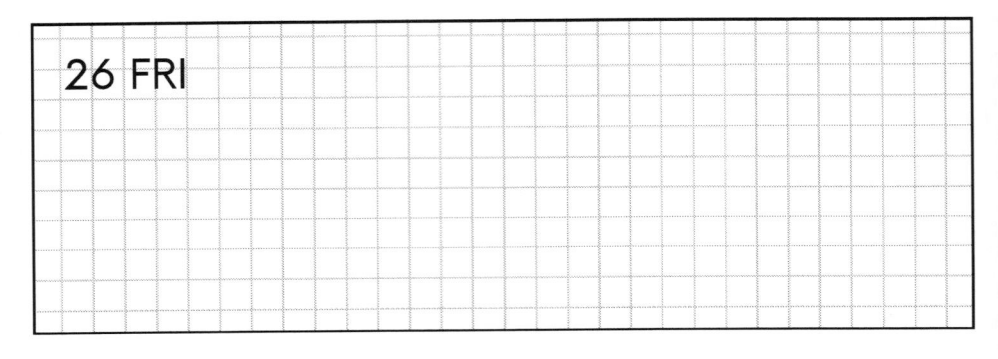

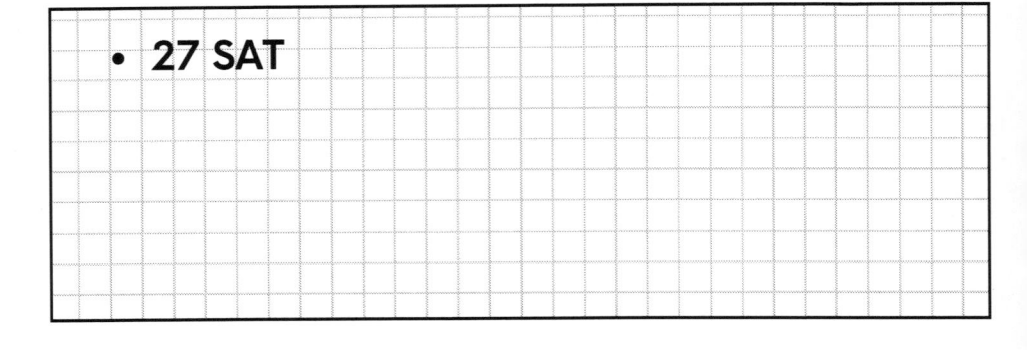

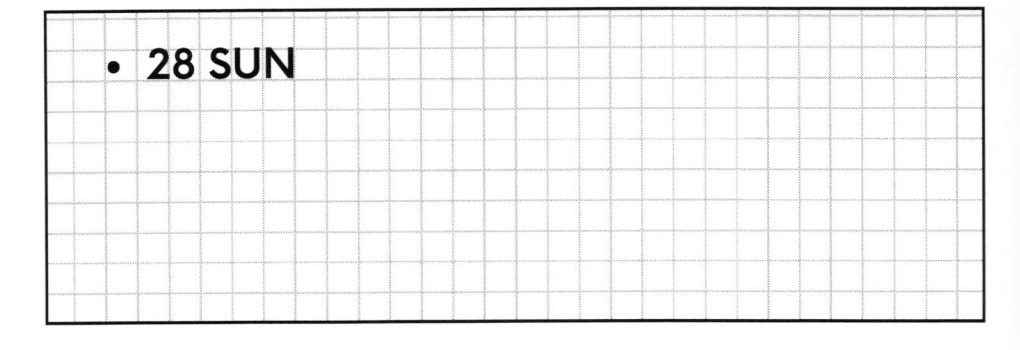

25 THU

26 FRI

- 27 SAT

- 28 SUN

DATE	START	BREAK	BREAK	FINISH	TOTAL HOURS

- VEHICLE INFORMATION
- START LOCATION
- END LOCATION
- PURPOSE

START	END	BUSINESS MILES	PERSONAL MILES

DATE	START	BREAK	BREAK	FINISH	TOTAL HOURS

- VEHICLE INFORMATION
- START LOCATION
- END LOCATION
- PURPOSE

START	END	BUSINESS MILES	PERSONAL MILES

DATE	START	BREAK	BREAK	FINISH	TOTAL HOURS

- VEHICLE INFORMATION
- START LOCATION
- END LOCATION
- PURPOSE

START	END	BUSINESS MILES	PERSONAL MILES

DATE	START	BREAK	BREAK	FINISH	TOTAL HOURS

- VEHICLE INFORMATION
- START LOCATION
- END LOCATION
- PURPOSE

START	END	BUSINESS MILES	PERSONAL MILES

AUGUST/SEPTEMBER 2022

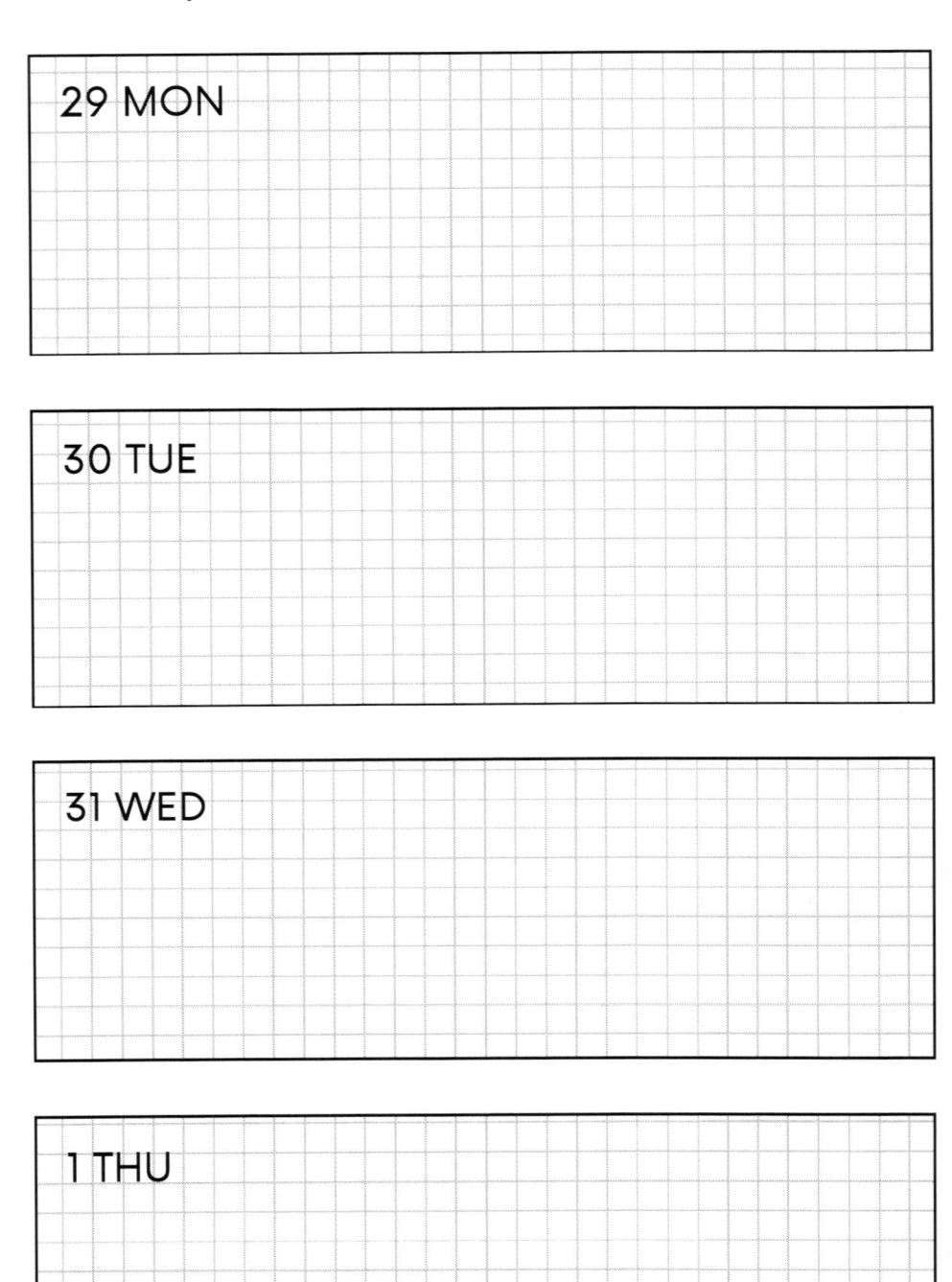

29 MON

30 TUE

31 WED

1 THU

DATE	START	BREAK	BREAK	FINISH	TOTAL HOURS

- VEHICLE INFORMATION
- START LOCATION
- END LOCATION
- PURPOSE

START	END	BUSINESS MILES	PERSONAL MILES

DATE	START	BREAK	BREAK	FINISH	TOTAL HOURS

- VEHICLE INFORMATION
- START LOCATION
- END LOCATION
- PURPOSE

START	END	BUSINESS MILES	PERSONAL MILES

DATE	START	BREAK	BREAK	FINISH	TOTAL HOURS

- VEHICLE INFORMATION
- START LOCATION
- END LOCATION
- PURPOSE

START	END	BUSINESS MILES	PERSONAL MILES

DATE	START	BREAK	BREAK	FINISH	TOTAL HOURS

- VEHICLE INFORMATION
- START LOCATION
- END LOCATION
- PURPOSE

START	END	BUSINESS MILES	PERSONAL MILES

SEPTEMBER 2022

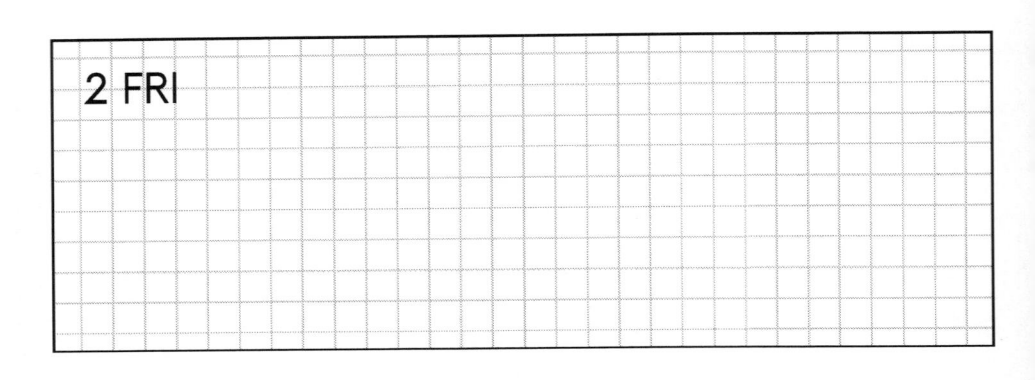

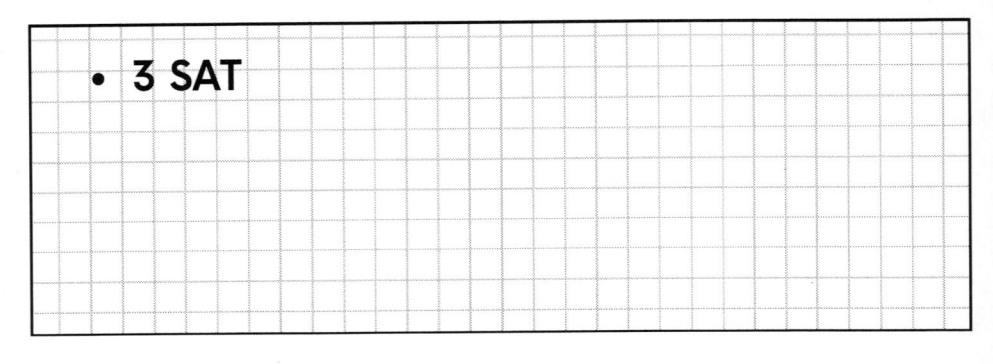

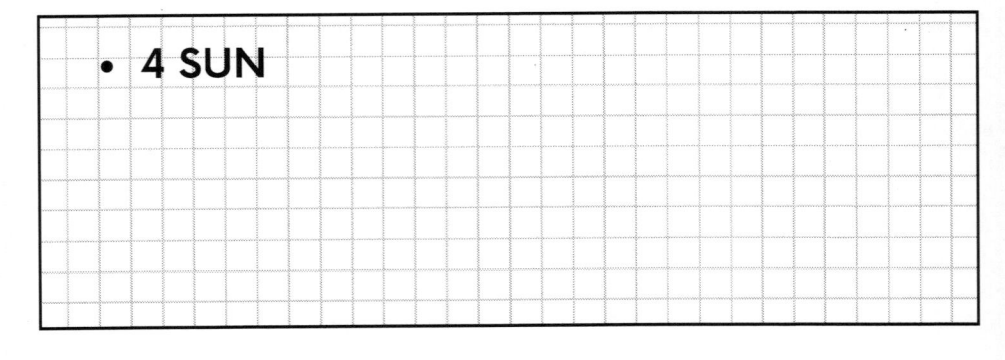

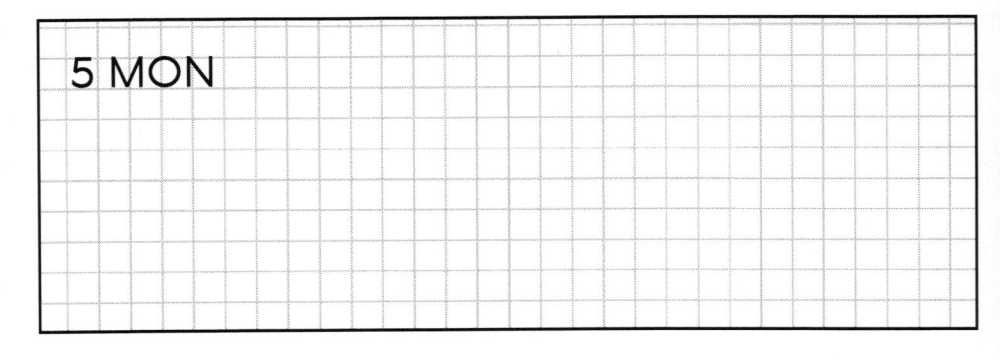

2 FRI

- 3 SAT

- 4 SUN

5 MON

DATE	START	BREAK	BREAK	FINISH	TOTAL HOURS

- VEHICLE INFORMATION
- START LOCATION
- END LOCATION
- PURPOSE

START	END	BUSINESS MILES	PERSONAL MILES

DATE	START	BREAK	BREAK	FINISH	TOTAL HOURS

- VEHICLE INFORMATION
- START LOCATION
- END LOCATION
- PURPOSE

START	END	BUSINESS MILES	PERSONAL MILES

DATE	START	BREAK	BREAK	FINISH	TOTAL HOURS

- VEHICLE INFORMATION
- START LOCATION
- END LOCATION
- PURPOSE

START	END	BUSINESS MILES	PERSONAL MILES

DATE	START	BREAK	BREAK	FINISH	TOTAL HOURS

- VEHICLE INFORMATION
- START LOCATION
- END LOCATION
- PURPOSE

START	END	BUSINESS MILES	PERSONAL MILES

SEPTEMBER 2022

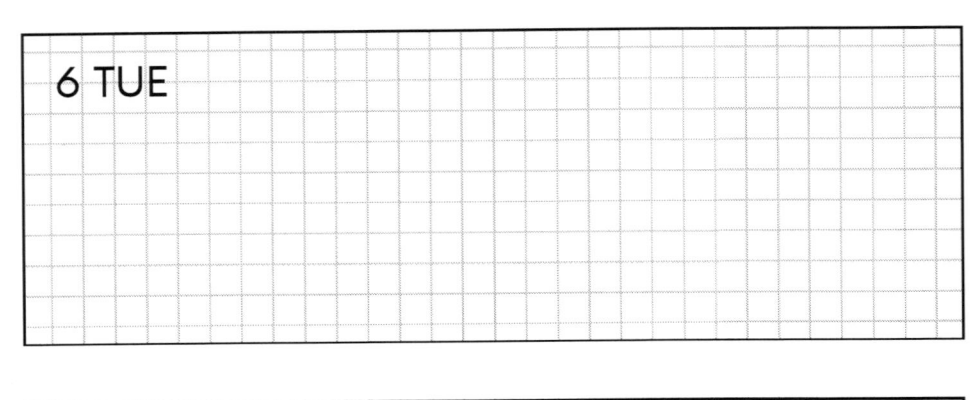

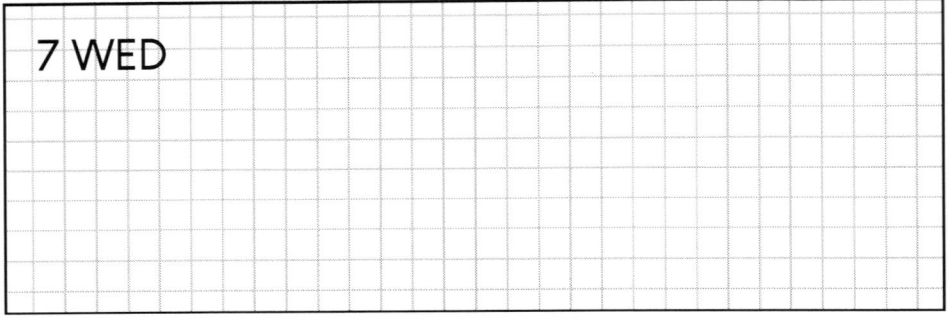

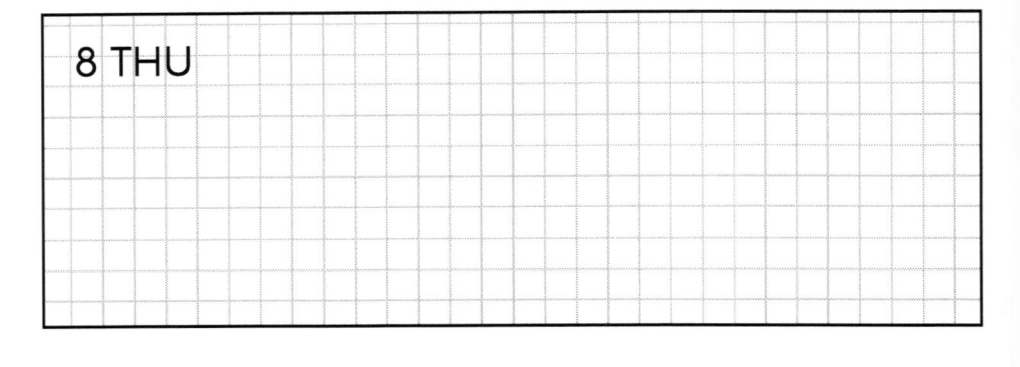

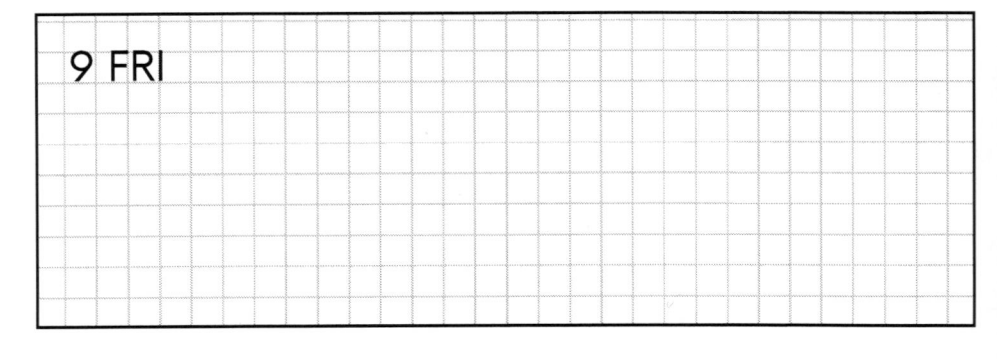

6 TUE

7 WED

8 THU

9 FRI

DATE	START	BREAK	BREAK	FINISH	TOTAL HOURS

- VEHICLE INFORMATION
- START LOCATION
- END LOCATION
- PURPOSE

START	END	BUSINESS MILES	PERSONAL MILES

DATE	START	BREAK	BREAK	FINISH	TOTAL HOURS

- VEHICLE INFORMATION
- START LOCATION
- END LOCATION
- PURPOSE

START	END	BUSINESS MILES	PERSONAL MILES

DATE	START	BREAK	BREAK	FINISH	TOTAL HOURS

- VEHICLE INFORMATION
- START LOCATION
- END LOCATION
- PURPOSE

START	END	BUSINESS MILES	PERSONAL MILES

DATE	START	BREAK	BREAK	FINISH	TOTAL HOURS

- VEHICLE INFORMATION
- START LOCATION
- END LOCATION
- PURPOSE

START	END	BUSINESS MILES	PERSONAL MILES

SEPTEMBER   2022

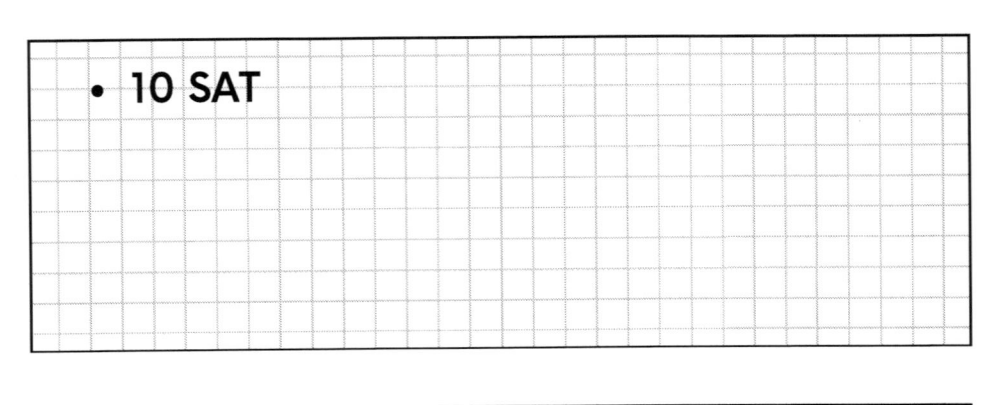

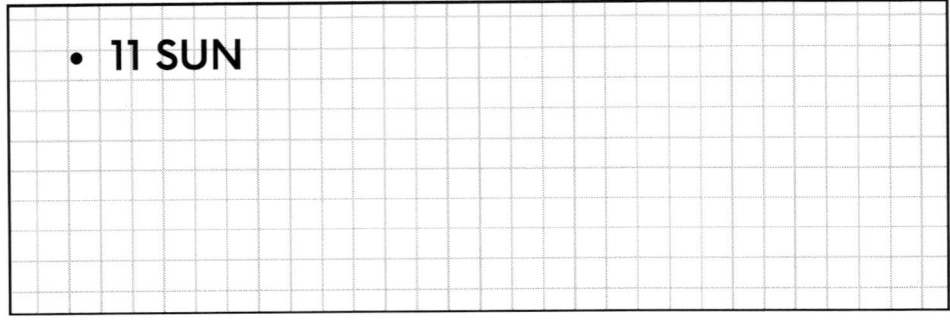

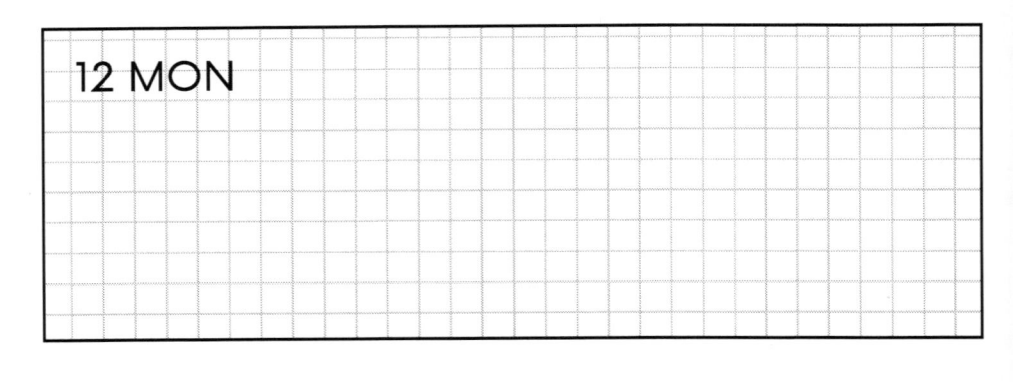

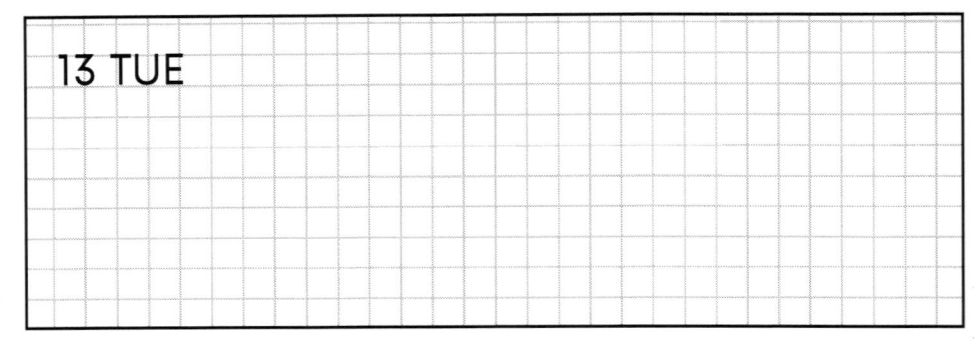

- **10 SAT**

- **11 SUN**

12 MON

13 TUE

DATE	START	BREAK	BREAK	FINISH	TOTAL HOURS

- VEHICLE INFORMATION
- START LOCATION
- END LOCATION
- PURPOSE

START	END	BUSINESS MILES	PERSONAL MILES

DATE	START	BREAK	BREAK	FINISH	TOTAL HOURS

- VEHICLE INFORMATION
- START LOCATION
- END LOCATION
- PURPOSE

START	END	BUSINESS MILES	PERSONAL MILES

DATE	START	BREAK	BREAK	FINISH	TOTAL HOURS

- VEHICLE INFORMATION
- START LOCATION
- END LOCATION
- PURPOSE

START	END	BUSINESS MILES	PERSONAL MILES

DATE	START	BREAK	BREAK	FINISH	TOTAL HOURS

- VEHICLE INFORMATION
- START LOCATION
- END LOCATION
- PURPOSE

START	END	BUSINESS MILES	PERSONAL MILES

SEPTEMBER 2022

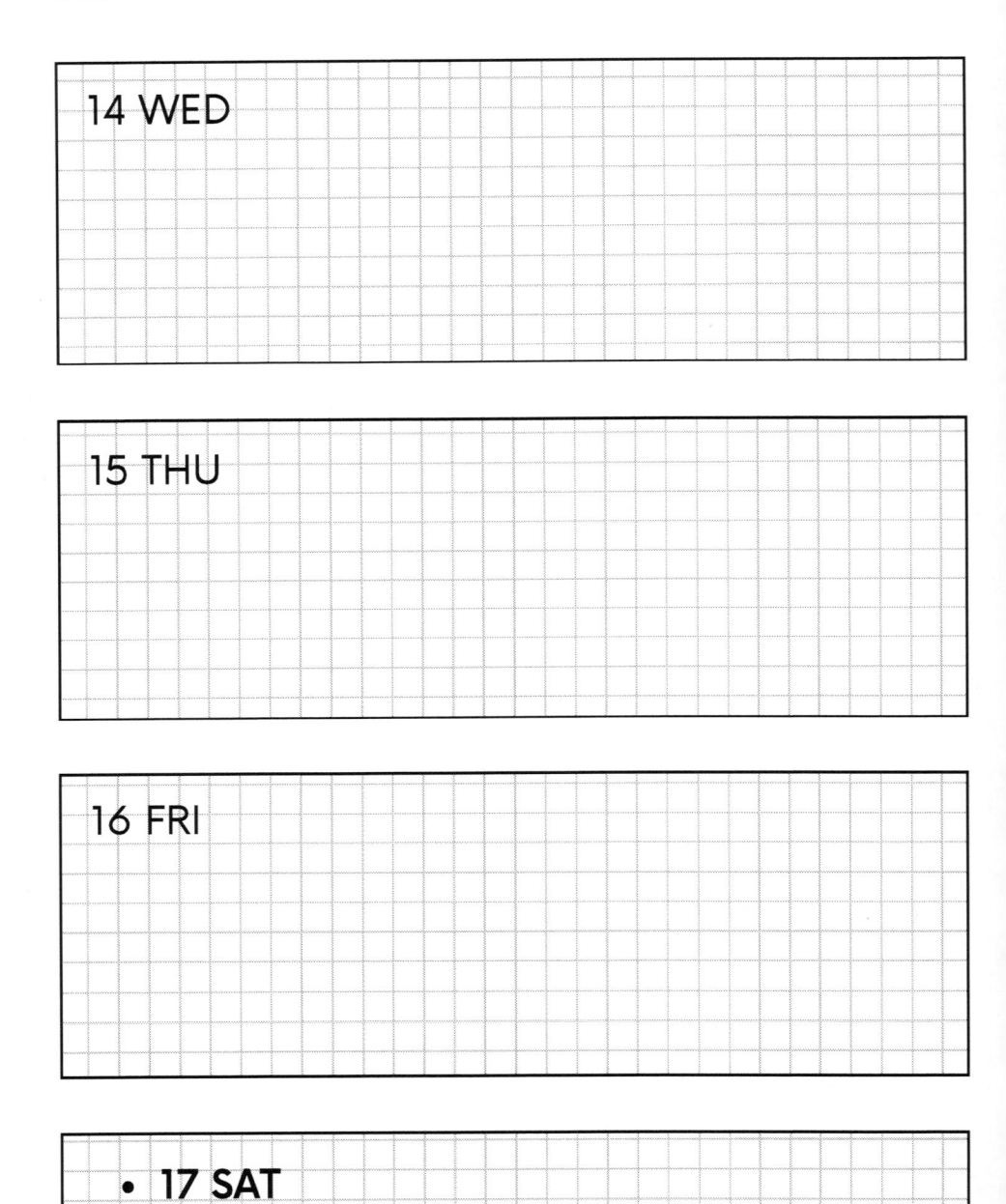

14 WED

15 THU

16 FRI

- **17 SAT**

DATE	START	BREAK	BREAK	FINISH	TOTAL HOURS

- VEHICLE INFORMATION
- START LOCATION
- END LOCATION
- PURPOSE

START	END	BUSINESS MILES	PERSONAL MILES

DATE	START	BREAK	BREAK	FINISH	TOTAL HOURS

- VEHICLE INFORMATION
- START LOCATION
- END LOCATION
- PURPOSE

START	END	BUSINESS MILES	PERSONAL MILES

DATE	START	BREAK	BREAK	FINISH	TOTAL HOURS

- VEHICLE INFORMATION
- START LOCATION
- END LOCATION
- PURPOSE

START	END	BUSINESS MILES	PERSONAL MILES

DATE	START	BREAK	BREAK	FINISH	TOTAL HOURS

- VEHICLE INFORMATION
- START LOCATION
- END LOCATION
- PURPOSE

START	END	BUSINESS MILES	PERSONAL MILES

SEPTEMBER   2022

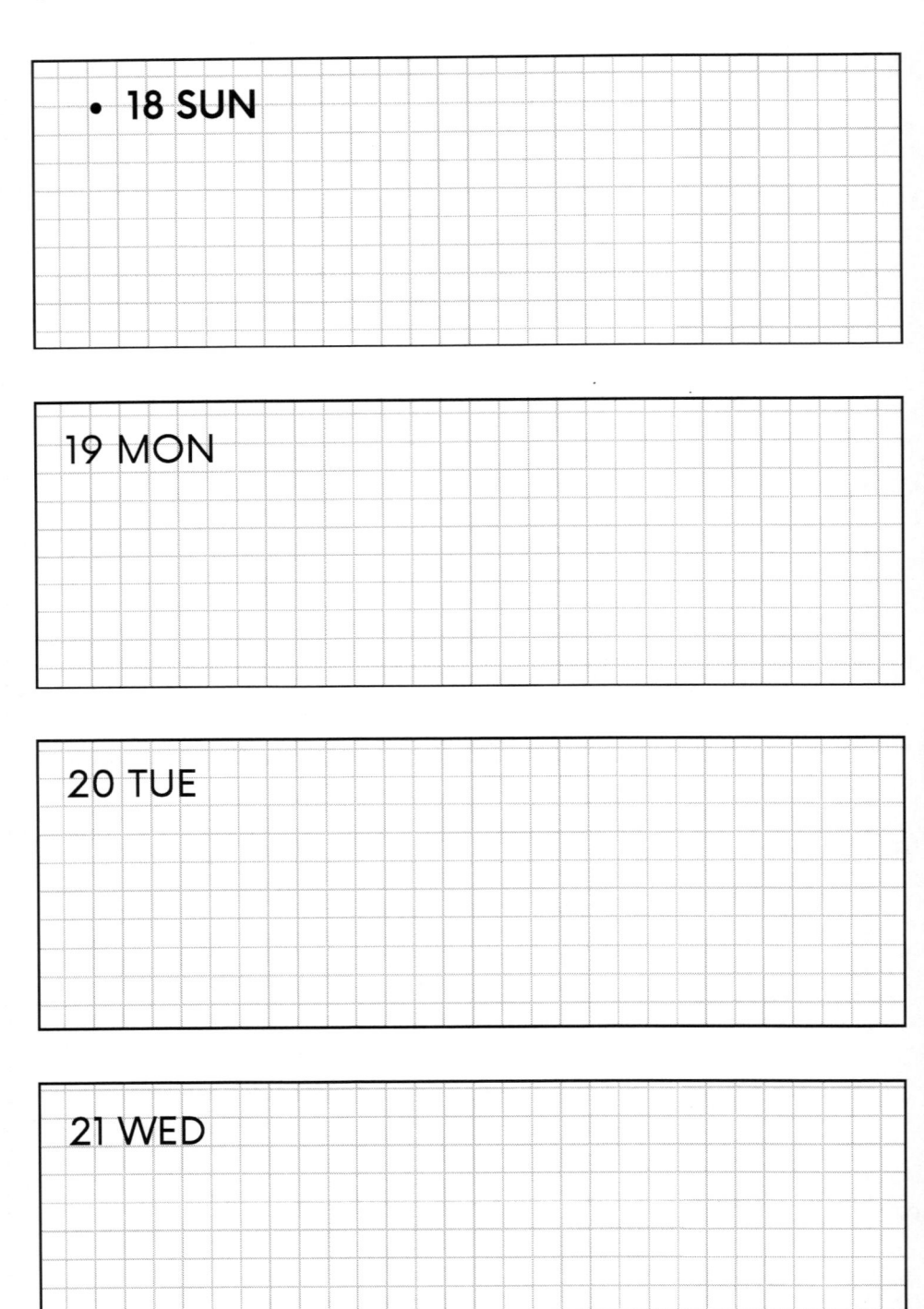

- **18 SUN**

19 MON

20 TUE

21 WED

DATE	START	BREAK	BREAK	FINISH	TOTAL HOURS

- VEHICLE INFORMATION
- START LOCATION
- END LOCATION
- PURPOSE

START	END	BUSINESS MILES	PERSONAL MILES

DATE	START	BREAK	BREAK	FINISH	TOTAL HOURS

- VEHICLE INFORMATION
- START LOCATION
- END LOCATION
- PURPOSE

START	END	BUSINESS MILES	PERSONAL MILES

DATE	START	BREAK	BREAK	FINISH	TOTAL HOURS

- VEHICLE INFORMATION
- START LOCATION
- END LOCATION
- PURPOSE

START	END	BUSINESS MILES	PERSONAL MILES

DATE	START	BREAK	BREAK	FINISH	TOTAL HOURS

- VEHICLE INFORMATION
- START LOCATION
- END LOCATION
- PURPOSE

START	END	BUSINESS MILES	PERSONAL MILES

SEPTEMBER 2022

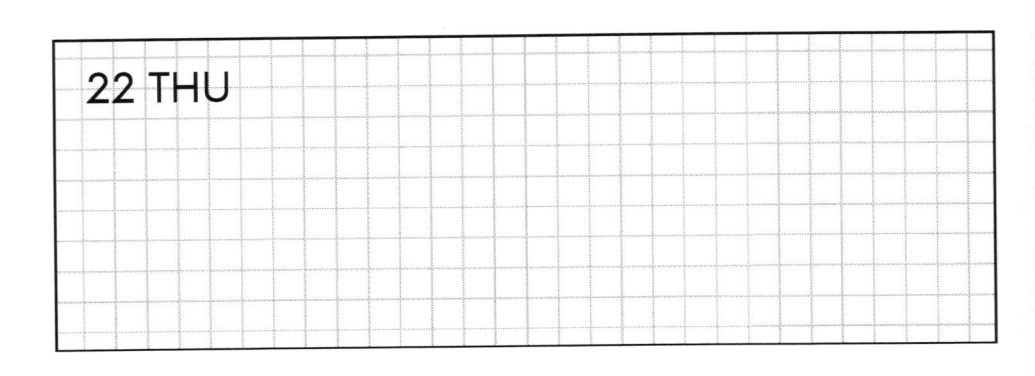

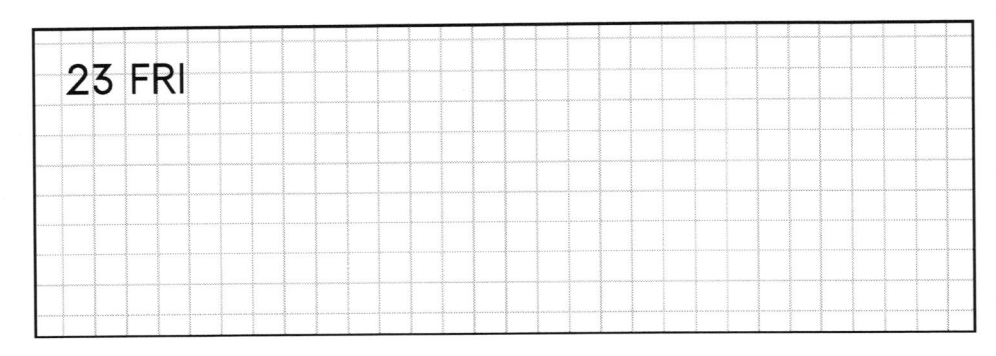

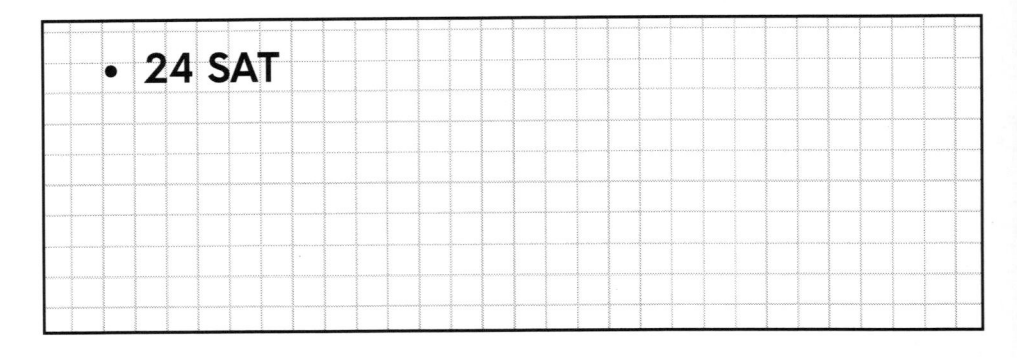

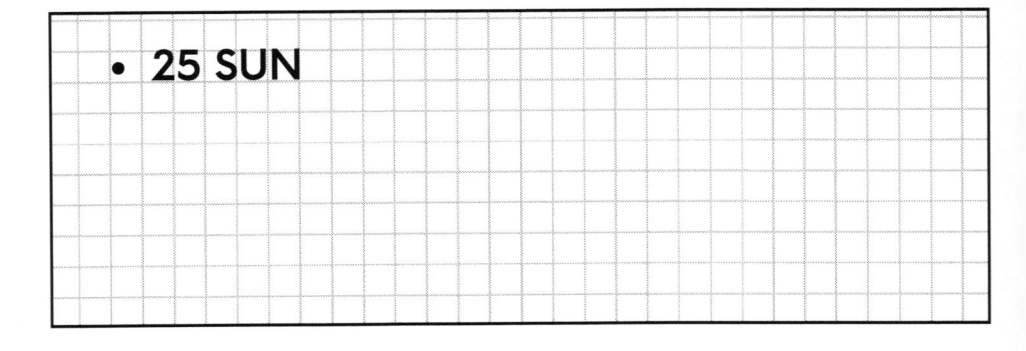

22 THU

23 FRI

- **24 SAT**

- **25 SUN**

DATE	START	BREAK	BREAK	FINISH	TOTAL HOURS

- VEHICLE INFORMATION
- START LOCATION
- END LOCATION
- PURPOSE

START	END	BUSINESS MILES	PERSONAL MILES

DATE	START	BREAK	BREAK	FINISH	TOTAL HOURS

- VEHICLE INFORMATION
- START LOCATION
- END LOCATION
- PURPOSE

START	END	BUSINESS MILES	PERSONAL MILES

DATE	START	BREAK	BREAK	FINISH	TOTAL HOURS

- VEHICLE INFORMATION
- START LOCATION
- END LOCATION
- PURPOSE

START	END	BUSINESS MILES	PERSONAL MILES

DATE	START	BREAK	BREAK	FINISH	TOTAL HOURS

- VEHICLE INFORMATION
- START LOCATION
- END LOCATION
- PURPOSE

START	END	BUSINESS MILES	PERSONAL MILES

SEPTEMBER 2022

26 MON

27 TUE

28 WED

29 THU

DATE	START	BREAK	BREAK	FINISH	TOTAL HOURS

- VEHICLE INFORMATION
- START LOCATION
- END LOCATION
- PURPOSE

START	END	BUSINESS MILES	PERSONAL MILES

DATE	START	BREAK	BREAK	FINISH	TOTAL HOURS

- VEHICLE INFORMATION
- START LOCATION
- END LOCATION
- PURPOSE

START	END	BUSINESS MILES	PERSONAL MILES

DATE	START	BREAK	BREAK	FINISH	TOTAL HOURS

- VEHICLE INFORMATION
- START LOCATION
- END LOCATION
- PURPOSE

START	END	BUSINESS MILES	PERSONAL MILES

DATE	START	BREAK	BREAK	FINISH	TOTAL HOURS

- VEHICLE INFORMATION
- START LOCATION
- END LOCATION
- PURPOSE

START	END	BUSINESS MILES	PERSONAL MILES

SEPTEMBER/OCTOBER   2022

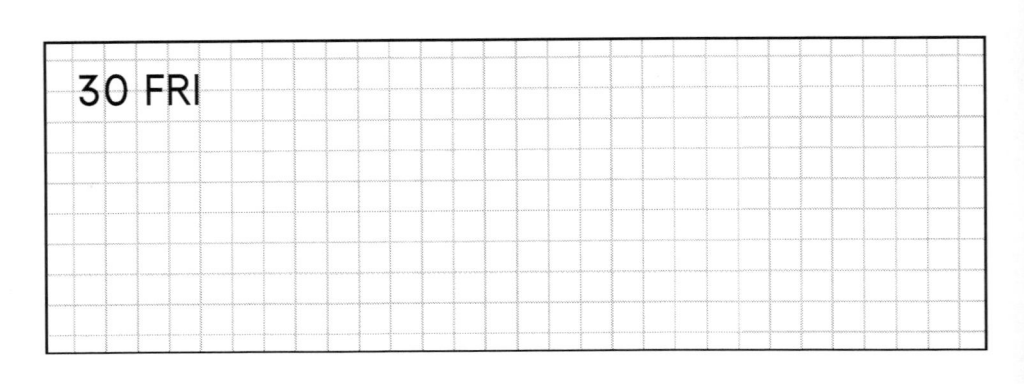

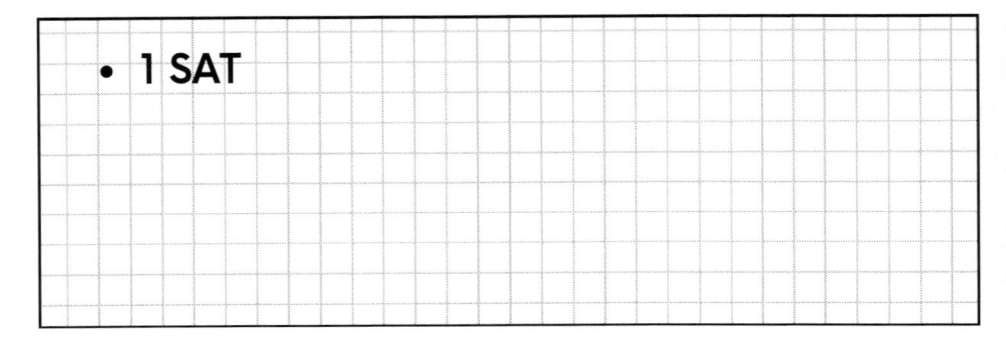

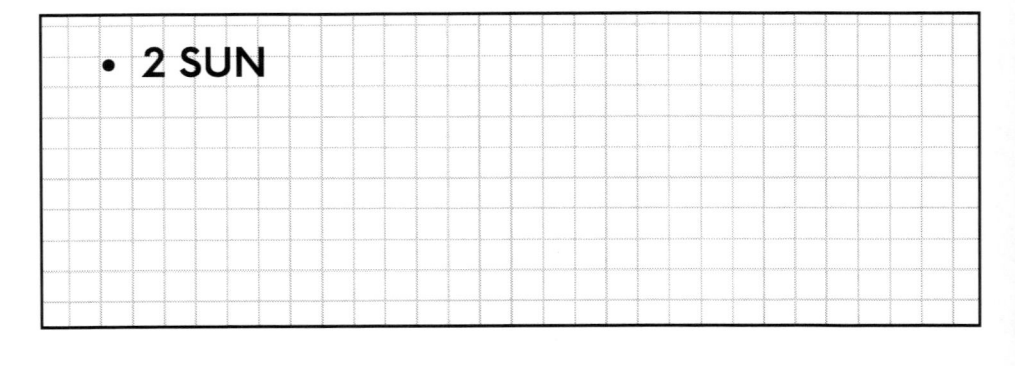

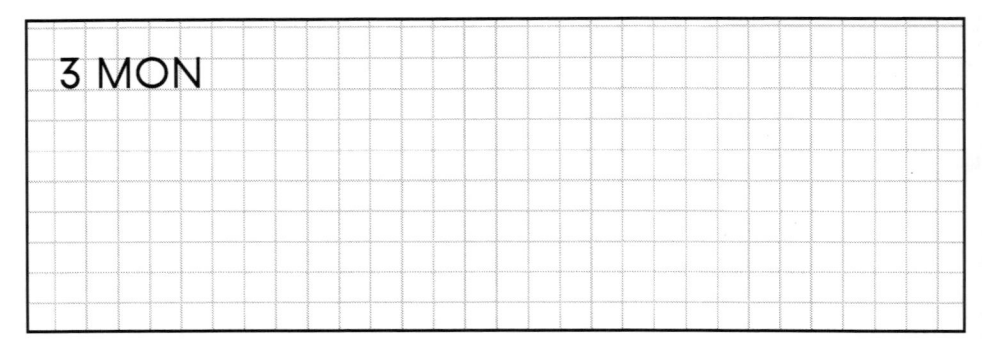

30 FRI

• 1 SAT

• 2 SUN

3 MON

DATE	START	BREAK	BREAK	FINISH	TOTAL HOURS

- VEHICLE INFORMATION
- START LOCATION
- END LOCATION
- PURPOSE

START	END	BUSINESS MILES	PERSONAL MILES

DATE	START	BREAK	BREAK	FINISH	TOTAL HOURS

- VEHICLE INFORMATION
- START LOCATION
- END LOCATION
- PURPOSE

START	END	BUSINESS MILES	PERSONAL MILES

DATE	START	BREAK	BREAK	FINISH	TOTAL HOURS

- VEHICLE INFORMATION
- START LOCATION
- END LOCATION
- PURPOSE

START	END	BUSINESS MILES	PERSONAL MILES

DATE	START	BREAK	BREAK	FINISH	TOTAL HOURS

- VEHICLE INFORMATION
- START LOCATION
- END LOCATION
- PURPOSE

START	END	BUSINESS MILES	PERSONAL MILES

OCTOBER 2022

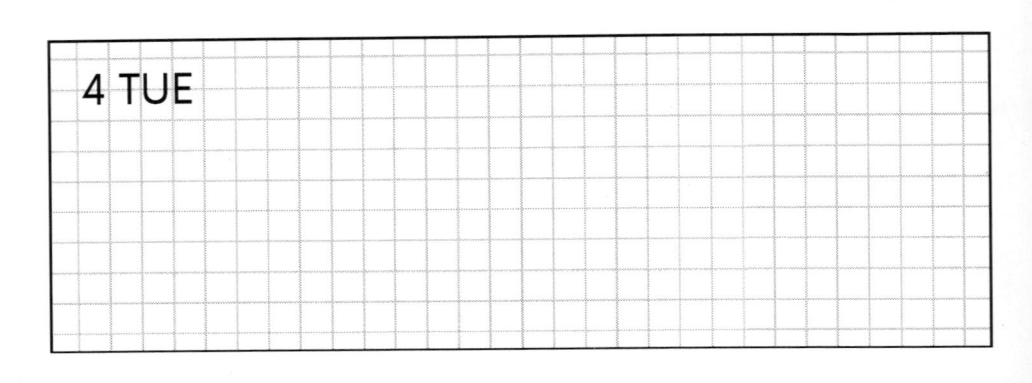

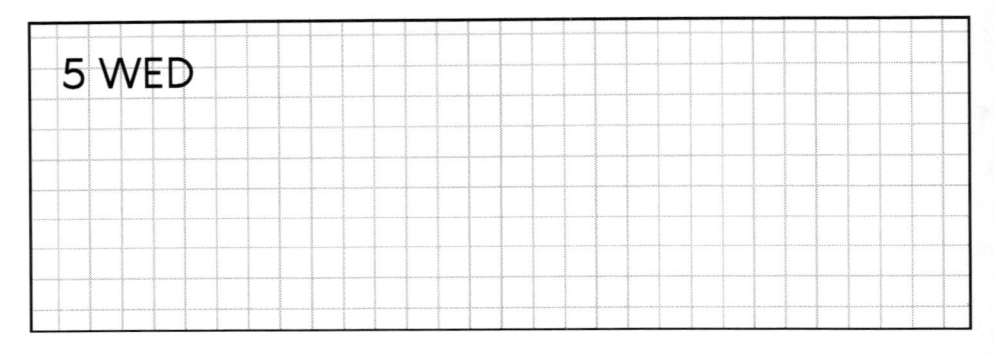

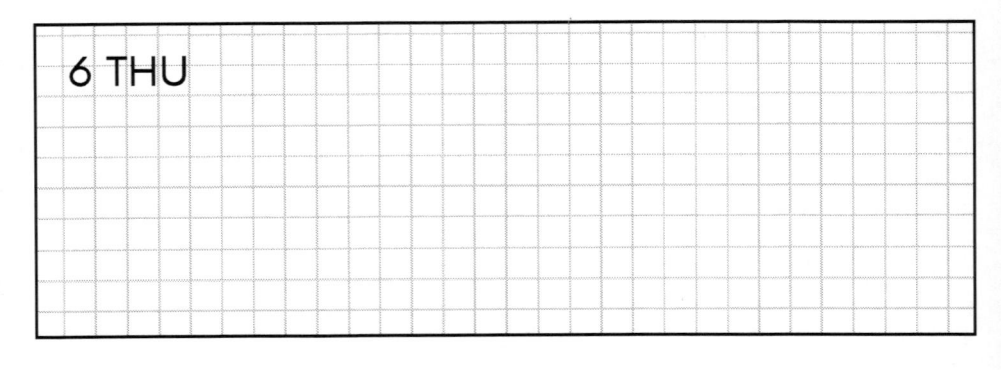

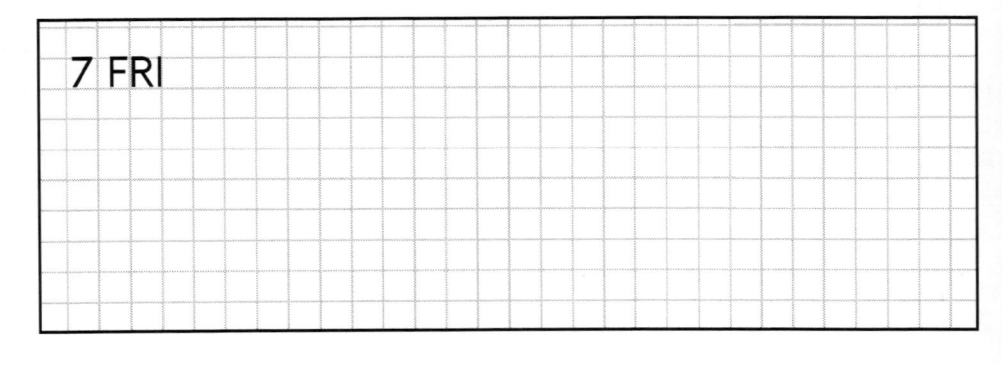

4 TUE

5 WED

6 THU

7 FRI

DATE	START	BREAK	BREAK	FINISH	TOTAL HOURS

- VEHICLE INFORMATION
- START LOCATION
- END LOCATION
- PURPOSE

START	END	BUSINESS MILES	PERSONAL MILES

DATE	START	BREAK	BREAK	FINISH	TOTAL HOURS

- VEHICLE INFORMATION
- START LOCATION
- END LOCATION
- PURPOSE

START	END	BUSINESS MILES	PERSONAL MILES

DATE	START	BREAK	BREAK	FINISH	TOTAL HOURS

- VEHICLE INFORMATION
- START LOCATION
- END LOCATION
- PURPOSE

START	END	BUSINESS MILES	PERSONAL MILES

DATE	START	BREAK	BREAK	FINISH	TOTAL HOURS

- VEHICLE INFORMATION
- START LOCATION
- END LOCATION
- PURPOSE

START	END	BUSINESS MILES	PERSONAL MILES

OCTOBER   2022

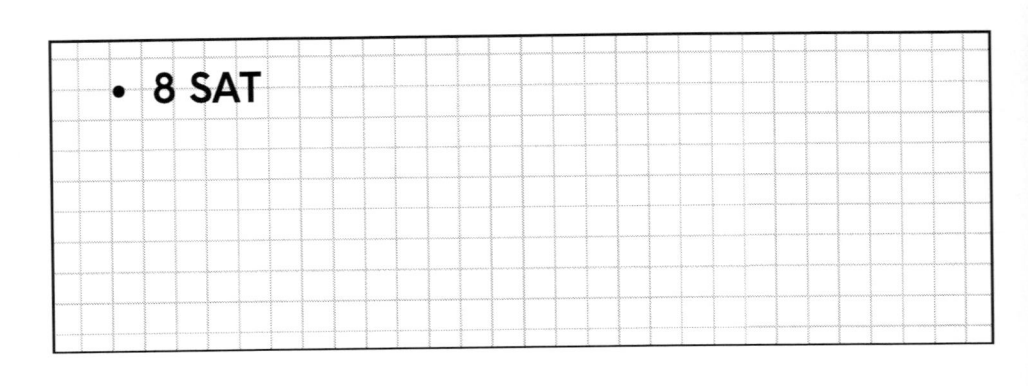

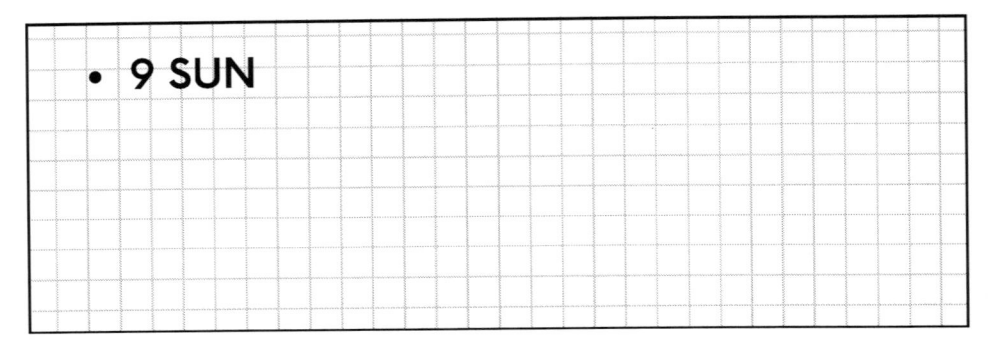

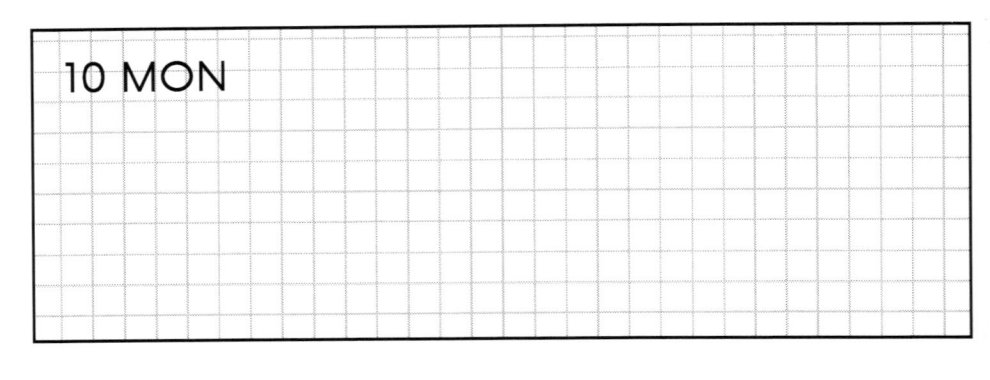

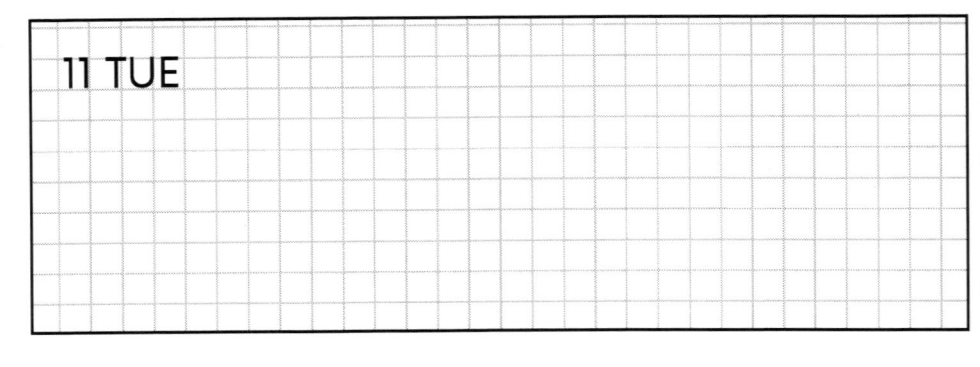

- **8 SAT**

- **9 SUN**

10 MON

11 TUE

DATE	START	BREAK	BREAK	FINISH	TOTAL HOURS

- VEHICLE INFORMATION
- START LOCATION
- END LOCATION
- PURPOSE

START	END	BUSINESS MILES	PERSONAL MILES

DATE	START	BREAK	BREAK	FINISH	TOTAL HOURS

- VEHICLE INFORMATION
- START LOCATION
- END LOCATION
- PURPOSE

START	END	BUSINESS MILES	PERSONAL MILES

DATE	START	BREAK	BREAK	FINISH	TOTAL HOURS

- VEHICLE INFORMATION
- START LOCATION
- END LOCATION
- PURPOSE

START	END	BUSINESS MILES	PERSONAL MILES

DATE	START	BREAK	BREAK	FINISH	TOTAL HOURS

- VEHICLE INFORMATION
- START LOCATION
- END LOCATION
- PURPOSE

START	END	BUSINESS MILES	PERSONAL MILES

OCTOBER 2022

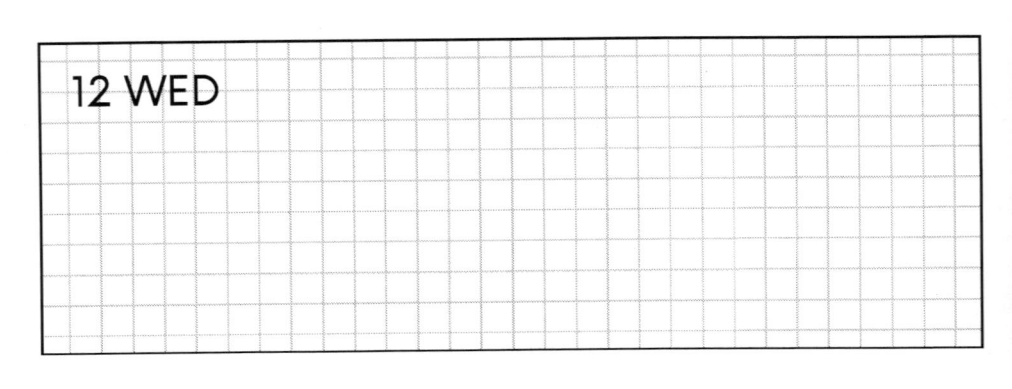

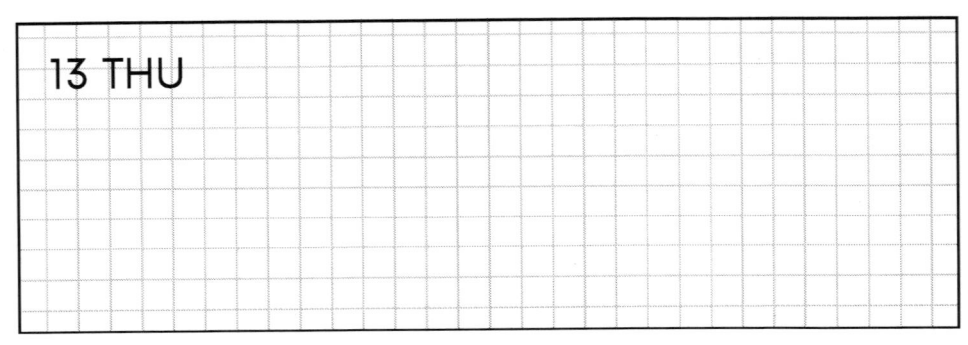

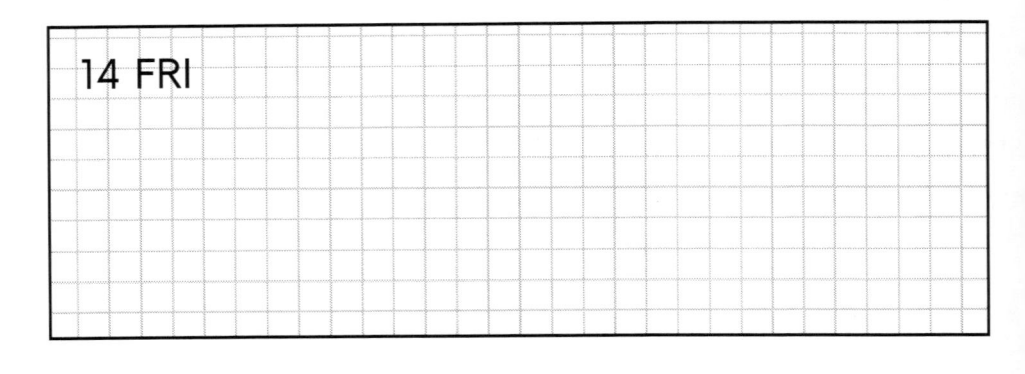

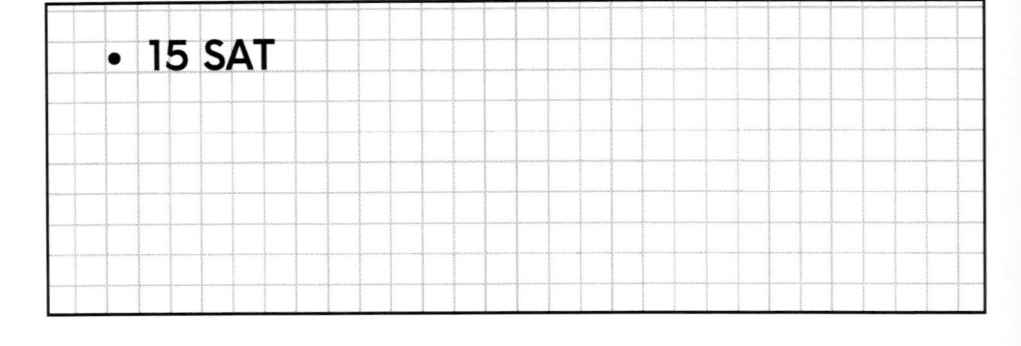

12 WED

13 THU

14 FRI

- ### 15 SAT

DATE	START	BREAK	BREAK	FINISH	TOTAL HOURS

- VEHICLE INFORMATION
- START LOCATION
- END LOCATION
- PURPOSE

START	END	BUSINESS MILES	PERSONAL MILES

DATE	START	BREAK	BREAK	FINISH	TOTAL HOURS

- VEHICLE INFORMATION
- START LOCATION
- END LOCATION
- PURPOSE

START	END	BUSINESS MILES	PERSONAL MILES

DATE	START	BREAK	BREAK	FINISH	TOTAL HOURS

- VEHICLE INFORMATION
- START LOCATION
- END LOCATION
- PURPOSE

START	END	BUSINESS MILES	PERSONAL MILES

DATE	START	BREAK	BREAK	FINISH	TOTAL HOURS

- VEHICLE INFORMATION
- START LOCATION
- END LOCATION
- PURPOSE

START	END	BUSINESS MILES	PERSONAL MILES

OCTOBER 2022

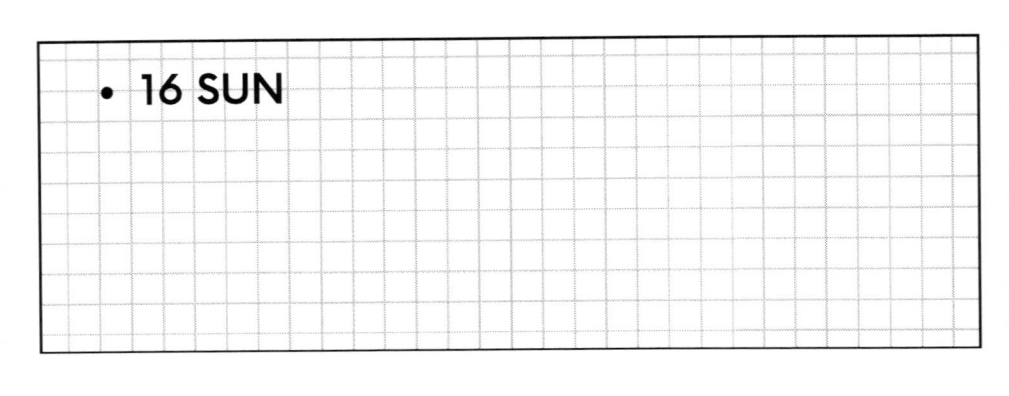

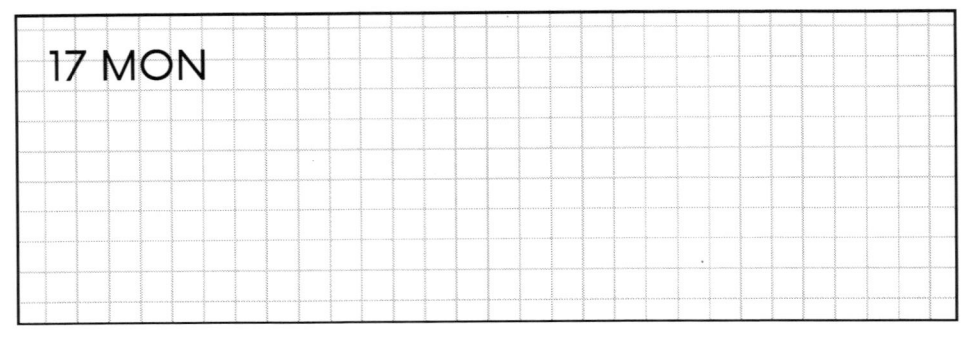

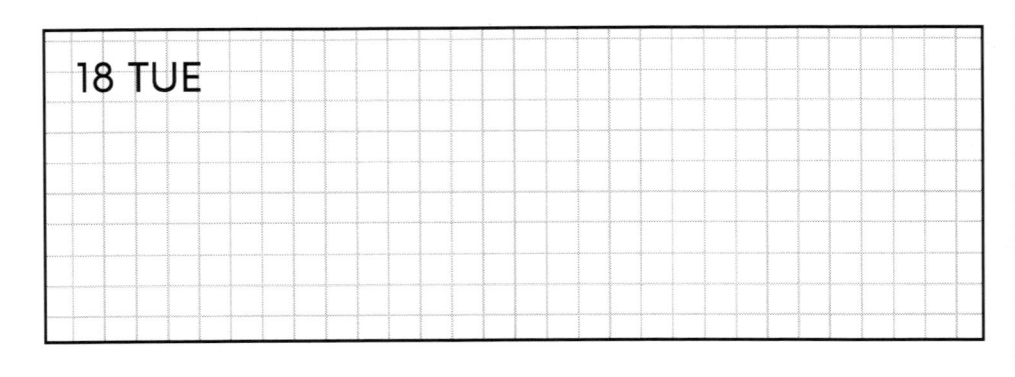

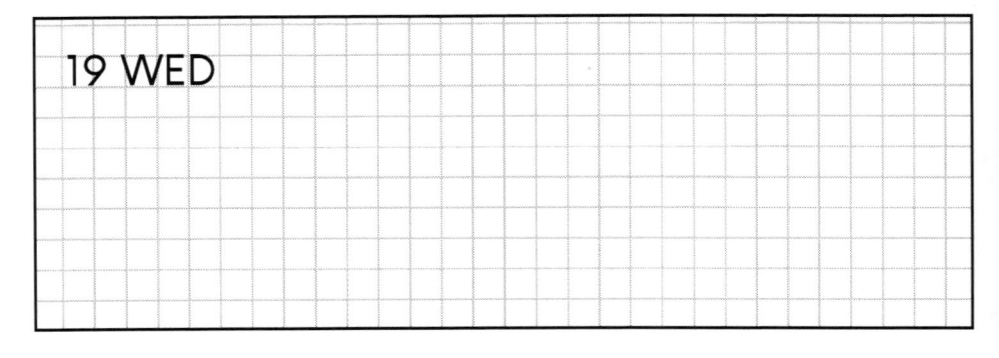

- **16 SUN**

17 MON

18 TUE

19 WED

DATE	START	BREAK	BREAK	FINISH	TOTAL HOURS

- VEHICLE INFORMATION
- START LOCATION
- END LOCATION
- PURPOSE

START	END	BUSINESS MILES	PERSONAL MILES

DATE	START	BREAK	BREAK	FINISH	TOTAL HOURS

- VEHICLE INFORMATION
- START LOCATION
- END LOCATION
- PURPOSE

START	END	BUSINESS MILES	PERSONAL MILES

DATE	START	BREAK	BREAK	FINISH	TOTAL HOURS

- VEHICLE INFORMATION
- START LOCATION
- END LOCATION
- PURPOSE

START	END	BUSINESS MILES	PERSONAL MILES

DATE	START	BREAK	BREAK	FINISH	TOTAL HOURS

- VEHICLE INFORMATION
- START LOCATION
- END LOCATION
- PURPOSE

START	END	BUSINESS MILES	PERSONAL MILES

OCTOBER 2022

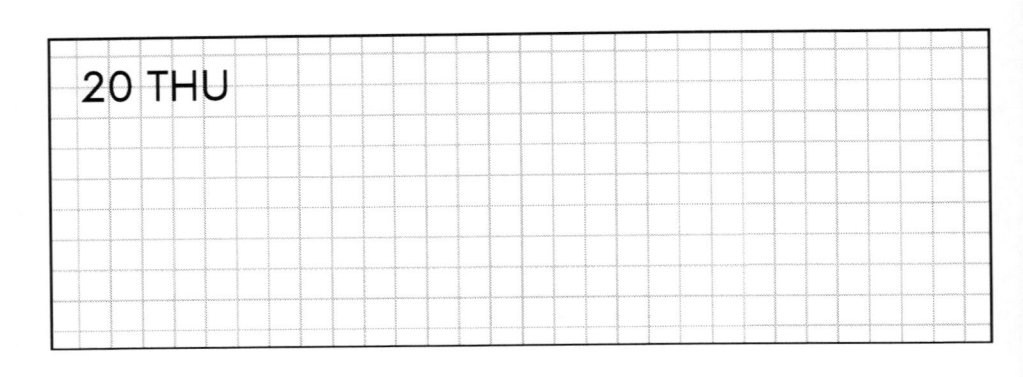

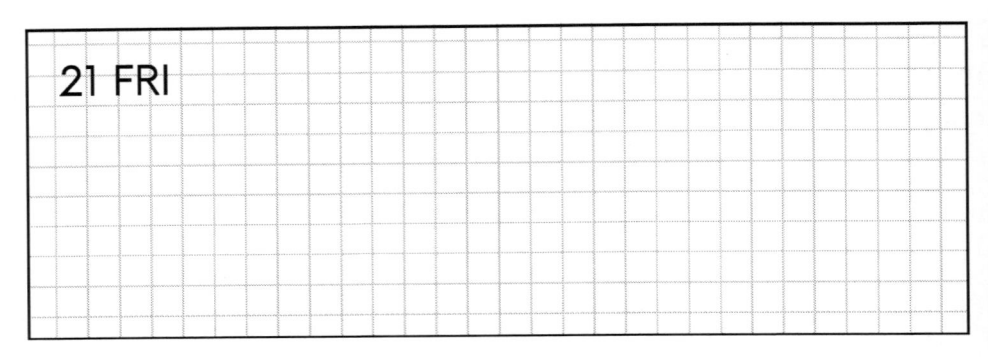

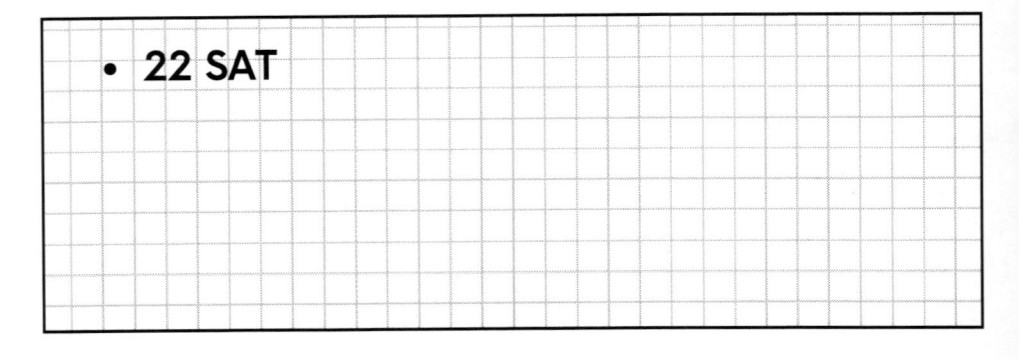

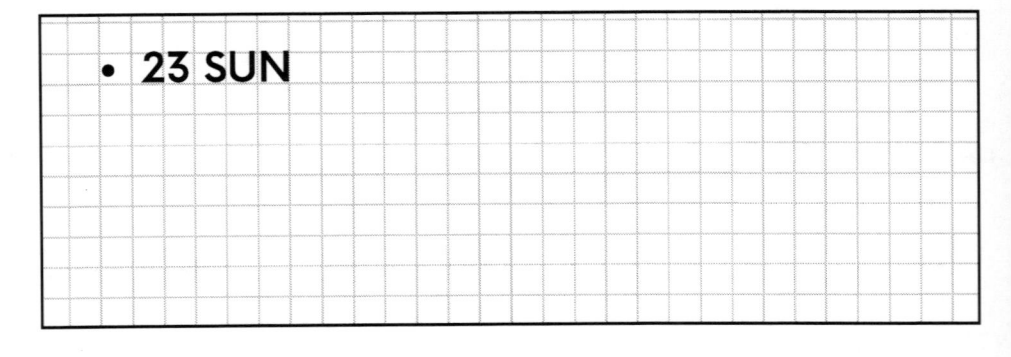

20 THU

21 FRI

- **22 SAT**

- **23 SUN**

DATE	START	BREAK	BREAK	FINISH	TOTAL HOURS

- VEHICLE INFORMATION
- START LOCATION
- END LOCATION
- PURPOSE

START	END	BUSINESS MILES	PERSONAL MILES

DATE	START	BREAK	BREAK	FINISH	TOTAL HOURS

- VEHICLE INFORMATION
- START LOCATION
- END LOCATION
- PURPOSE

START	END	BUSINESS MILES	PERSONAL MILES

DATE	START	BREAK	BREAK	FINISH	TOTAL HOURS

- VEHICLE INFORMATION
- START LOCATION
- END LOCATION
- PURPOSE

START	END	BUSINESS MILES	PERSONAL MILES

DATE	START	BREAK	BREAK	FINISH	TOTAL HOURS

- VEHICLE INFORMATION
- START LOCATION
- END LOCATION
- PURPOSE

START	END	BUSINESS MILES	PERSONAL MILES

OCTOBER 2022

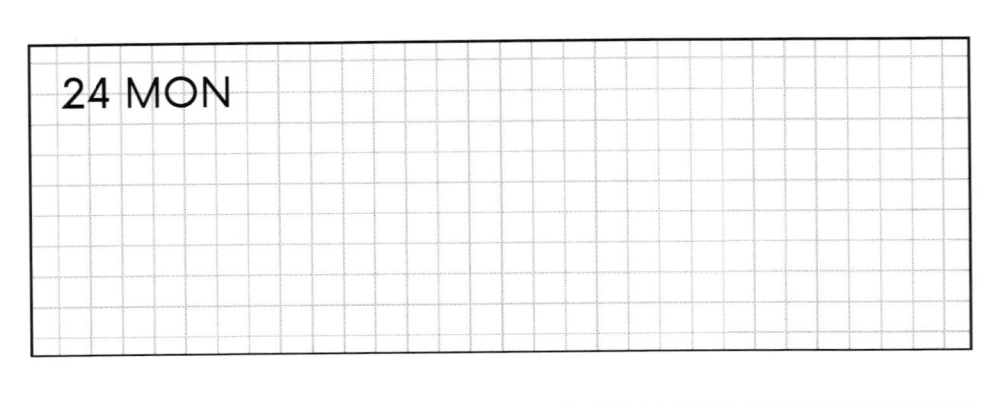

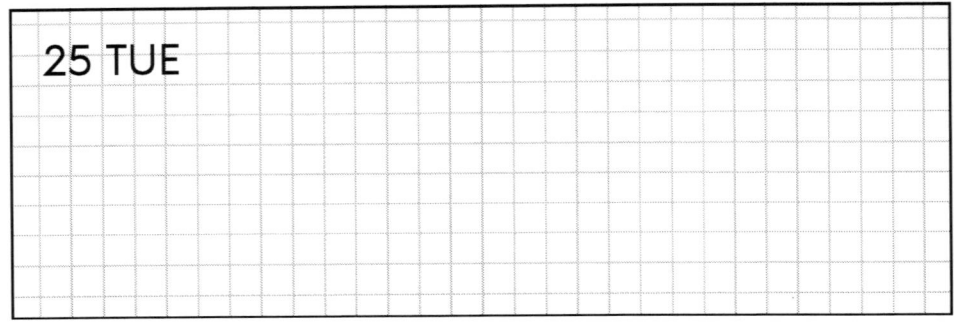

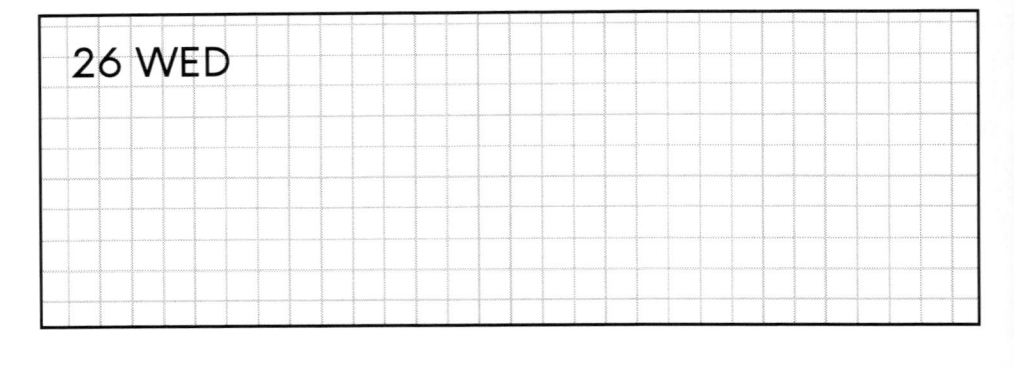

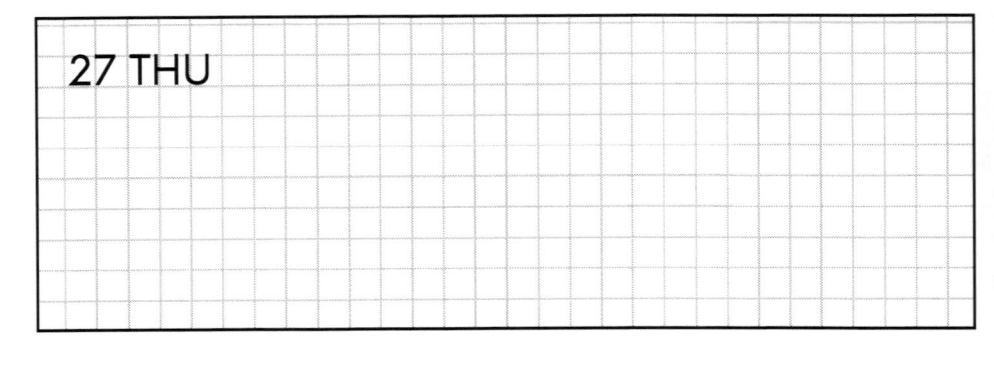

24 MON

25 TUE

26 WED

27 THU

DATE	START	BREAK	BREAK	FINISH	TOTAL HOURS

- VEHICLE INFORMATION
- START LOCATION
- END LOCATION
- PURPOSE

START	END	BUSINESS MILES	PERSONAL MILES

DATE	START	BREAK	BREAK	FINISH	TOTAL HOURS

- VEHICLE INFORMATION
- START LOCATION
- END LOCATION
- PURPOSE

START	END	BUSINESS MILES	PERSONAL MILES

DATE	START	BREAK	BREAK	FINISH	TOTAL HOURS

- VEHICLE INFORMATION
- START LOCATION
- END LOCATION
- PURPOSE

START	END	BUSINESS MILES	PERSONAL MILES

DATE	START	BREAK	BREAK	FINISH	TOTAL HOURS

- VEHICLE INFORMATION
- START LOCATION
- END LOCATION
- PURPOSE

START	END	BUSINESS MILES	PERSONAL MILES

OCTOBER 2022

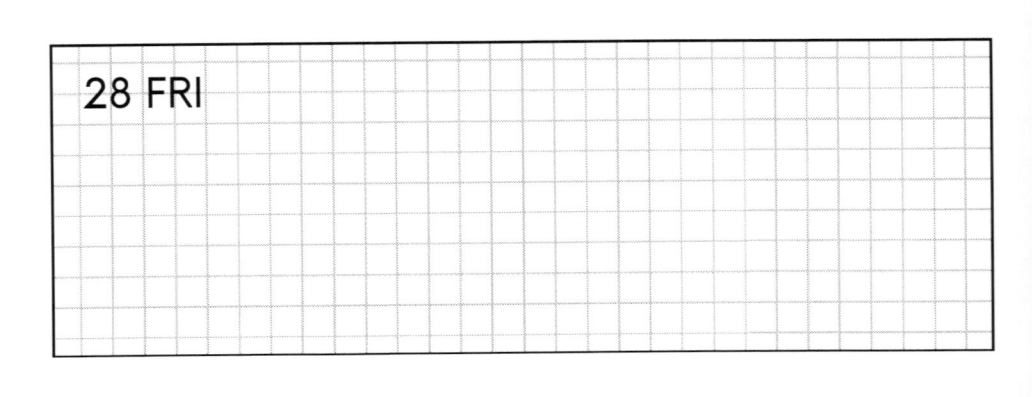

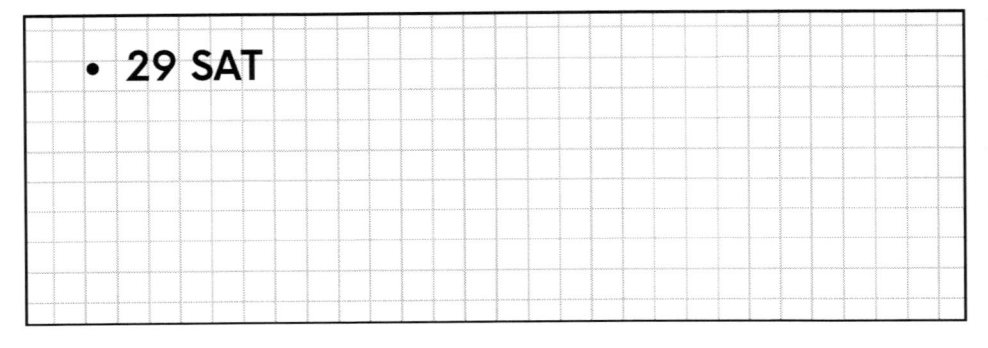

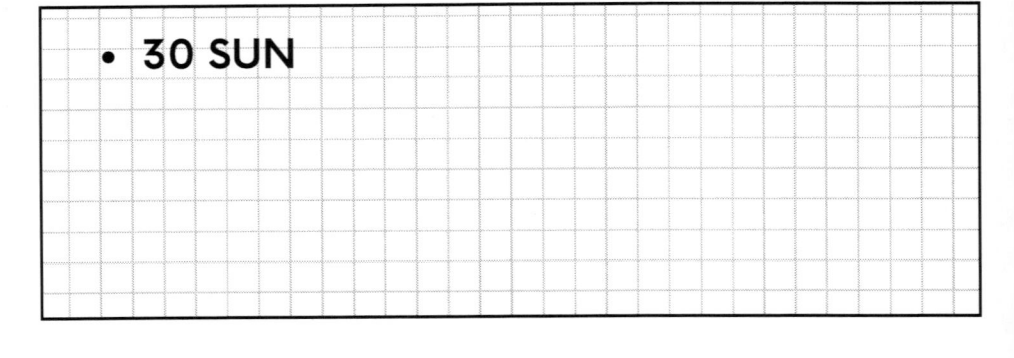

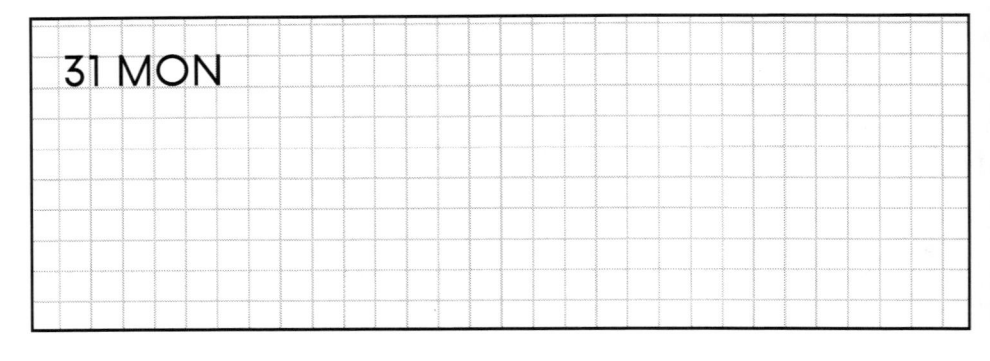

28 FRI

- **29 SAT**

- **30 SUN**

31 MON

DATE	START	BREAK	BREAK	FINISH	TOTAL HOURS

- VEHICLE INFORMATION
- START LOCATION
- END LOCATION
- PURPOSE

START	END	BUSINESS MILES	PERSONAL MILES

DATE	START	BREAK	BREAK	FINISH	TOTAL HOURS

- VEHICLE INFORMATION
- START LOCATION
- END LOCATION
- PURPOSE

START	END	BUSINESS MILES	PERSONAL MILES

DATE	START	BREAK	BREAK	FINISH	TOTAL HOURS

- VEHICLE INFORMATION
- START LOCATION
- END LOCATION
- PURPOSE

START	END	BUSINESS MILES	PERSONAL MILES

DATE	START	BREAK	BREAK	FINISH	TOTAL HOURS

- VEHICLE INFORMATION
- START LOCATION
- END LOCATION
- PURPOSE

START	END	BUSINESS MILES	PERSONAL MILES

NOVEMBER 2022

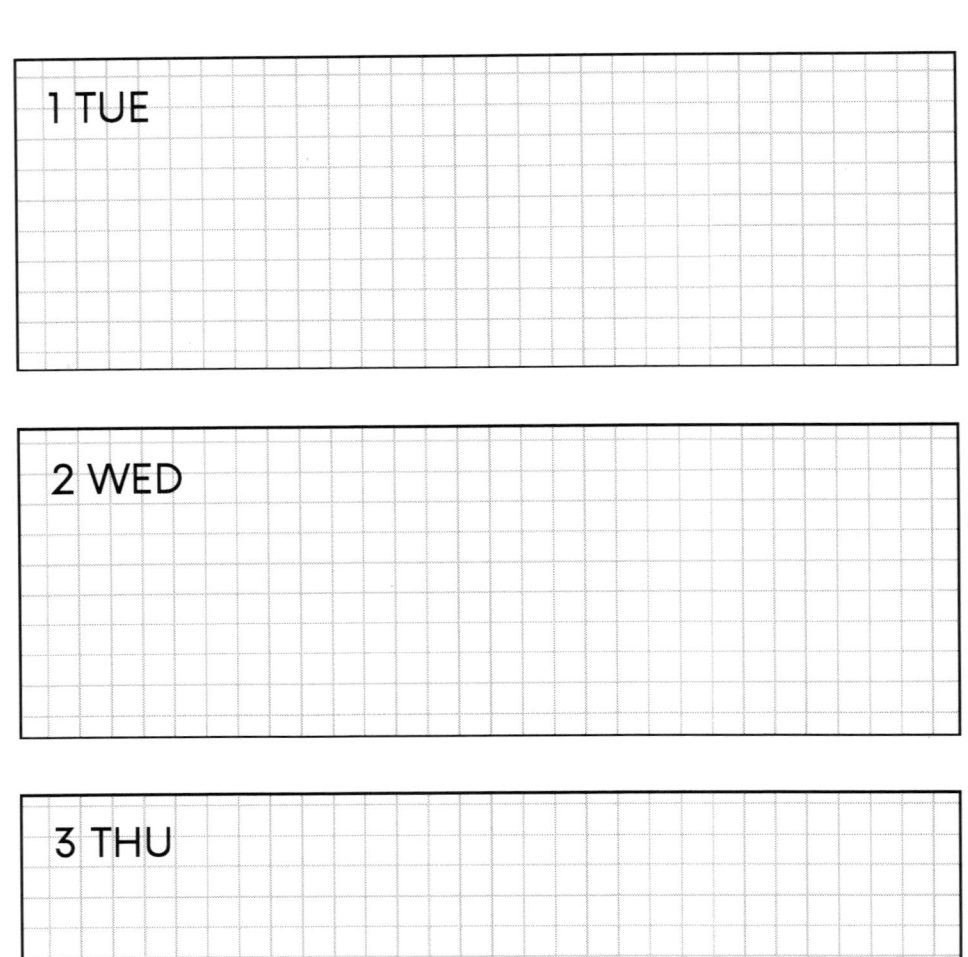

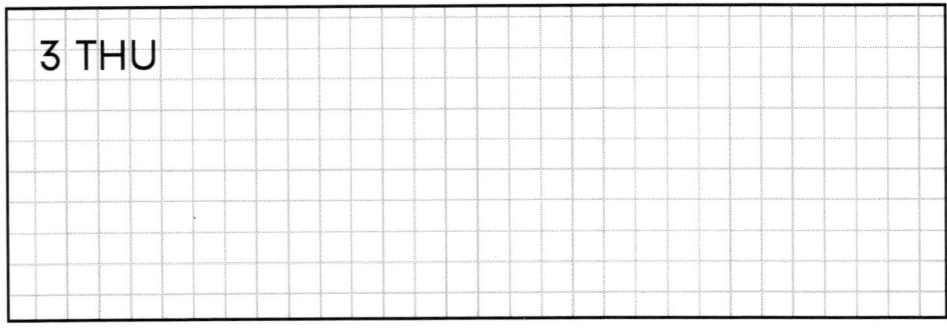

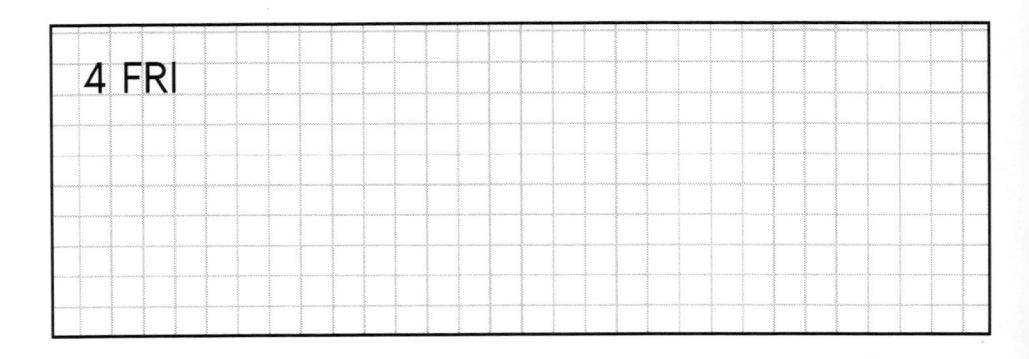

1 TUE

2 WED

3 THU

4 FRI

DATE	START	BREAK	BREAK	FINISH	TOTAL HOURS

- VEHICLE INFORMATION
- START LOCATION
- END LOCATION
- PURPOSE

START	END	BUSINESS MILES	PERSONAL MILES

DATE	START	BREAK	BREAK	FINISH	TOTAL HOURS

- VEHICLE INFORMATION
- START LOCATION
- END LOCATION
- PURPOSE

START	END	BUSINESS MILES	PERSONAL MILES

DATE	START	BREAK	BREAK	FINISH	TOTAL HOURS

- VEHICLE INFORMATION
- START LOCATION
- END LOCATION
- PURPOSE

START	END	BUSINESS MILES	PERSONAL MILES

DATE	START	BREAK	BREAK	FINISH	TOTAL HOURS

- VEHICLE INFORMATION
- START LOCATION
- END LOCATION
- PURPOSE

START	END	BUSINESS MILES	PERSONAL MILES

NOVEMBER   2022

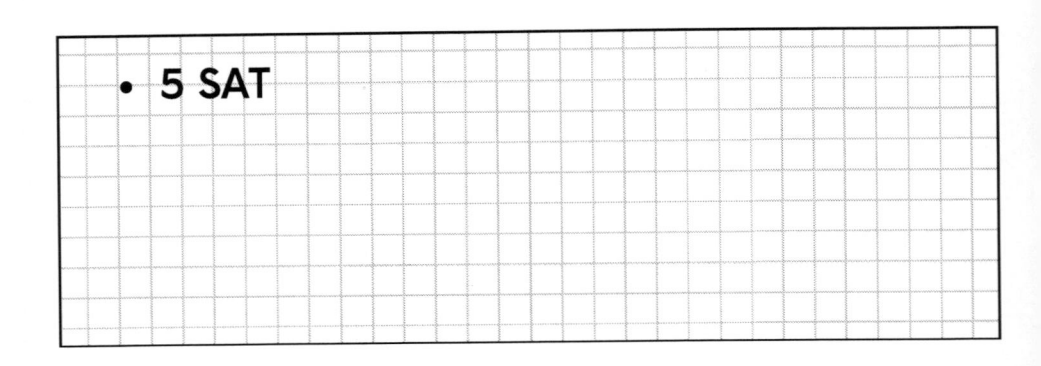

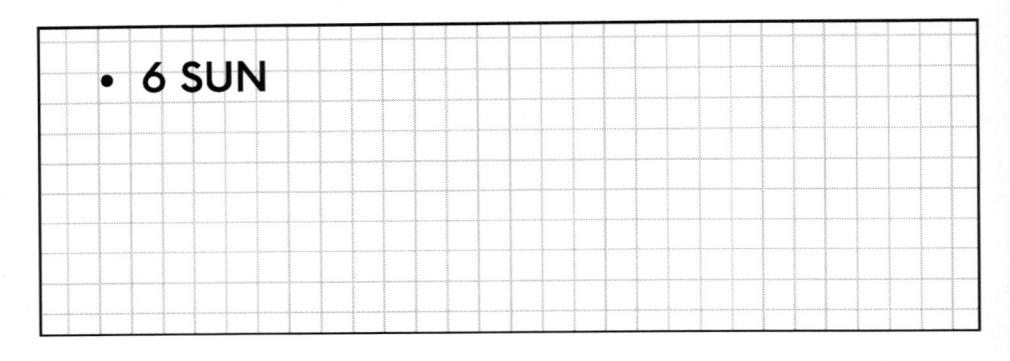

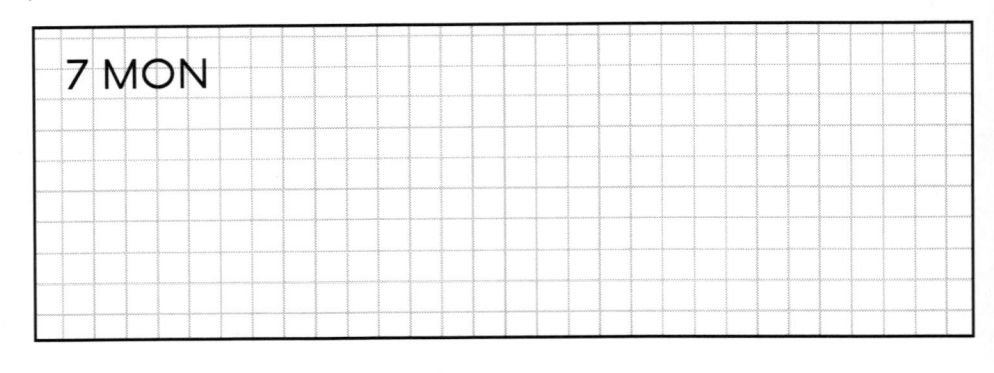

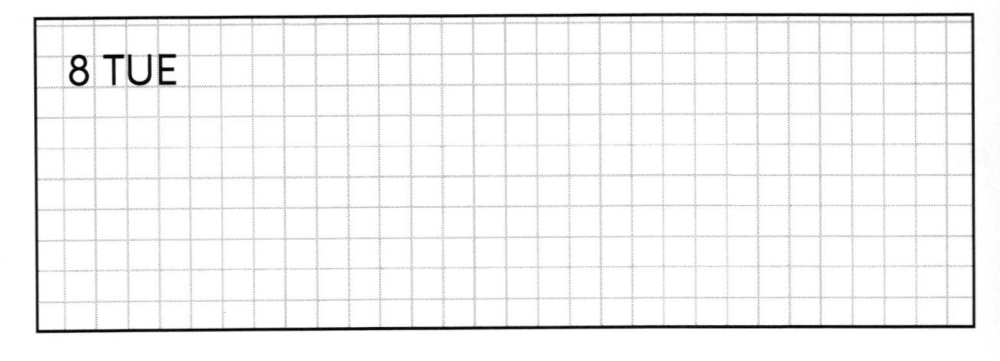

- **5 SAT**

- **6 SUN**

7 MON

8 TUE

DATE	START	BREAK	BREAK	FINISH	TOTAL HOURS

- VEHICLE INFORMATION
- START LOCATION
- END LOCATION
- PURPOSE

START	END	BUSINESS MILES	PERSONAL MILES

DATE	START	BREAK	BREAK	FINISH	TOTAL HOURS

- VEHICLE INFORMATION
- START LOCATION
- END LOCATION
- PURPOSE

START	END	BUSINESS MILES	PERSONAL MILES

DATE	START	BREAK	BREAK	FINISH	TOTAL HOURS

- VEHICLE INFORMATION
- START LOCATION
- END LOCATION
- PURPOSE

START	END	BUSINESS MILES	PERSONAL MILES

DATE	START	BREAK	BREAK	FINISH	TOTAL HOURS

- VEHICLE INFORMATION
- START LOCATION
- END LOCATION
- PURPOSE

START	END	BUSINESS MILES	PERSONAL MILES

NOVEMBER   2022

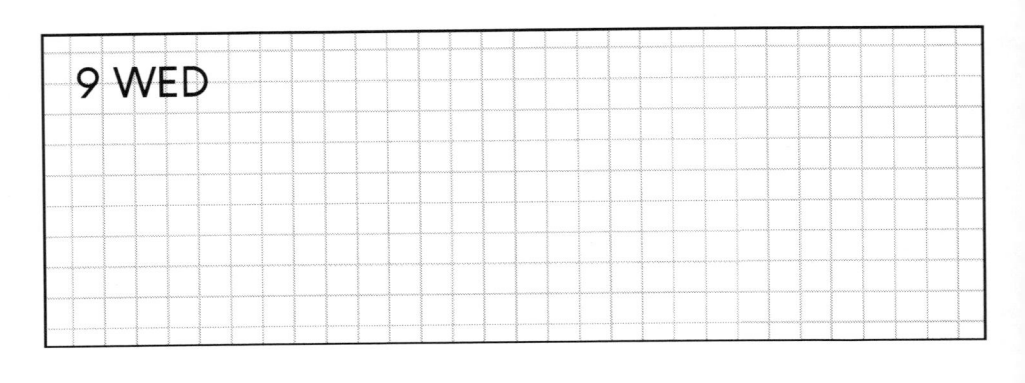

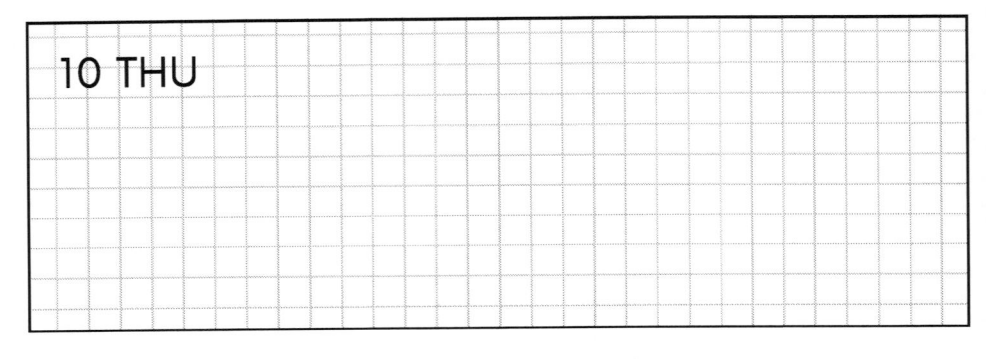

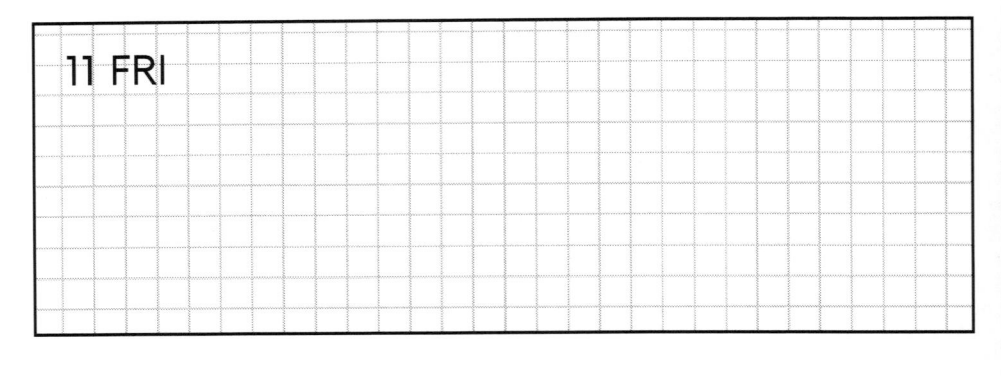

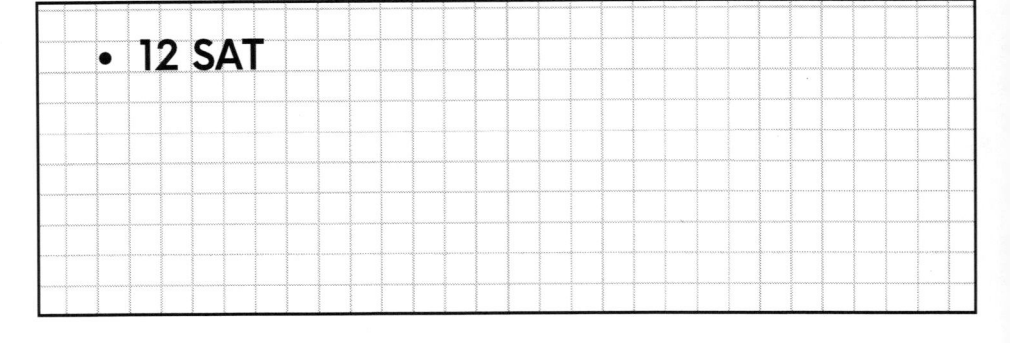

9 WED

10 THU

11 FRI

- **12 SAT**

DATE	START	BREAK	BREAK	FINISH	TOTAL HOURS

- VEHICLE INFORMATION
- START LOCATION
- END LOCATION
- PURPOSE

START	END	BUSINESS MILES	PERSONAL MILES

DATE	START	BREAK	BREAK	FINISH	TOTAL HOURS

- VEHICLE INFORMATION
- START LOCATION
- END LOCATION
- PURPOSE

START	END	BUSINESS MILES	PERSONAL MILES

DATE	START	BREAK	BREAK	FINISH	TOTAL HOURS

- VEHICLE INFORMATION
- START LOCATION
- END LOCATION
- PURPOSE

START	END	BUSINESS MILES	PERSONAL MILES

DATE	START	BREAK	BREAK	FINISH	TOTAL HOURS

- VEHICLE INFORMATION
- START LOCATION
- END LOCATION
- PURPOSE

START	END	BUSINESS MILES	PERSONAL MILES

NOVEMBER 2022

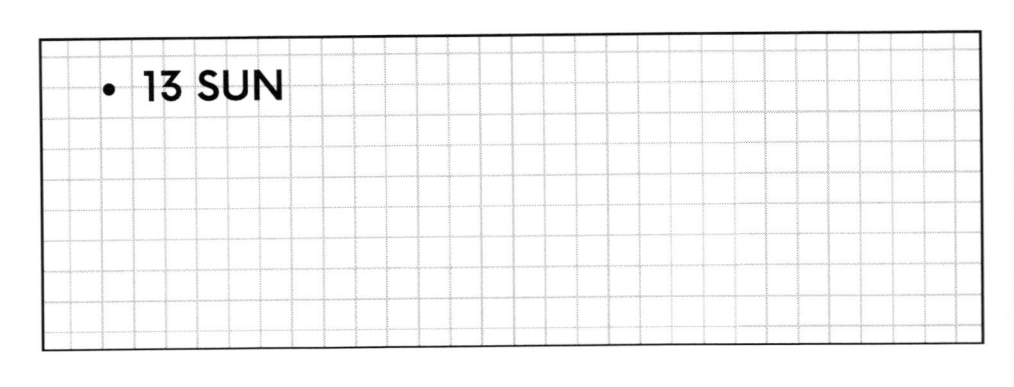

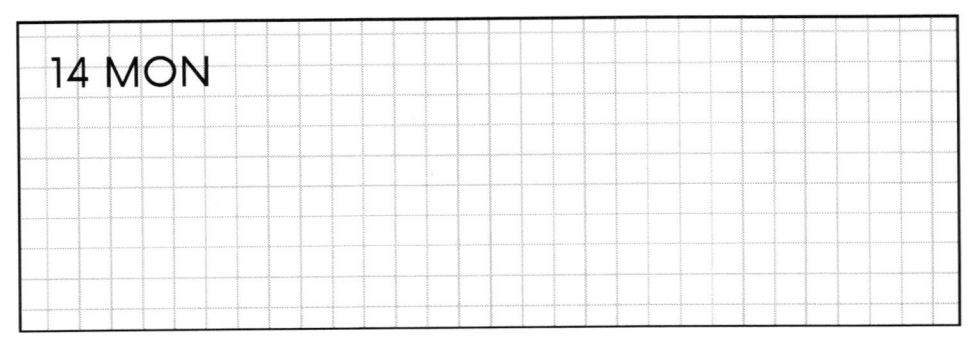

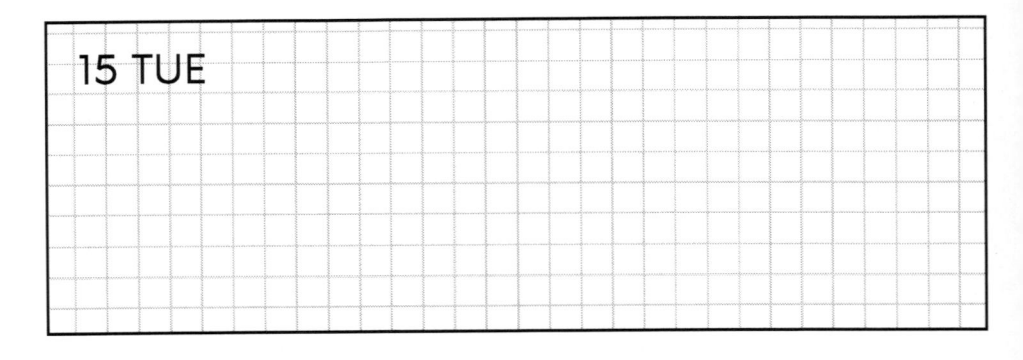

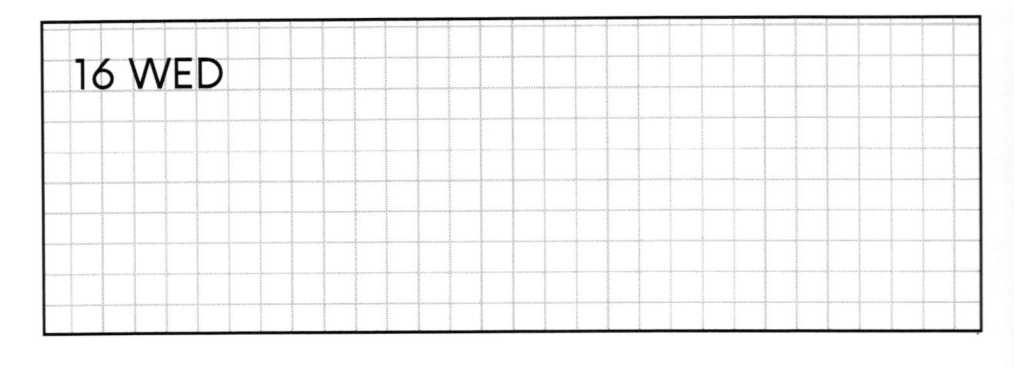

- **13 SUN**

14 MON

15 TUE

16 WED

DATE	START	BREAK	BREAK	FINISH	TOTAL HOURS

- VEHICLE INFORMATION
- START LOCATION
- END LOCATION
- PURPOSE

START	END	BUSINESS MILES	PERSONAL MILES

DATE	START	BREAK	BREAK	FINISH	TOTAL HOURS

- VEHICLE INFORMATION
- START LOCATION
- END LOCATION
- PURPOSE

START	END	BUSINESS MILES	PERSONAL MILES

DATE	START	BREAK	BREAK	FINISH	TOTAL HOURS

- VEHICLE INFORMATION
- START LOCATION
- END LOCATION
- PURPOSE

START	END	BUSINESS MILES	PERSONAL MILES

DATE	START	BREAK	BREAK	FINISH	TOTAL HOURS

- VEHICLE INFORMATION
- START LOCATION
- END LOCATION
- PURPOSE

START	END	BUSINESS MILES	PERSONAL MILES

NOVEMBER 2022

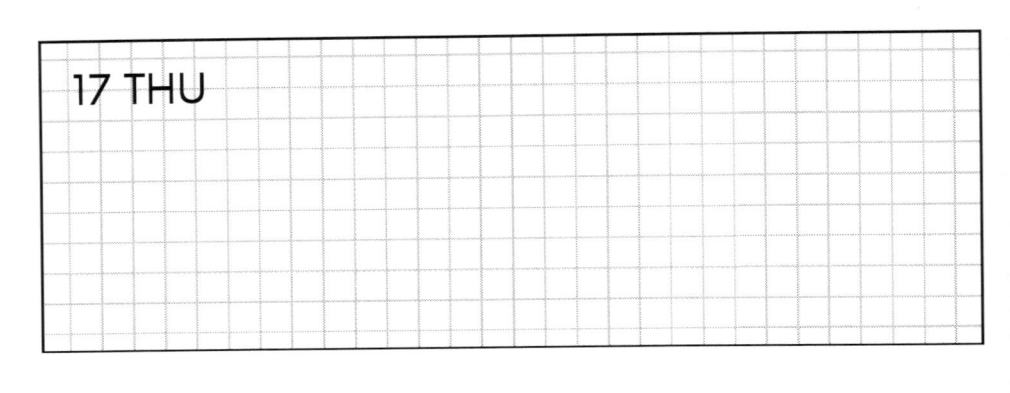

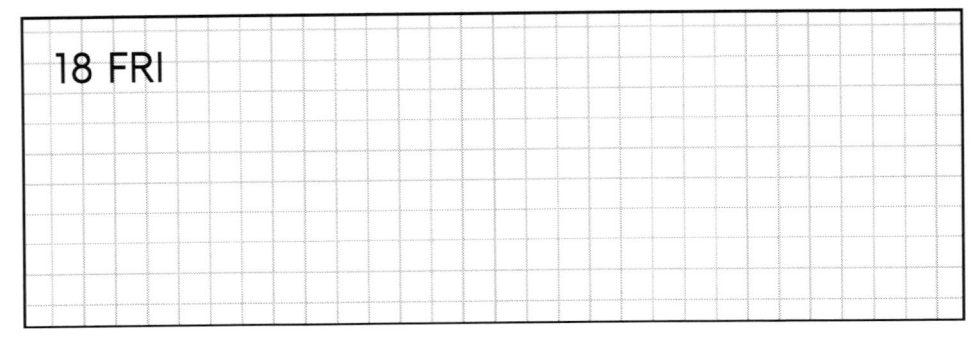

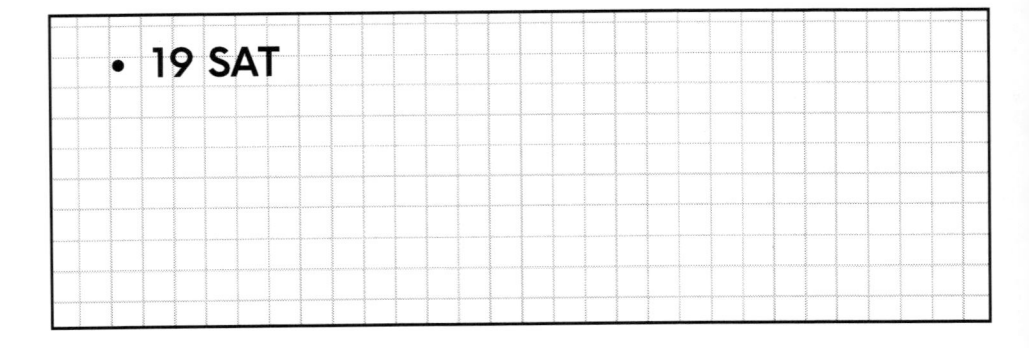

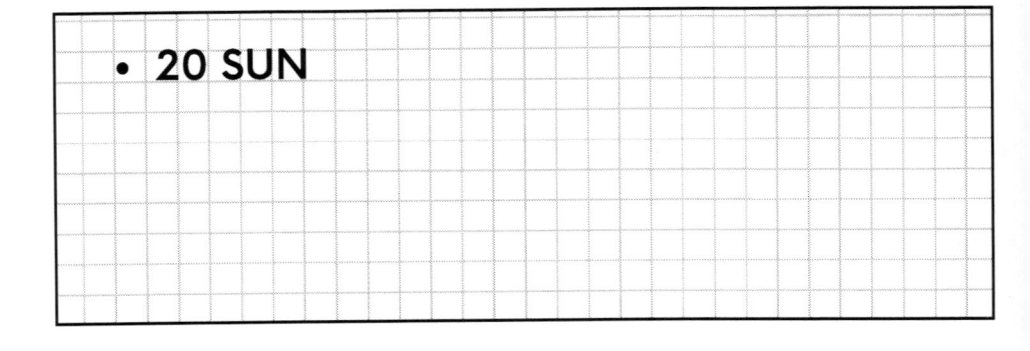

17 THU

18 FRI

- **19 SAT**

- **20 SUN**

DATE	START	BREAK	BREAK	FINISH	TOTAL HOURS

- VEHICLE INFORMATION
- START LOCATION
- END LOCATION
- PURPOSE

START	END	BUSINESS MILES	PERSONAL MILES

DATE	START	BREAK	BREAK	FINISH	TOTAL HOURS

- VEHICLE INFORMATION
- START LOCATION
- END LOCATION
- PURPOSE

START	END	BUSINESS MILES	PERSONAL MILES

DATE	START	BREAK	BREAK	FINISH	TOTAL HOURS

- VEHICLE INFORMATION
- START LOCATION
- END LOCATION
- PURPOSE

START	END	BUSINESS MILES	PERSONAL MILES

DATE	START	BREAK	BREAK	FINISH	TOTAL HOURS

- VEHICLE INFORMATION
- START LOCATION
- END LOCATION
- PURPOSE

START	END	BUSINESS MILES	PERSONAL MILES

NOVEMBER 2022

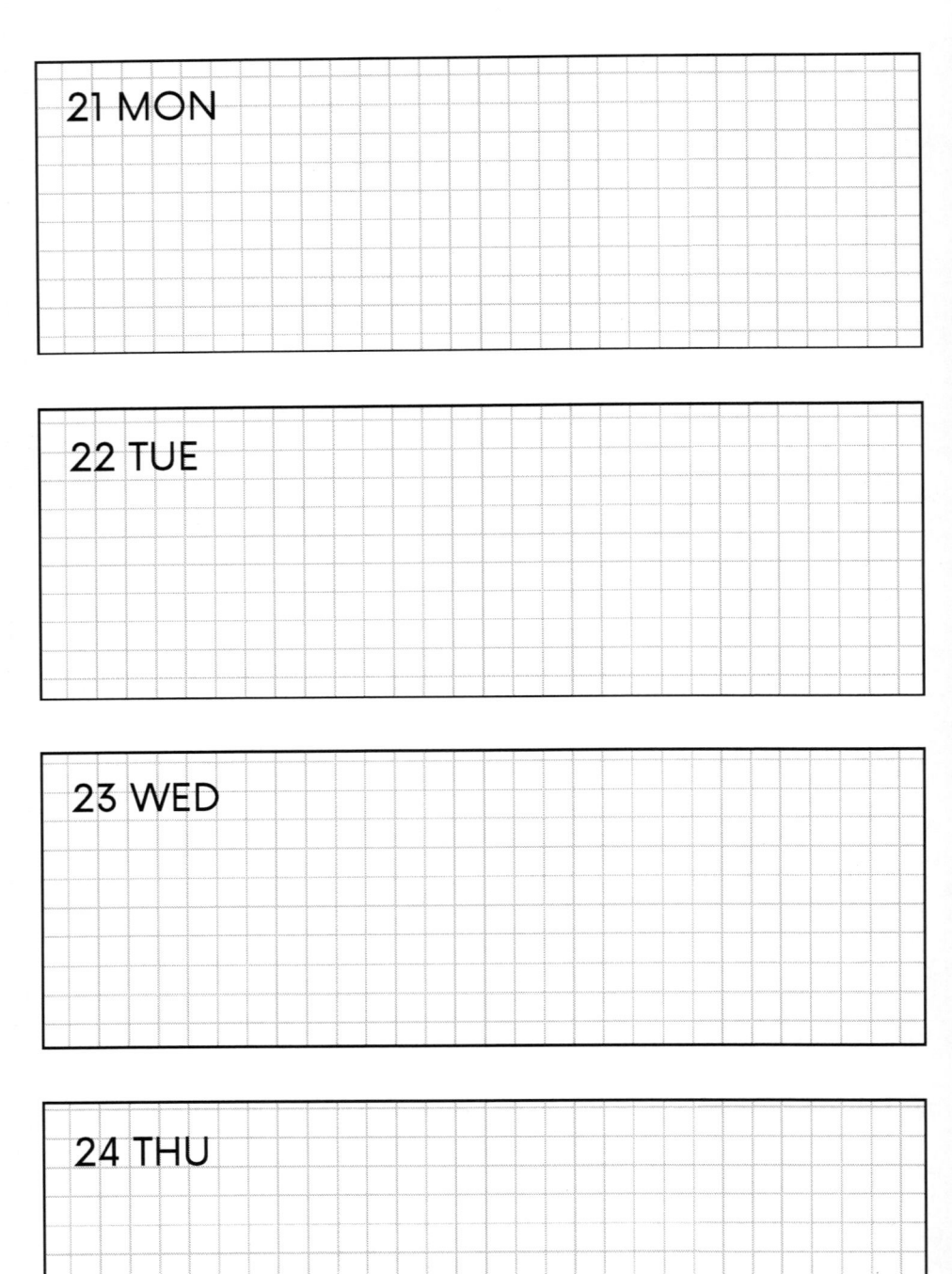

21 MON

22 TUE

23 WED

24 THU

DATE	START	BREAK	BREAK	FINISH	TOTAL HOURS

- VEHICLE INFORMATION
- START LOCATION
- END LOCATION
- PURPOSE

START	END	BUSINESS MILES	PERSONAL MILES

DATE	START	BREAK	BREAK	FINISH	TOTAL HOURS

- VEHICLE INFORMATION
- START LOCATION
- END LOCATION
- PURPOSE

START	END	BUSINESS MILES	PERSONAL MILES

DATE	START	BREAK	BREAK	FINISH	TOTAL HOURS

- VEHICLE INFORMATION
- START LOCATION
- END LOCATION
- PURPOSE

START	END	BUSINESS MILES	PERSONAL MILES

DATE	START	BREAK	BREAK	FINISH	TOTAL HOURS

- VEHICLE INFORMATION
- START LOCATION
- END LOCATION
- PURPOSE

START	END	BUSINESS MILES	PERSONAL MILES

NOVEMBER 2022

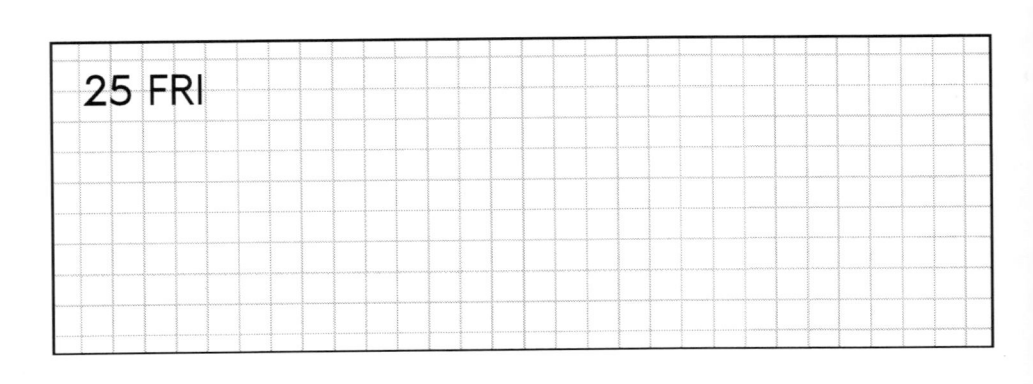

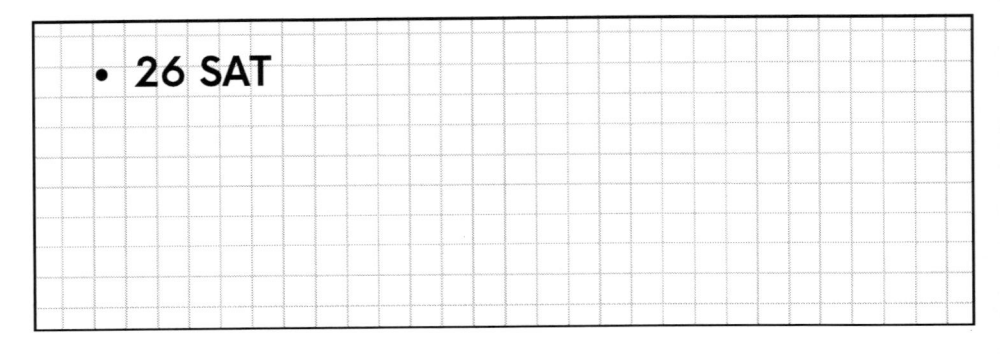

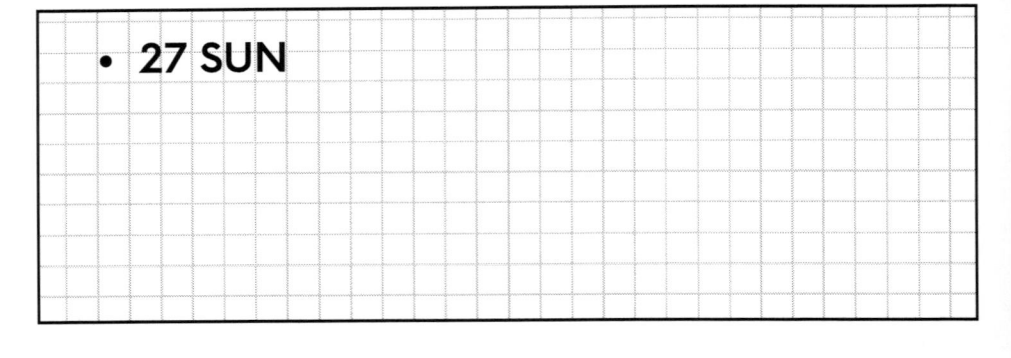

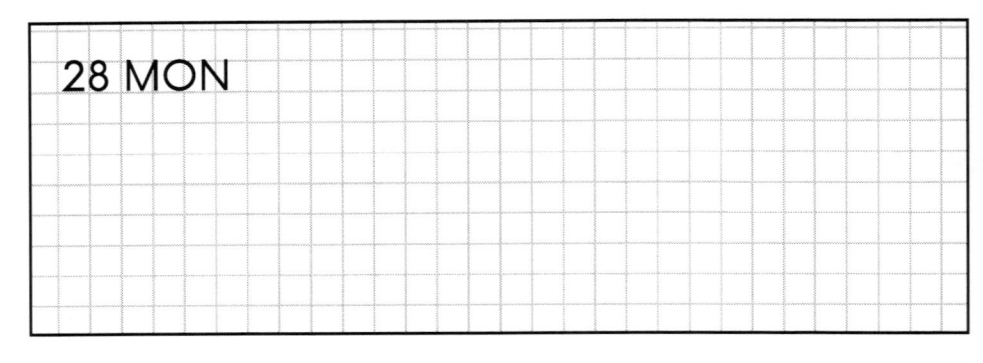

25 FRI

- **26 SAT**

- **27 SUN**

28 MON

DATE	START	BREAK	BREAK	FINISH	TOTAL HOURS

- VEHICLE INFORMATION
- START LOCATION
- END LOCATION
- PURPOSE

START	END	BUSINESS MILES	PERSONAL MILES

DATE	START	BREAK	BREAK	FINISH	TOTAL HOURS

- VEHICLE INFORMATION
- START LOCATION
- END LOCATION
- PURPOSE

START	END	BUSINESS MILES	PERSONAL MILES

DATE	START	BREAK	BREAK	FINISH	TOTAL HOURS

- VEHICLE INFORMATION
- START LOCATION
- END LOCATION
- PURPOSE

START	END	BUSINESS MILES	PERSONAL MILES

DATE	START	BREAK	BREAK	FINISH	TOTAL HOURS

- VEHICLE INFORMATION
- START LOCATION
- END LOCATION
- PURPOSE

START	END	BUSINESS MILES	PERSONAL MILES

NOVEMBER/DECEMBER 2022

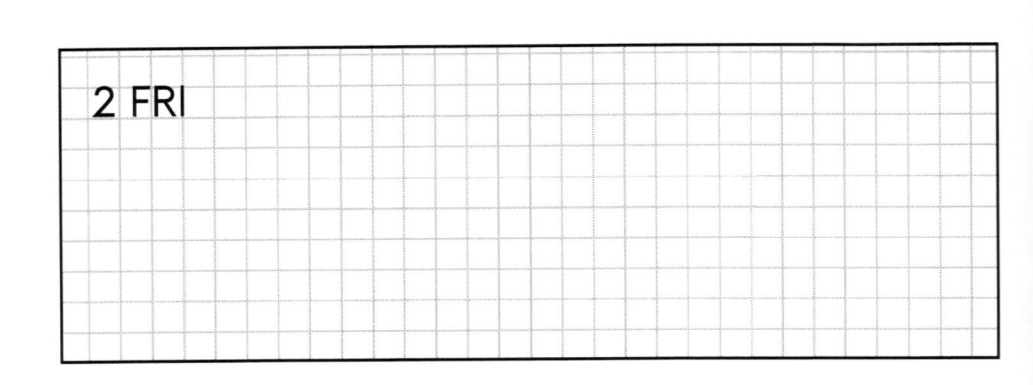

29 TUE

30 WED

1 THU

2 FRI

DATE	START	BREAK	BREAK	FINISH	TOTAL HOURS

- VEHICLE INFORMATION
- START LOCATION
- END LOCATION
- PURPOSE

START	END	BUSINESS MILES	PERSONAL MILES

DATE	START	BREAK	BREAK	FINISH	TOTAL HOURS

- VEHICLE INFORMATION
- START LOCATION
- END LOCATION
- PURPOSE

START	END	BUSINESS MILES	PERSONAL MILES

DATE	START	BREAK	BREAK	FINISH	TOTAL HOURS

- VEHICLE INFORMATION
- START LOCATION
- END LOCATION
- PURPOSE

START	END	BUSINESS MILES	PERSONAL MILES

DATE	START	BREAK	BREAK	FINISH	TOTAL HOURS

- VEHICLE INFORMATION
- START LOCATION
- END LOCATION
- PURPOSE

START	END	BUSINESS MILES	PERSONAL MILES

DECEMBER 2022

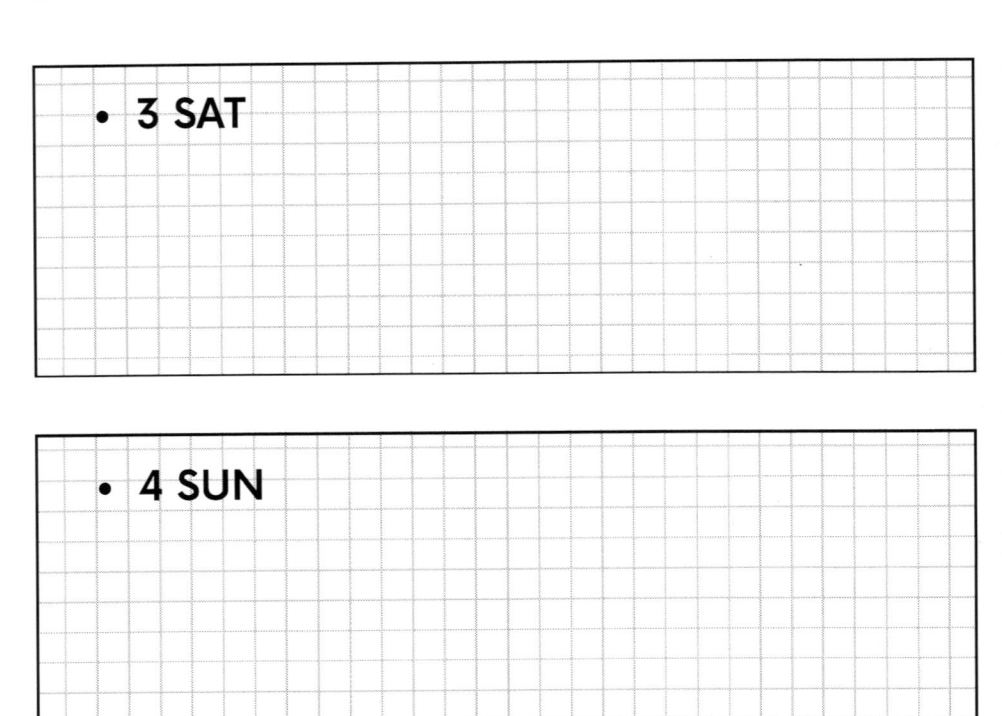

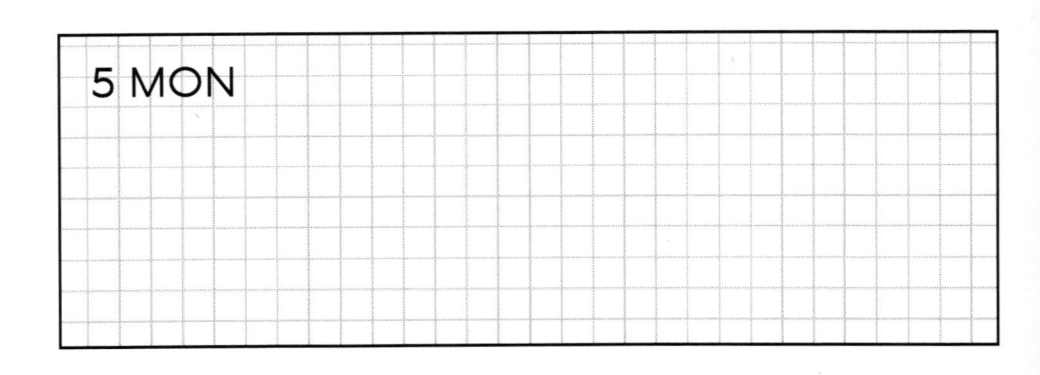

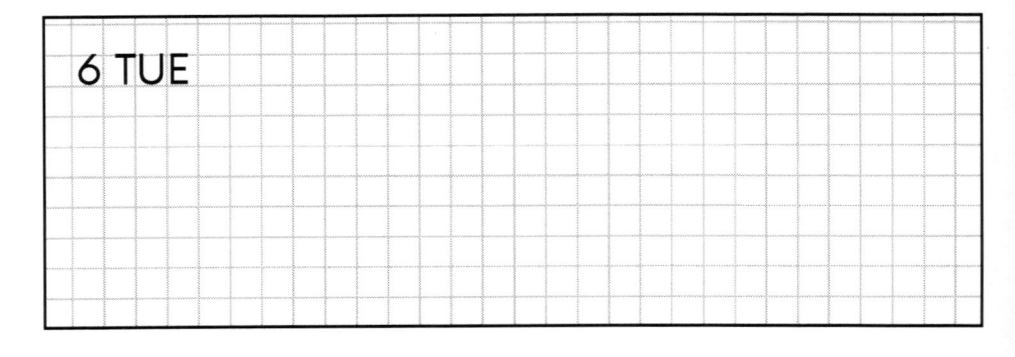

- **3 SAT**

- **4 SUN**

5 MON

6 TUE

DATE	START	BREAK	BREAK	FINISH	TOTAL HOURS

- VEHICLE INFORMATION
- START LOCATION
- END LOCATION
- PURPOSE

START	END	BUSINESS MILES	PERSONAL MILES

DATE	START	BREAK	BREAK	FINISH	TOTAL HOURS

- VEHICLE INFORMATION
- START LOCATION
- END LOCATION
- PURPOSE

START	END	BUSINESS MILES	PERSONAL MILES

DATE	START	BREAK	BREAK	FINISH	TOTAL HOURS

- VEHICLE INFORMATION
- START LOCATION
- END LOCATION
- PURPOSE

START	END	BUSINESS MILES	PERSONAL MILES

DATE	START	BREAK	BREAK	FINISH	TOTAL HOURS

- VEHICLE INFORMATION
- START LOCATION
- END LOCATION
- PURPOSE

START	END	BUSINESS MILES	PERSONAL MILES

DECEMBER   2022

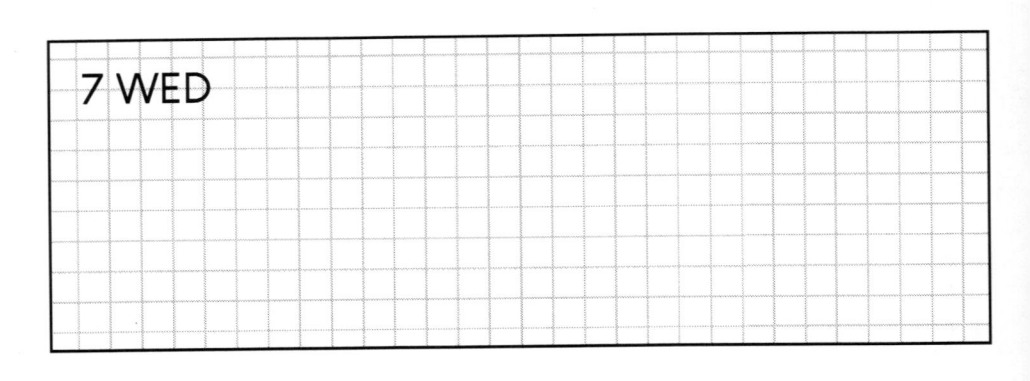

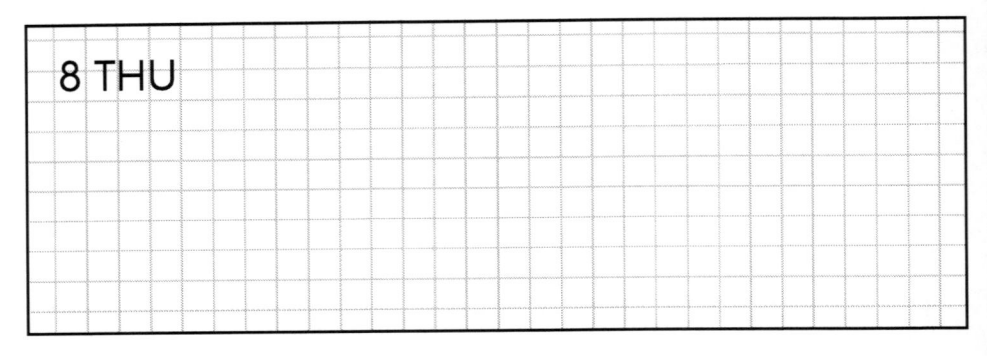

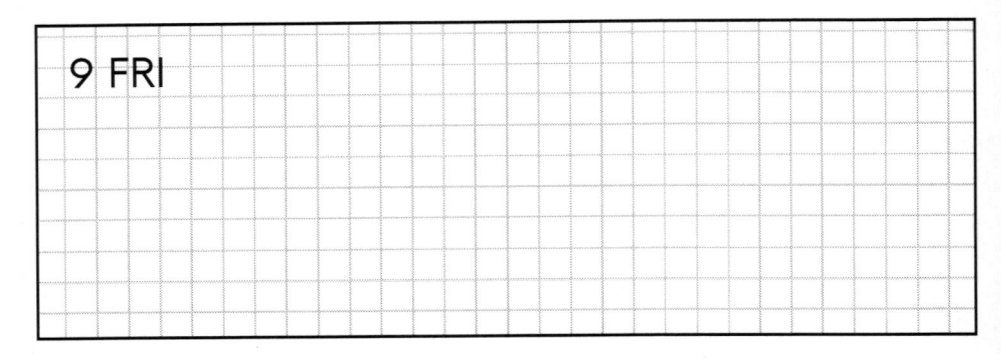

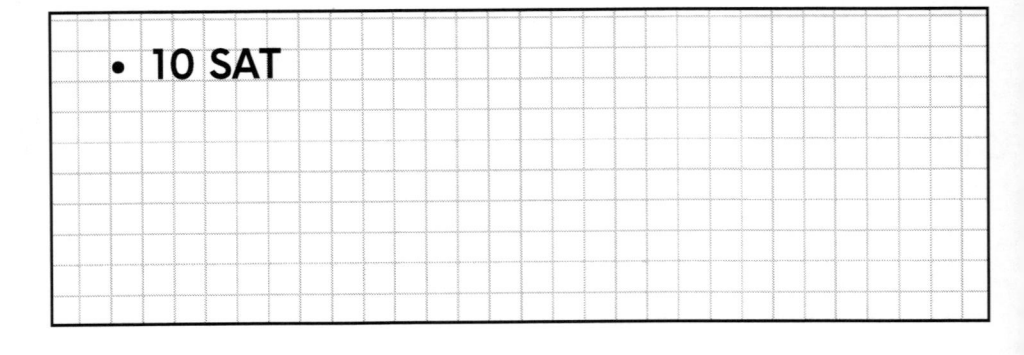

7 WED

8 THU

9 FRI

- **10 SAT**

DATE	START	BREAK	BREAK	FINISH	TOTAL HOURS

- **VEHICLE INFORMATION**
- **START LOCATION**
- **END LOCATION**
- **PURPOSE**

START	END	BUSINESS MILES	PERSONAL MILES

DATE	START	BREAK	BREAK	FINISH	TOTAL HOURS

- **VEHICLE INFORMATION**
- **START LOCATION**
- **END LOCATION**
- **PURPOSE**

START	END	BUSINESS MILES	PERSONAL MILES

DATE	START	BREAK	BREAK	FINISH	TOTAL HOURS

- **VEHICLE INFORMATION**
- **START LOCATION**
- **END LOCATION**
- **PURPOSE**

START	END	BUSINESS MILES	PERSONAL MILES

DATE	START	BREAK	BREAK	FINISH	TOTAL HOURS

- **VEHICLE INFORMATION**
- **START LOCATION**
- **END LOCATION**
- **PURPOSE**

START	END	BUSINESS MILES	PERSONAL MILES

DECEMBER 2022

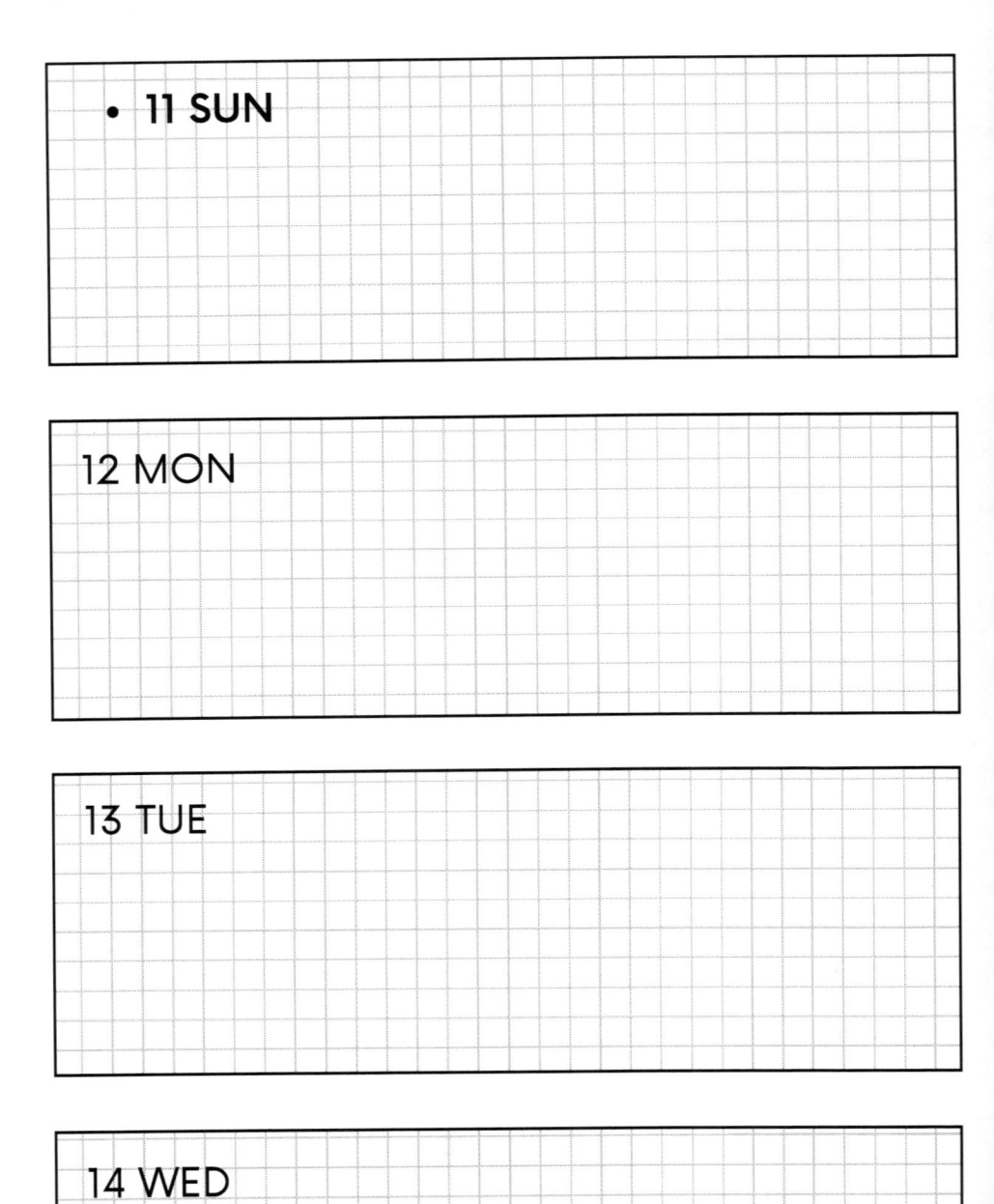

- **11 SUN**

12 MON

13 TUE

14 WED

DATE	START	BREAK	BREAK	FINISH	TOTAL HOURS

- VEHICLE INFORMATION
- START LOCATION
- END LOCATION
- PURPOSE

START	END	BUSINESS MILES	PERSONAL MILES

DATE	START	BREAK	BREAK	FINISH	TOTAL HOURS

- VEHICLE INFORMATION
- START LOCATION
- END LOCATION
- PURPOSE

START	END	BUSINESS MILES	PERSONAL MILES

DATE	START	BREAK	BREAK	FINISH	TOTAL HOURS

- VEHICLE INFORMATION
- START LOCATION
- END LOCATION
- PURPOSE

START	END	BUSINESS MILES	PERSONAL MILES

DATE	START	BREAK	BREAK	FINISH	TOTAL HOURS

- VEHICLE INFORMATION
- START LOCATION
- END LOCATION
- PURPOSE

START	END	BUSINESS MILES	PERSONAL MILES

DECEMBER 2022

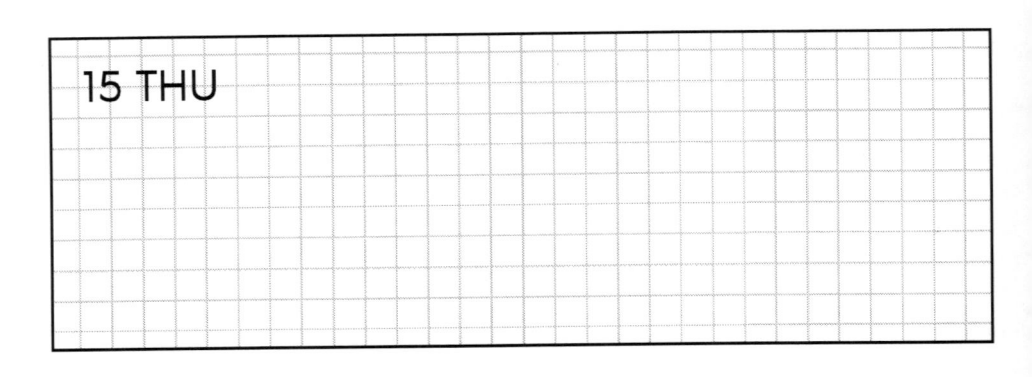

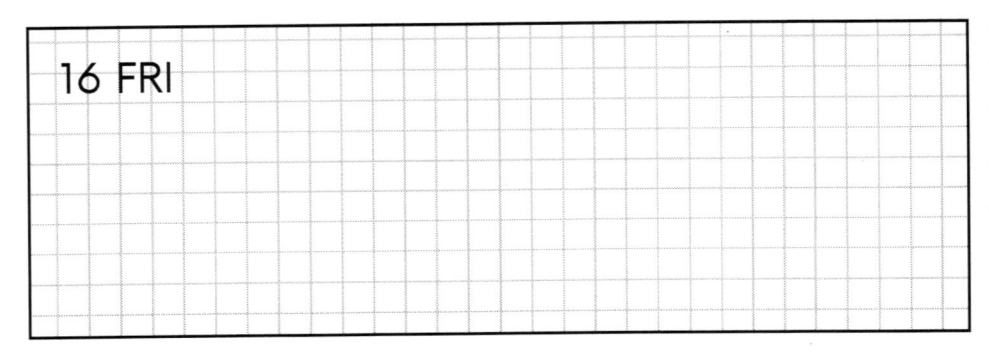

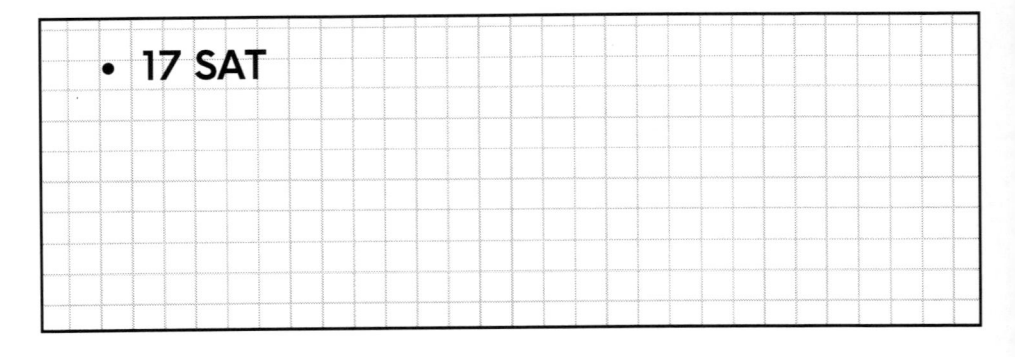

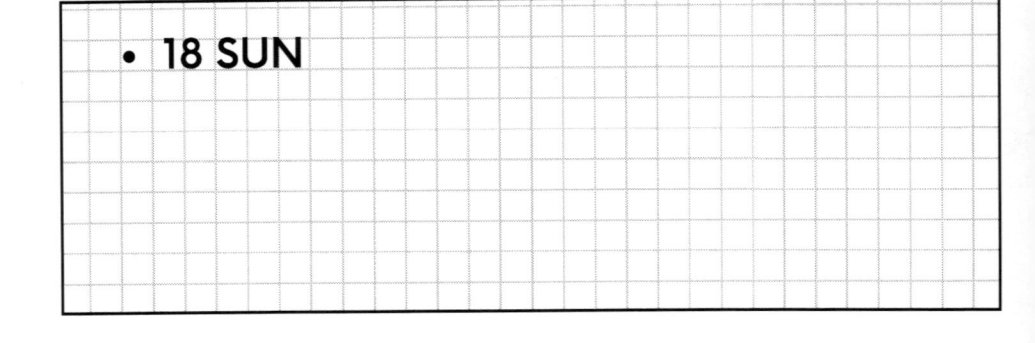

15 THU

16 FRI

- **17 SAT**

- **18 SUN**

DATE	START	BREAK	BREAK	FINISH	TOTAL HOURS

- VEHICLE INFORMATION
- START LOCATION
- END LOCATION
- PURPOSE

START	END	BUSINESS MILES	PERSONAL MILES

DATE	START	BREAK	BREAK	FINISH	TOTAL HOURS

- VEHICLE INFORMATION
- START LOCATION
- END LOCATION
- PURPOSE

START	END	BUSINESS MILES	PERSONAL MILES

DATE	START	BREAK	BREAK	FINISH	TOTAL HOURS

- VEHICLE INFORMATION
- START LOCATION
- END LOCATION
- PURPOSE

START	END	BUSINESS MILES	PERSONAL MILES

DATE	START	BREAK	BREAK	FINISH	TOTAL HOURS

- VEHICLE INFORMATION
- START LOCATION
- END LOCATION
- PURPOSE

START	END	BUSINESS MILES	PERSONAL MILES

DECEMBER   2022

19 MON

20 TUE

21 WED

22 THU

DATE	START	BREAK	BREAK	FINISH	TOTAL HOURS

- VEHICLE INFORMATION
- START LOCATION
- END LOCATION
- PURPOSE

START	END	BUSINESS MILES	PERSONAL MILES

DATE	START	BREAK	BREAK	FINISH	TOTAL HOURS

- VEHICLE INFORMATION
- START LOCATION
- END LOCATION
- PURPOSE

START	END	BUSINESS MILES	PERSONAL MILES

DATE	START	BREAK	BREAK	FINISH	TOTAL HOURS

- VEHICLE INFORMATION
- START LOCATION
- END LOCATION
- PURPOSE

START	END	BUSINESS MILES	PERSONAL MILES

DATE	START	BREAK	BREAK	FINISH	TOTAL HOURS

- VEHICLE INFORMATION
- START LOCATION
- END LOCATION
- PURPOSE

START	END	BUSINESS MILES	PERSONAL MILES

DECEMBER 2022

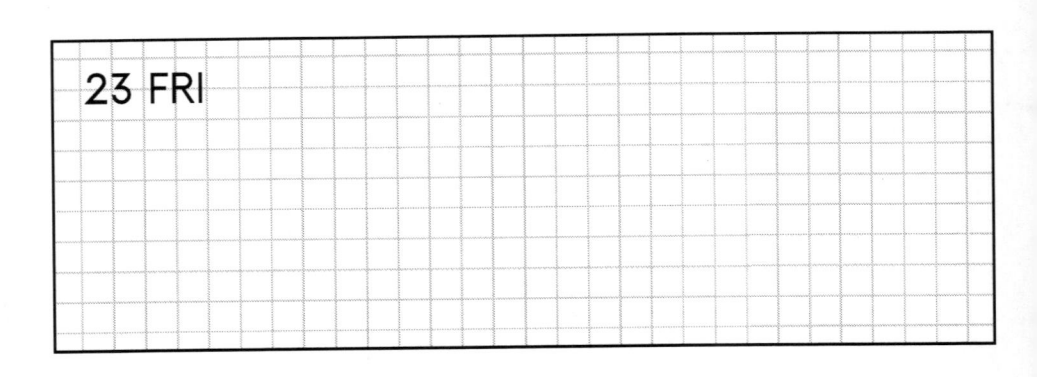

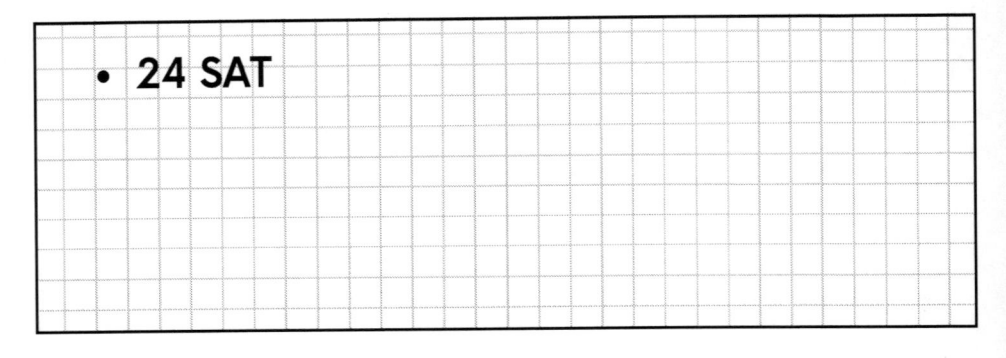

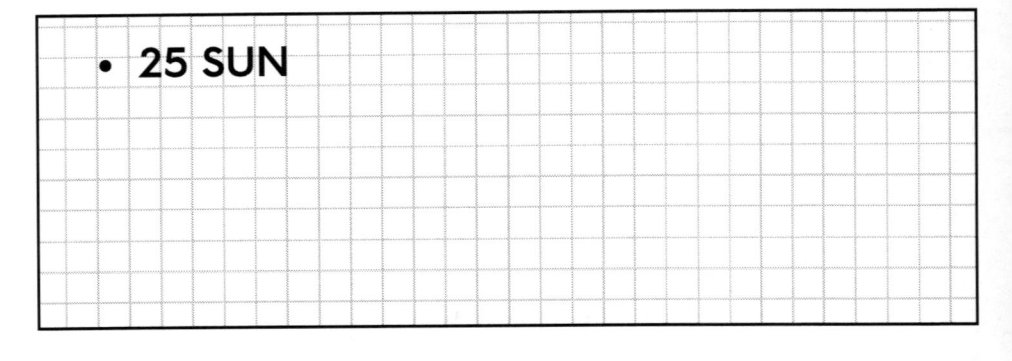

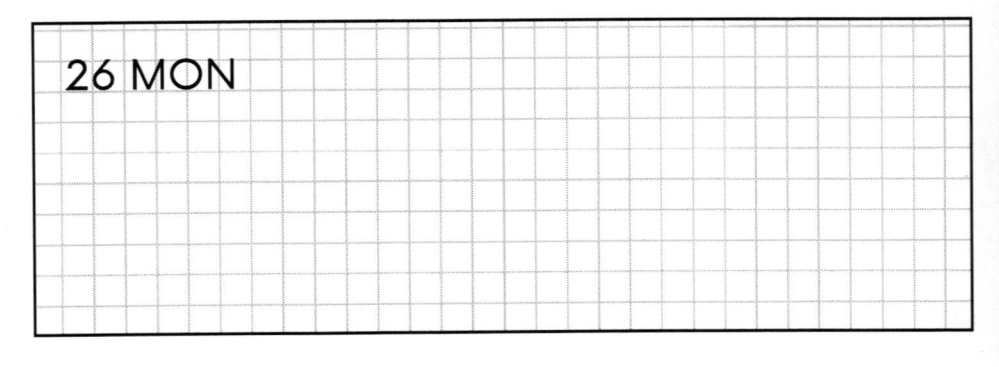

23 FRI

- **24 SAT**

- **25 SUN**

26 MON

DATE	START	BREAK	BREAK	FINISH	TOTAL HOURS

- **VEHICLE INFORMATION**
- **START LOCATION**
- **END LOCATION**
- **PURPOSE**

START	END	BUSINESS MILES	PERSONAL MILES

DATE	START	BREAK	BREAK	FINISH	TOTAL HOURS

- **VEHICLE INFORMATION**
- **START LOCATION**
- **END LOCATION**
- **PURPOSE**

START	END	BUSINESS MILES	PERSONAL MILES

DATE	START	BREAK	BREAK	FINISH	TOTAL HOURS

- **VEHICLE INFORMATION**
- **START LOCATION**
- **END LOCATION**
- **PURPOSE**

START	END	BUSINESS MILES	PERSONAL MILES

DATE	START	BREAK	BREAK	FINISH	TOTAL HOURS

- **VEHICLE INFORMATION**
- **START LOCATION**
- **END LOCATION**
- **PURPOSE**

START	END	BUSINESS MILES	PERSONAL MILES

DECEMBER 2022

27 TUE

28 WED

29 THU

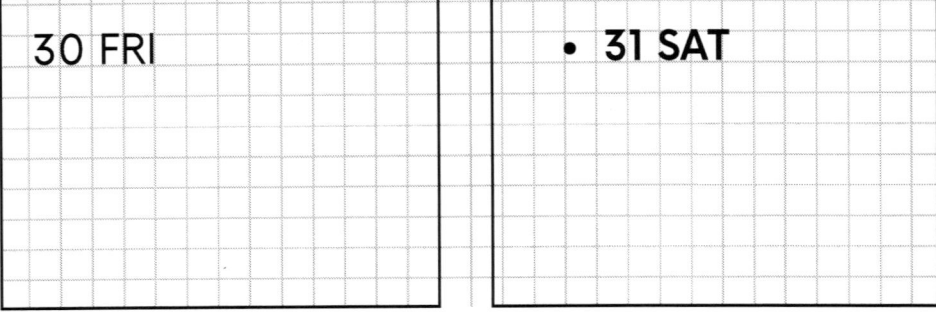

30 FRI

- ### 31 SAT

2022 CALENDAR / PLANNER

January

S	M	T	W	T	F	S
						1
2	3	4	5	6	7	8
9	10	11	12	13	14	15
16	17	18	19	20	21	22
23	24	25	26	27	28	29
30	31					

February

S	M	T	W	T	F	S
		1	2	3	4	5
6	7	8	9	10	11	12
13	14	15	16	17	18	19
20	21	22	23	24	25	26
27	28					

May

S	M	T	W	T	F	S
1	2	3	4	5	6	7
8	9	10	11	12	13	14
15	16	17	18	19	20	21
22	23	24	25	26	27	28
29	30	31				

June

S	M	T	W	T	F	S
			1	2	3	4
5	6	7	8	9	10	11
12	13	14	15	16	17	18
19	20	21	22	23	24	25
26	27	28	29	30		

September

S	M	T	W	T	F	S
				1	2	3
4	5	6	7	8	9	10
11	12	13	14	15	16	17
18	19	20	21	22	23	24
25	26	27	28	29	30	

October

S	M	T	W	T	F	S
						1
2	3	4	5	6	7	8
9	10	11	12	13	14	15
16	17	18	19	20	21	22
23	24	25	26	27	28	29
30	31					

March

S	M	T	W	T	F	S
		1	2	3	4	5
6	7	8	9	10	11	12
13	14	15	16	17	18	19
20	21	22	23	24	25	26
27	28	29	30	31		

April

S	M	T	W	T	F	S
					1	2
3	4	5	6	7	8	9
10	11	12	13	14	15	16
17	18	19	20	21	22	23
24	25	26	27	28	29	30

July

S	M	T	W	T	F	S
					1	2
3	4	5	6	7	8	9
10	11	12	13	14	15	16
17	18	19	20	21	22	23
24	25	26	27	28	29	30
31						

August

S	M	T	W	T	F	S
	1	2	3	4	5	6
7	8	9	10	11	12	13
14	15	16	17	18	19	20
21	22	23	24	25	26	27
28	29	30	31			

November

S	M	T	W	T	F	S
		1	2	3	4	5
6	7	8	9	10	11	12
13	14	15	16	17	18	19
20	21	22	23	24	25	26
27	28	29	30			

December

S	M	T	W	T	F	S
				1	2	3
4	5	6	7	8	9	10
11	12	13	14	15	16	17
18	19	20	21	22	23	24
25	26	27	28	29	30	31

JANUARY 2022

SUN	MON	TUE	WED	THU	FRI	SAT
26	27	28	29	30	31	1
2	3	4	5	6	7	8
9	10	11	12	13	14	15
16	17	18	19	20	21	22
23	24	25	26	27	28	29
30	31	1	2	3	4	5

FEBRUARY 2022

SUN	MON	TUE	WED	THU	FRI	SAT
30	31	1	2	3	4	5
6	7	8	9	10	11	12
13	14	15	16	17	18	19
20	21	22	23	24	25	26
27	28	1	2	3	4	5
6	7	8	9	10	11	12

MARCH 2022

SUN	MON	TUE	WED	THU	FRI	SAT
27	28	1	2	3	4	5
6	7	8	9	10	11	12
13	14	15	16	17	18	19
20	21	22	23	24	25	26
27	28	29	30	31	1	2
3	4	5	6	7	8	9

APRIL 2022

SUN	MON	TUE	WED	THU	FRI	SAT
27	28	29	30	31	1	2
3	4	5	6	7	8	9
10	11	12	13	14	15	16
17	18	19	20	21	22	23
24	25	26	27	28	29	30
1	2	3	4	5	6	7

MAY 2022

SUN	MON	TUE	WED	THU	FRI	SAT
1	2	3	4	5	6	7
8	9	10	11	12	13	14
15	16	17	18	19	20	21
22	23	24	25	26	27	28
29	30	31				

JUNE 2022

SUN	MON	TUE	WED	THU	FRI	SAT
29	30	31	1	2	3	4
5	6	7	8	9	10	11
12	13	14	15	16	17	18
19	20	21	22	23	24	25
26	27	28	29	30	1	2
3	4	5	6	7	8	9

JULY 2022

SUN	MON	TUE	WED	THU	FRI	SAT
26	27	28	29	30	1	2
3	4	5	6	7	8	9
10	11	12	13	14	15	16
17	18	19	20	21	22	23
24	25	26	27	28	29	30
31	1	2	3	4	5	6

AUGUST 2022

SUN	MON	TUE	WED	THU	FRI	SAT
31	1	2	3	4	5	6
7	8	9	10	11	12	13
14	15	16	17	18	19	20
21	22	23	24	25	26	27
28	29	30	31	1	2	3
4	5	6	7	8	9	10

SEPTEMBER 2022

SUN	MON	TUE	WED	THU	FRI	SAT
28	29	30	31	1	2	3
4	5	6	7	8	9	10
11	12	13	14	15	16	17
18	19	20	21	22	23	24
25	26	27	28	29	30	1
2	3	4	5	6	7	8

OCTOBER 2022

SUN	MON	TUE	WED	THU	FRI	SAT
25	26	27	28	29	30	1
2	3	4	5	6	7	8
9	10	11	12	13	14	15
16	17	18	19	20	21	22
23	24	25	26	27	28	29
30	31	1	2	3	4	5

NOVEMBER 2022

SUN	MON	TUE	WED	THU	FRI	SAT
30	31	1	2	3	4	5
6	7	8	9	10	11	12
13	14	15	16	17	18	19
20	21	22	23	24	25	26
27	28	29	30	1	2	3
4	5	6	7	8	9	10

DECEMBER 2022

SUN	MON	TUE	WED	THU	FRI	SAT
27	28	29	30	1	2	3
4	5	6	7	8	9	10
11	12	13	14	15	16	17
18	19	20	21	22	23	24
25	26	27	28	29	30	31
1	2	3	4	5	6	7

NOTES

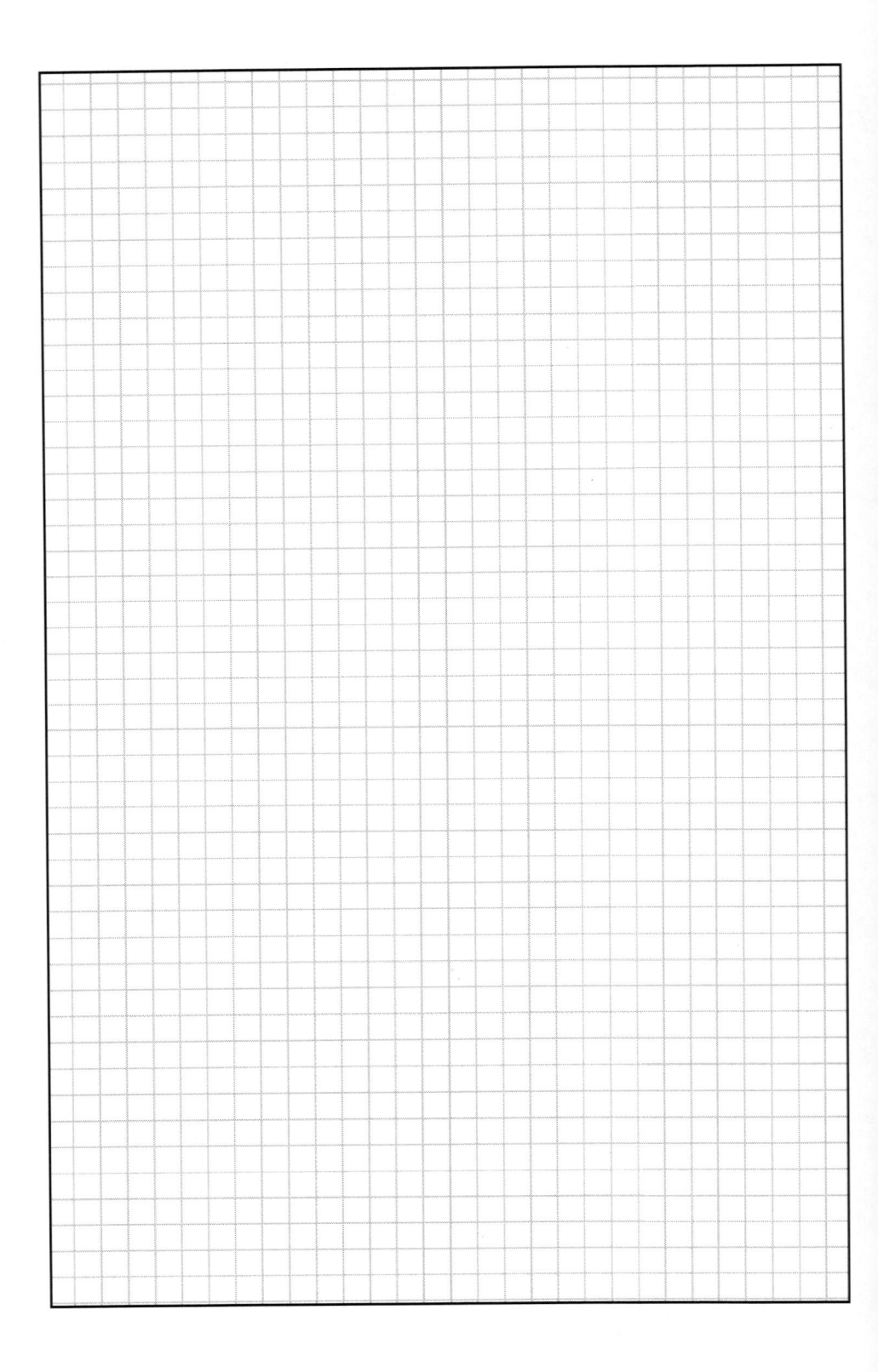

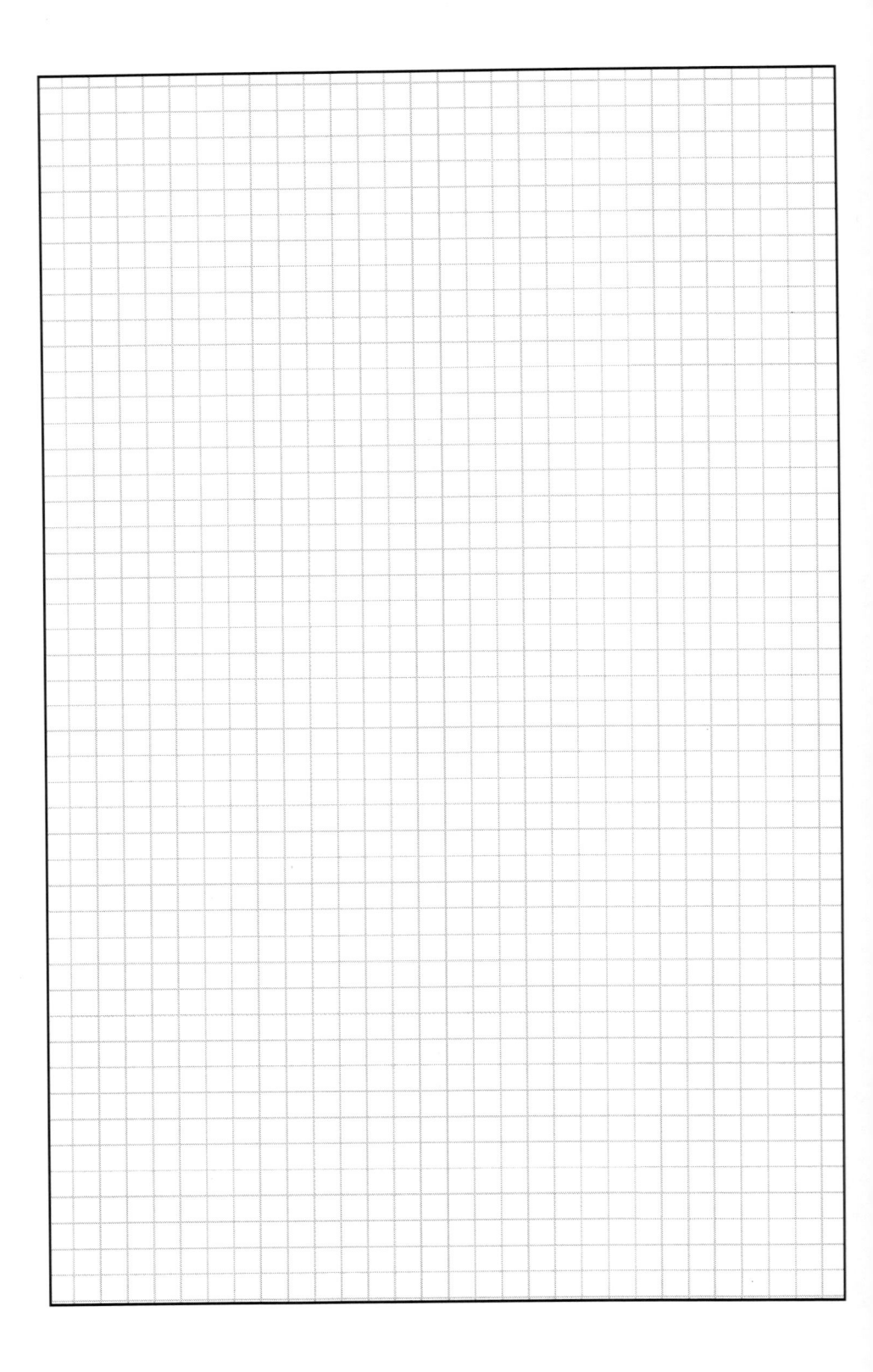

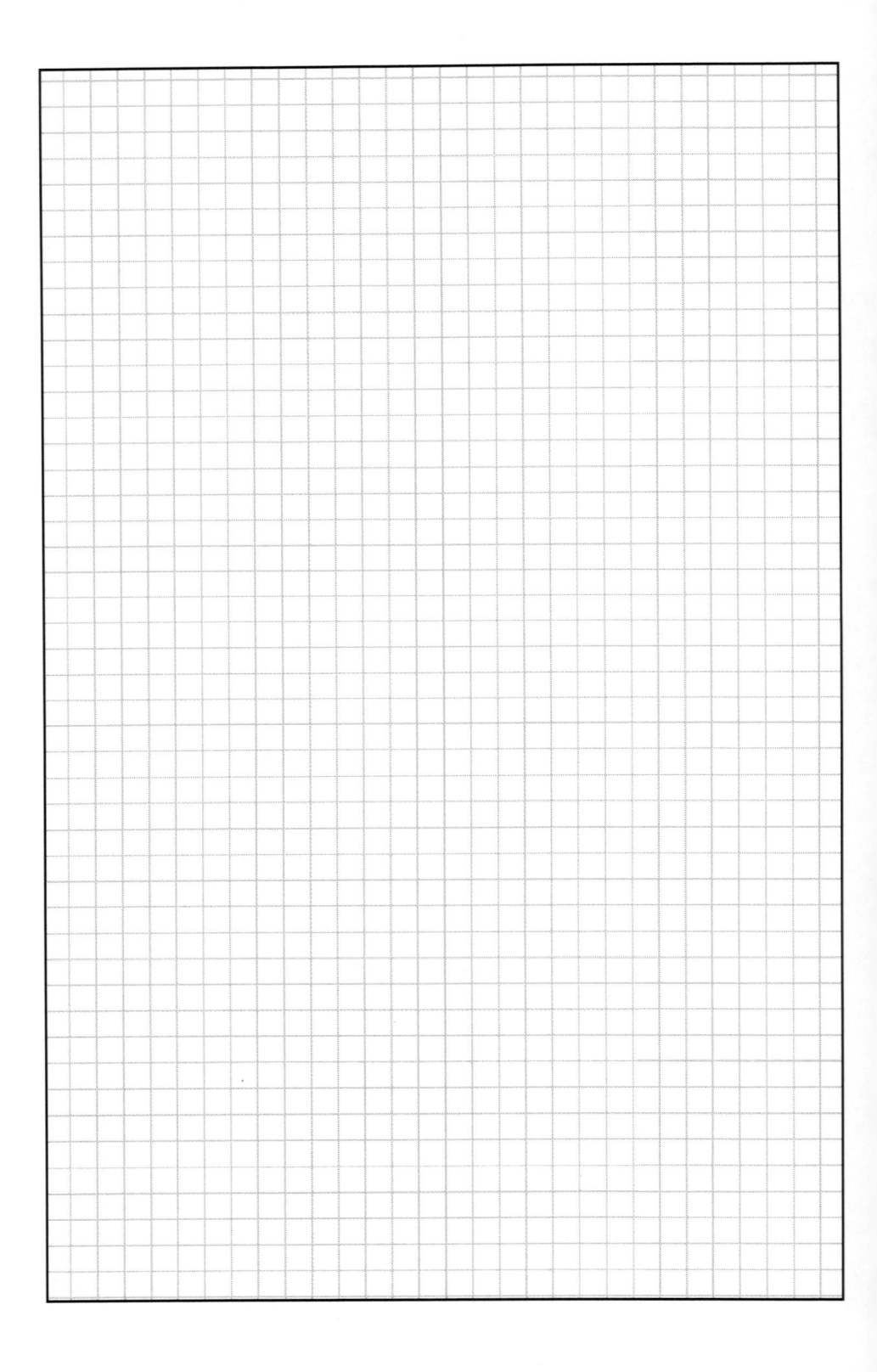

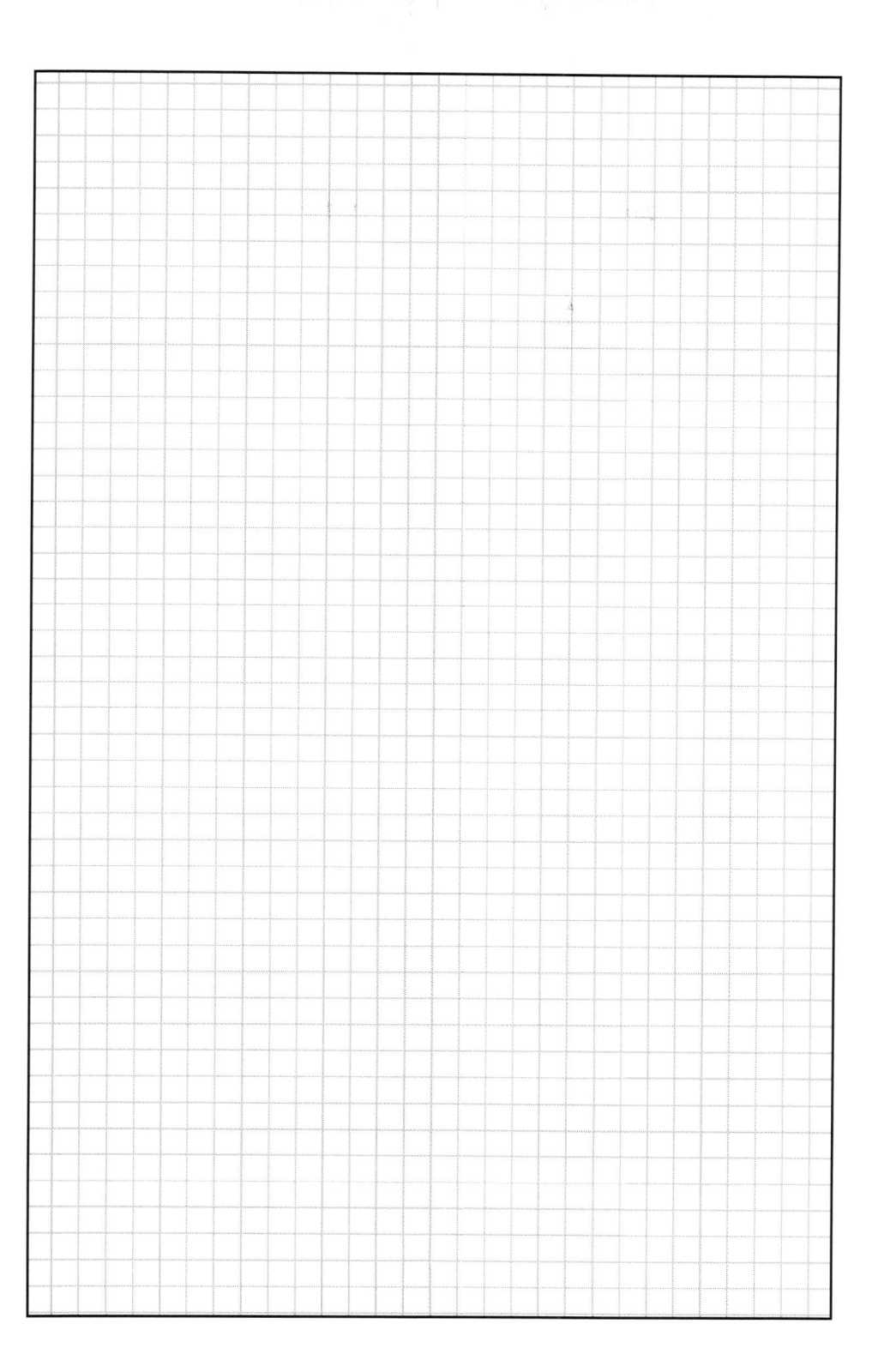

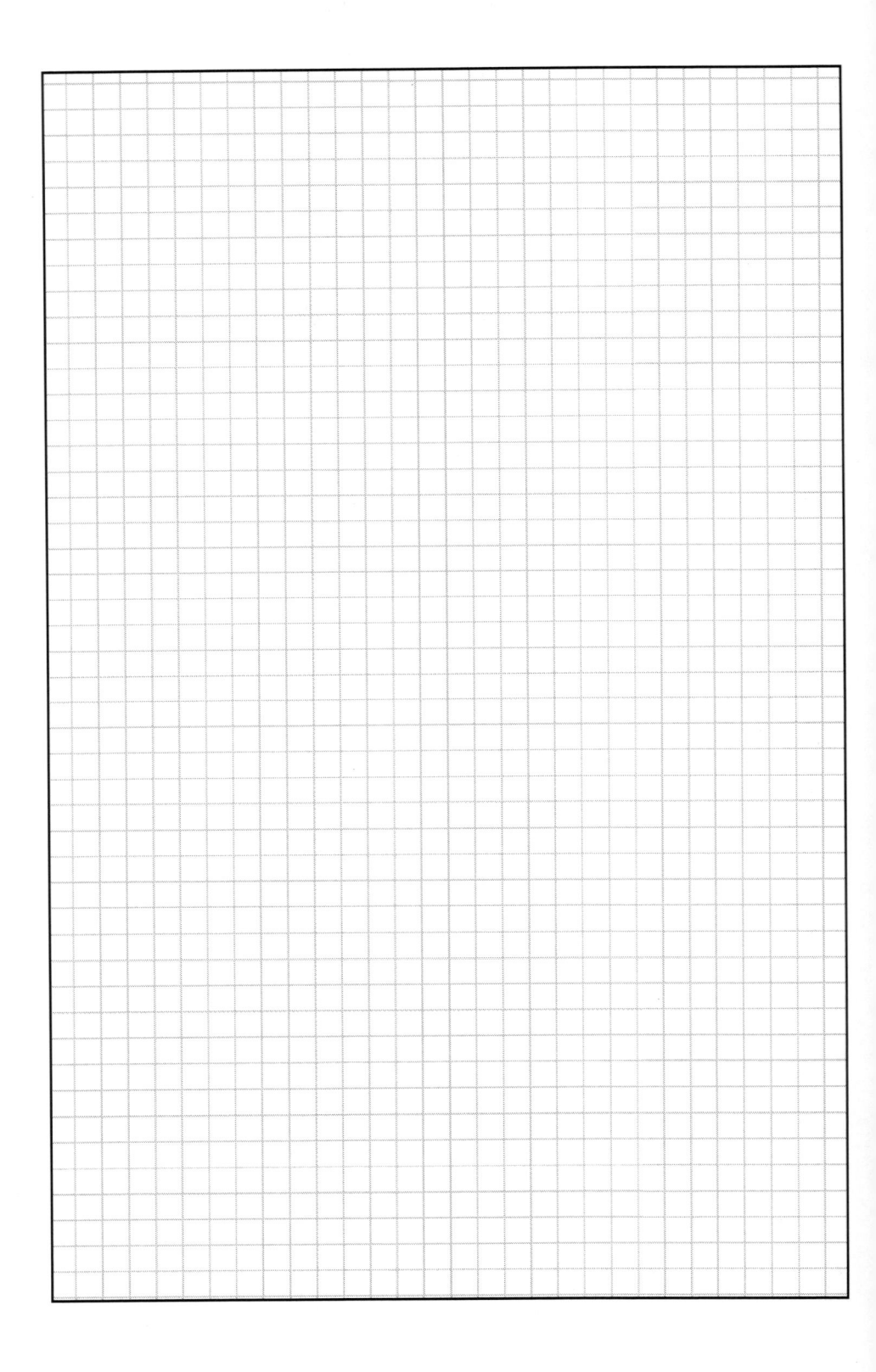

DOCUMENTS

Heavy goods vehicle (HGV) defect report form for drivers

Date: _____

Driver's name: _____

Vehicle no: _____

Trailer fleet/serial no.: _____

Odometer reading: _____

Daily or shift check (tick or cross) *Items refer to vehicle and trailer combinations

Fuel / oil leaks	
Battery security (condition)	
Tyres / wheel and wheel fixing	
Spray suppression	
Steering	
Security of load / Vehicle height	
Mirrors / Glass / Visibility	
Air build-up / Leaks	
Fuel / oil leaks	
Battery security (condition)	
Tyres / wheel and wheel fixing	
Spray suppression	
Steering	
Security of load / Vehicle height	
Mirrors / Glass / Visibility	
Air build-up / Leaks	
Reflectors / Markers	
Battery security (condition)	
Indicators / Side repeaters	
Wipers	

Washers	
Horn	
Excessive engine exhaust smoke	
AdBlue® if required	

Heavy goods vehicle (HGV) defect report form for drivers

REPORT DEFECTS HERE:

DEFECT ASSESSMENT AND RECTIFICATION:

DEFECTS REPORTED TO:

WRITE NIL HERE IF NO DEFECTS FOUND	DRIVER'S SIGNATURE:

DEFECTS RECTIFIED BY:

....

SIGNATURE: DATE:

....

Heavy goods vehicle (HGV) defect report form for drivers

Date: _____

Driver's name: _____

Vehicle no: _____

Trailer fleet/serial no.: _____

Odometer reading: _____

Daily or shift check (tick or cross)   *Items refer to vehicle and trailer combinations

Fuel / oil leaks		Washers	
Battery security (condition)			
Tyres / wheel and wheel fixing		Horn	
Spray suppression			
Steering		Excessive engine exhaust smoke	
Security of load / Vehicle height			
Mirrors / Glass / Visibility			
Air build-up / Leaks		AdBlue® if required	
Fuel / oil leaks			
Battery security (condition)			
Tyres / wheel and wheel fixing			
Spray suppression			
Steering			
Security of load / Vehicle height			
Mirrors / Glass / Visibility			
Air build-up / Leaks			
Reflectors / Markers			
Battery security (condition)			
Indicators / Side repeaters			
Wipers			

Heavy goods vehicle (HGV) defect report form for drivers

REPORT DEFECTS HERE:

DEFECT ASSESSMENT AND RECTIFICATION:

DEFECTS REPORTED TO:

WRITE NIL HERE IF NO DEFECTS FOUND	DRIVER'S SIGNATURE:

DEFECTS RECTIFIED BY:

....

SIGNATURE: DATE:

....

DRIVERS CHECKLIST
WHEN INVOLVED IN A ROAD ACCIDENT

Has the driver taken details from the other party involved (Name/Vehicle reg/Make of the car/Insurance provider/Mileage for truck/Time of accident/Location of accident).	
Take photos of the other person's vehicle involved.	
Photos of the road you were traveling on.	
Photos of any relevant road signs (for example tight turn ahead, slow down).	
Photos of the vehicle to show how many people were in the car.	
Photos showing weather condition.	
Photos of our vehicle after the collision showing the vehicle registration number.	
If safe to do so write the statement straight away so this is fresh in mind.	
Make sure the mobile number the other person gives you works in case they provide false information.	
If other person seems intimidating do not react, talk calmly and softly to calm the situation and if they are aggressive then call the police (in case they leave the scene of the accident).	

Driver		Vehicle Reg	
Time		Date		Supervisor	

ACCIDENT REPORT

Sketch of the incident

Name of the person involved	
Location of Accident	
Time		Date		Reported to Office	Y/N
Vehicle reg.		Make		Colour	
Insurance Company	
Address	
Mobile		Home	
Weather		Road condition	
Photos taken following checklist overleaf	Y/N
Names of other people involved	
Address		Mobile	
		Home	
		Vehicle reg.	
		Make	
		Colour	

ACCIDENT REPORT

Driver Statement

DRIVERS CHECKLIST
WHEN INVOLVED IN A ROAD ACCIDENT

Has the driver taken details from the other party involved (Name/Vehicle reg/Make of the car/Insurance provider/Mileage for truck/Time of accident/Location of accident).	
Take photos of the other person's vehicle involved.	
Photos of the road you were traveling on.	
Photos of any relevant road signs (for example tight turn ahead, slow down).	
Photos of the vehicle to show how many people were in the car.	
Photos showing weather condition.	
Photos of our vehicle after the collision showing the vehicle registration number.	
If safe to do so write the statement straight away so this is fresh in mind.	
Make sure the mobile number the other person gives you works in case they provide false information.	
If other person seems intimidating do not react, talk calmly and softly to calm the situation and if they are aggressive then call the police (in case they leave the scene of the accident).	

| Driver | | Vehicle Reg | |
| Time | | Date | | Supervisor | |

ACCIDENT REPORT

Sketch of the incident

Name of the person involved	
Location of Accident	
Time	Date	Reported to Office	Y/N
Vehicle reg.	Make	Colour	
Insurance Company	
Address	
Mobile	Home
Weather	Road condition
Photos taken following checklist overleaf	Y/N
Names of other people involved	
Address	Mobile
	Home
	Vehicle reg.
	Make
	Colour

ACCIDENT REPORT

Driver Statement

Printed in Great Britain
by Amazon